DATE DUE

			PRINTED IN U.S.A.

Authors & Artists for Young Adults

ISSN 1040-5682

Authors & Artists for Young Adults

VOLUME 29

Thomas McMahon
Editor

The Gale Group

DETROIT • SAN FRANCISCO • LONDON • BOSTON • WOODBRIDGE, CT

Thomas McMahon, *Editor*

Joyce Nakamura, *Managing Editor*
Hal May, *Publisher*

Diane Andreassi, Carol Brennan, Ken Cuthbertson, Catherine Goldstein,
J. Sydney Jones, Nancy Rampson, Gerard J. Senick, Diane Telgen, Brandon Trenz,
Kathleen Witman, *Sketchwriters/Contributing Editors*

Victoria B. Cariappa, *Research Manager*
Cheryl L. Warnock, *Project Coordinator*
Patricia Tsune Ballard, Wendy K. Festerling, *Research Assistants*

Susan M. Trosky, *Permissions Manager*
Maria L. Franklin, *Permissions Specialist*
Sarah Chesney, Edna Hedblad, Michele Lonoconus, *Permissions Associates*

Mary Beth Trimper, *Production Director*
Cindy Range, *Production Assistant*

Randy Bassett, *Image Database Supervisor*
Gary Leach, *Graphic Artist*
Robert Duncan, Michael Logusz, *Imaging Specialists*
Pamela A. Reed, *Imaging Coordinator*

The paper used in this publication meets the minimum requirements of
American National Standard for Information Sciences—Permanence Paper
for Printed Library Materials, ANSI Z39.48-1984.

Library of Congress Catalog Card Number 89-641100
ISBN 0-7876-2072-6
ISSN 1040-5682

10 9 8 7 6 5 4 3 2 1

Printed in the United States of America

Contents

Introduction

Authors and Artists for Young Adults is a reference series designed to serve the needs of middle school, junior high, and high school students interested in creative artists. Originally inspired by the need to bridge the gap between Gale's *Something about the Author,* created for children, and *Contemporary Authors,* intended for older students and adults, *Authors and Artists for Young Adults* has been expanded to cover not only an international scope of authors, but also a wide variety of other artists.

Although the emphasis of the series remains on the writer for young adults, we recognize that these readers have diverse interests covering a wide range of reading levels. The series therefore contains not only those creative artists who are of high interest to young adults, including cartoonists, photographers, music composers, bestselling authors of adult novels, media directors, producers, and performers, but also literary and artistic figures studied in academic curricula, such as influential novelists, playwrights, poets, and painters. The goal of *Authors and Artists for Young Adults* is to present this great diversity of creative artists in a format that is entertaining, informative, and understandable to the young adult reader.

Entry Format

Each volume of *Authors and Artists for Young Adults* will furnish in-depth coverage of twenty to twenty-five authors and artists. The typical entry consists of:

—A detailed biographical section that includes date of birth, marriage, children, education, and addresses.

—A comprehensive bibliography or filmography including publishers, producers, and years.

—Adaptations into other media forms.

—Works in progress.

—A distinctive essay featuring comments on an artist's life, career, artistic intentions, world views, and controversies.

—References for further reading.

—Extensive illustrations, photographs, movie stills, cartoons, book covers, and other relevant visual material.

A cumulative index to featured authors and artists appears in each volume.

Compilation Methods

The editors of *Authors and Artists for Young Adults* make every effort to secure information directly from the authors and artists through personal correspondence and interviews. Sketches on living authors and artists are sent to the biographee for review prior to publication. Any sketches not personally reviewed by biographees or their representatives are marked with an asterisk (*).

Highlights of Forthcoming Volumes

Among the authors and artists planned for future volumes are:

Sherwood Anderson	Franz Kafka	Lisa Scottoline
T. A. Barron	Trudy Krisher	J. Michael Straczynski
James Berry	Stanley Kubrick	Neil Simon
Dee Brown	Jacob Lawrence	Erika Tamar
Olive Ann Burns	Lois Lowry	Sheri S. Tepper
Judith Ortiz Cofer	Joan Miro	Joan D. Vinge
Robin Cook	Janette Oke	Cynthia Voigt
Diane Duane	Judith Ortiz Cofer	Will Weaver
Jean Ferris	Sara Paretsky	Connie Willis
Jack Finney	Nick Park	Oprah Winfrey
John Jakes	Jackson Pollack	Tad Williams
Francisco Jimenez	Tom Robbins	Kevin Williamson

Contact the Editor

We encourage our readers to examine the entire *AAYA* series. Please write and tell us if we can make AAYA even more helpful to you. Give your comments and suggestions to the editor:

BY MAIL: The Editor, *Authors and Artists for Young Adults*, 27500 Drake Rd., Farmington Hills, MI 48331-3535.

BY TELEPHONE: (800) 347-GALE

Authors & Artists for Young Adults

Cherie Bennett

■ Personal

Born October 6, 1960, in Buffalo, NY; daughter of Bennett Berman (a writer) and Roslyn (Ozur) Cantor (an educator); married Jeff Gottesfeld (a writer and producer), February 4, 1991. *Education:* University of Michigan, B.A. *Religion:* Jewish.

■ Addresses

Home and office—P.O. Box 150326, Nashville, TN 37215. *Agents*—Curtis Brown Ltd., 10 Astor Place, New York, NY 10003; Writers and Artists Agency, 19 West 44th St., New York, NY 10036; Metropolitan Talent, Inc., 4526 Wilshire Blvd., Los Angeles, CA 90010; Don Buchwald & Associates, 10 East 44th St., New York, NY 10017.

■ Career

Author, playwright, and syndicated columnist. Performer in Broadway, Off-Broadway, and re-gional theater productions, including *Grease* and *When You Comin' Back, Red Ryder.* Theater director at regional and off-Broadway productions, including *Anne Frank & Me.* Has performed as a vocalist, singing backup for John Cougar Mellencamp and in her play, *Honk Tonk Angels.* Has appeared on television and radio talk shows and as a lecturer in schools. *Member:* Writers Guild East, Dramatists Guild, PEN American Center.

■ Awards, Honors

First Night award for best new play, RCI Festival of Emerging American Theater award, and Wing Walker Award, all 1993, and first place, Jackie White Memorial National Competition, 1995, all for *John Lennon and Me;* Children's Choice designation, Children's Book Council, and American Library Association distinction, both 1994, both for *Did You Hear about Amber?;* Dallas Shortfest! award, 1994, for *Sex and Rage in a Soho Loft;* Sholem Aleichem Commission award, 1994, and Bonderman Biennial award and First Night award, both 1995, all for *Anne Frank and Me;* New Visions/New Voices award, Kennedy Center for the Performing Arts, 1996, for *Cyra and Rocky;* New Visions/New Voices award, Kennedy Center for the Performing Arts, 1998, for *Searching for David's Heart;* first place, Jackie White Memorial Children's Playwriting Competition, 1998, for *Zink: The Myth, The Legend, The Zebra.*

■ Writings

FOR YOUNG ADULTS

Life in the Fat Lane (novel), Delacorte, 1998.

YOUNG ADULT NOVELS; MASS MARKET

Good-Bye, Best Friend (also see below), HarperCollins (New York), 1993.
Girls in Love, Scholastic (New York), 1996.
Bridesmaids, Scholastic, 1996.
Searching for David's Heart, Scholastic, 1998.

Also author of *With a Face Like Mine*, c. 1980.

YOUNG ADULT NOVELS; THE "SUNSET ISLAND" SERIES

Sunset Island, Berkley (New York), 1991.
Sunset Kiss, Berkley, 1991.
Sunset Dreams, Berkley, 1991.
Sunset Farewell, Berkley, 1991.
Sunset Reunion, Berkley, 1991.
Sunset Heat, Berkley, 1992.
Sunset Paradise, Berkley, 1992.
Sunset Promises, Berkley, 1992.
Sunset Scandal, Berkley, 1992.
Sunset Secrets, Berkley, 1992.
Sunset Whispers, Berkley, 1992.
Sunset after Dark, Berkley, 1993.
Sunset after Hours, Berkley, 1993.
Sunset after Midnight, Berkley, 1993.
Sunset Deceptions, Berkley, 1993.
Sunset Embrace, Berkley, 1993.
Sunset on the Road, Berkley, 1993.
Sunset Surf, Berkley, 1993.
Sunset Wishes, Berkley, 1993.
Sunset Touch, Berkley, 1993.
Sunset Wedding, Berkley, 1993.
Sunset Fantasy, Berkley, 1994.
Sunset Fire, Berkley, 1994.
Sunset Glitter, Berkley, 1994.
Sunset Heart, Berkley, 1994.
Sunset Illusions, Berkley, 1994.
Sunset Magic, Berkley, 1994.
Sunset Passion, Berkley, 1994.
Sunset Revenge, Berkley, 1994.
Sunset Sensation, Berkley, 1994.
Sunset Stranger, Berkley, 1994.
Sunset Fling, Berkley, 1995.
Sunset Love, Berkley, 1995.
Sunset Spirit, Berkley, 1995.
Sunset Tears, Berkley, 1995.
Sunset Forever, Berkley, 1997.

JUVENILE NOVELS; THE "CLUB SUNSET ISLAND" TRILOGY

Too Many Boys!, Berkley, 1994.
Dixie's First Kiss, Berkley, 1994.
Tori's Crush, Berkley, 1994.

YOUNG ADULT NOVELS; THE "SURVIVING SIXTEEN" TRILOGY

Did You Hear about Amber?, Puffin, 1993.
The Fall of the Perfect Girl, Puffin, 1993.
Only Love Can Break Your Heart, Puffin, 1994.

YOUNG ADULT NOVELS; THE "WILD HEARTS" SERIES

Hot Winter Nights, Pocket Books, 1994.
On the Edge, Pocket Books, 1994.
Passionate Kisses, Pocket Books, 1994.
Wild Hearts, Pocket Books, 1994.
Wild Hearts Forever, Pocket Books, 1994.
Wild Hearts on Fire, Pocket Books, 1994.

YOUNG ADULT NOVELS; THE "TEEN ANGELS" SERIES; CO-WRITTEN WITH HUSBAND, JEFF GOTTESFELD

Heaven Can't Wait, Avon, 1996.
Love Never Dies, Avon, 1996.
Angel Kisses, Avon, 1996.
Heaven Help Us!, Avon, 1996.
Nightmare in Heaven, Avon, 1996.
Love without End, Avon, 1996.

YOUNG ADULT NOVELS; THE "HOPE HOSPITAL" SERIES

Get Well Soon, Little Sister, Troll Communications, 1996.
The Initiation, Troll Communications, 1996.
The Accident, Troll Communications, 1997.

YOUNG ADULT NOVELS: THE "TRASH" SERIES; CO-WRITTEN WITH HUSBAND, JEFF GOTTESFELD

Trash, Berkley, 1997.
Trash: Love, Lies, and Video, Berkley, 1997.
Trash: Good Girls, Bad Boys, Berkley, 1997.
Dirty Big Secrets, Berkley, 1997.
Trash: The Evil Twin, Berkley, 1997.
Trash: Truth or Scare, Berkley, 1998.

PLAYS

Honky Tonk Angels, produced in New York City, 1988, Boston, MA, 1990, and Charlotte, NC, 1991-92.

John Lennon and Me (also known as *Candy Store Window*; adapted from her novel *Good-Bye, Best Friend*; produced in Nashville, TN, 1993), Dramatic Publishing (Woodstock, IL), 1996.

Sex and Rage in a Soho Loft, produced in Nashville, 1994, Dallas, TX, 1994, and Columbia, SC, 1995.

Anne Frank and Me (produced in Nashville, 1995, produced off-Broadway, American Jewish Theater, 1996), Dramatic Publishing, 1997.

Cyra and Rocky (based on *Cyrano de Bergerac* by Edmund Rostand; produced in Washington, DC, at Kennedy Center for the Performing Arts, 1996), Dramatic Publishing, 1997.

Zink the So-Called Zebra (produced in Milwaukee, WI, 1997), Dramatic Publishing, 1998.

Searching for David's Heart (play; adapted from novel of the same name), produced in Washington, DC, at Kennedy Center for the Preforming Arts, 1998.

Author of screenplays *Angel from Montgomery* (New Line Cinema), 1993, and *Wild Hearts* (Lantana Publications), 1995.

OTHER

Also author of *Samantha Tyler's Younger Sister* (in German translation only), Cora-Verlag Press (Germany). Author of nationally syndicated advice column, "Hey Cherie!" Author of novels in series "The Party Line," under the pseudonym Carrie Austen. Creator and monitor of America Online's first online reader-written young adult novel, *Horror Ink*, 1997. Has written for National Broadcasting Company (NBC) television daytime drama *Another World*. Bennett's works have been translated into several languages, including French, German, Spanish, and Swedish.

■ **Adaptations**

Several novels and plays have been optioned for film and television, including *Honky Tonk Angels, John Lennon & Me, Wild Hearts, Teen Angels, Anne Frank & Me, Hope Hospital*, and *Cyra and Rocky*.

■ **Work in Progress**

A novelization of *Anne Frank & Me*; a new young adult fiction series entitled "Pageant" for Berkley.

■ **Sidelights**

A popular columnist and novelist read by young teens around the United States, Nashville-based author Cherie Bennett is as enthusiastic about entertaining her young audience as she is about the city she calls home. A former Broadway actress and singer, Bennett spends much of her non-writing time outside Tennessee, visiting with groups of teen girls in different parts of the United States. The upbeat author's discussions with adolescents are a constant reminder that growing up is a difficult time. "They [teen girls] worry most whether they are cute enough or thin

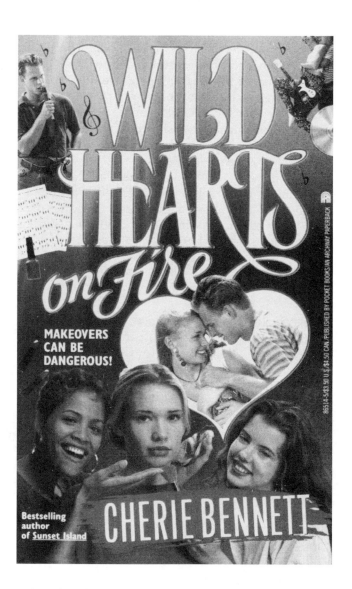

When friends give her a new make-over, Kimmy Carrier becomes torn between the old Kimmy versus the new Kimmy in this 1994 novel.

enough," Bennett explained to *React for Teens* contributor Karen Pritzker. "Their lives become smaller. If I can write one book that saves a girl from that, I'm happy."

Born in 1960, Bennett spent her childhood years in Michigan, the only girl in a show-biz family. Her father worked as a writer for television shows, including *Twilight Zone, Route 66,* and Sid Caesar's *Show of Shows.* She explained to *Blast!* contributor Laura Matter that she started writing at a young age. "I wrote really, really bad poetry when I was a teenager," Bennett admitted. "This should give hope to kids out there who write poetry and think, 'This isn't any good.' I mean, my poetry stunk."

Bennett published her first novel, *With a Face Like Mine,* while she was a student at the University of Michigan at the beginning of the 1980s. However, it wasn't until she had graduated from college and spent several years in New York City as a singer and dancer that she returned to her writing seriously, first as a playwright. Bennett's play *Honky Tonk Angels* provided her with an introduction to the city she would one day call home. Featuring a group of women with dreams of becoming country music singing sensations, the play was produced in Nashville in 1988 and sold to Tri Star Pictures in 1992.

Series Prove Popular

Bennett's long-running "Sunset Island" series of young adult novels, which she introduced in 1991, features teens Sam, Emma, and Carrie on a summer vacation that never ends. Taking place on an island off the coast of Maine, the novels follow the teens' efforts to find time for fun and friends while working as summer au pairs for vacationing families. In 1994 Bennett published the "Club Sunset Island" companion trilogy for younger readers. Featuring the novels *Too Many Boys, Dixie's First Kiss,* and *Tori's Crush,* the three-novel series features preteen protagonists coping with their first romantic experiences.

Other Bennett-penned series popular with teen readers include "Surviving Sixteen," a trilogy that debuted in 1993, and "Wild Hearts," which began in 1994. In *Wild Hearts,* the opening novel of the latter series, country music provides the backdrop to a New York City teen's growing appre-

Teen angel Nicole visits Earth to prevent a sixteen-year-old-girl from becoming pregnant in this 1996 novel from the "Teen Angels" series.

ciation for her new hometown of Nashville. Street-smart and cosmopolitan newcomer Jane McVay and her new friends—Savannah, Kimmy, and Sandra—eventually decide to form the band Wild Hearts, which serves as the series' focus. "Nashville provides a distinctive setting," noted a *Publishers Weekly* reviewer, who added that "Jane's wisecracking, first-person narrative . . . sets a rapid tempo." Silvia Makowski, in her review of the series premier in *Voice of Youth Advocates,* commented that "Bennett is in top form with this first installment. . . . Teens will feel sad and bad for [Jane] and identify with her predicament, caught between two exotic city cultures."

Comprised of the novels *Did You Hear about Amber?*, *The Fall of the Perfect Girl*, and *Only Love Can Break Your Heart*, the "Surviving Sixteen" trilogy was praised by reviewers for its humor and lively style. Bennett's first-hand experience with rheumatoid arthritis serves as inspiration for her book *Did You Hear about Amber?* The novel follows the beautiful but snobbish Amber, who makes up for living on the poor side of town by excelling at dance. Her talent and good looks gain her entry into the in-crowd until a diagnosis of rheumatoid arthritis cuts Amber's dreams of a career as a dancer short at age sixteen. In *The Fall of the Perfect Girl*, Bennett introduces readers to another teen with a less-than-ideal personality: Suzanne Elizabeth Wentworth Lafayette. As the length of her name might suggest, Bennett's protagonist is wealthy, worldly, and very spoiled. But the sixteen-year-old's perfect life comes crashing down around her after an indiscretion in her politically prominent father's past is publicly revealed. The family is scandalized with the discovery that Suzanne has a half-sister, Patsy, by her father's old girlfriend, and Suzanne's socialite mother indignantly leaves her husband. While noting that most readers will not find much to sympathize with in the novel's haughty heroine, Elaine S. Patterson stated in *Kliatt* that "girls should enjoy . . . [watching] Suzanne becoming more thoughtful and mature." Noting that the novel was a "refreshing change of pace," *Voice of Youth Advocates* critic Beth Andersen maintained that *The Fall of the Perfect Girl* "is a good story about decent teens behaving in believable ways that do *not* involve substance abuse or promiscuity."

Bennett's "Teen Angels" novels, created and co-authored by her writer-producer husband, Jeff Gottesfeld, concern three older teens who meet untimely deaths and wind up in Teen Heaven, sent there by "Big Guy . . . when they still had lessons of life to learn." The series begins with 1996's *Heaven Can't Wait*, as Cisco, Melody, and Nicole attempt to earn "Angel Points" by helping self-destructive musician Shayne Stone straighten out his life and end his dependance on drugs and alcohol. Averting a teen pregnancy becomes the focus of *Love Never Dies*, as angel Nicole is sent to "Ground Zero" (Earth) to convince a sixteen-year-old that motherhood should wait, no matter how much she loves her boyfriend. Observing that the series contains nondenominational references to religion despite its subject matter, Holly M. Ward, writing in *Voice of Youth Advocates*, praised

If you enjoy the works of Cherie Bennett, you may also want to check out the following books and films:

Ilene Cooper, *My Co-Star, My Enemy*, 1993.
Sonia Levitin, *A Season for Unicorns*, 1986.
Cynthia Voigt, *Izzy, Willy Nilly*, 1986.
Circle of Friends, a film starring Minnie Driver and Chris O'Donnell, 1994.

the "Teen Angels" books as a "cute idea." Ward summarized the overall works as "light romance with the idea that one can make a positive difference in another's life." Similar in theme are Bennett's "Hope Hospital" books, which feature a trio of thirteen-year-olds who volunteer at a hospital in Hope, Michigan, and discover a great deal about life, death, and, of course, boys.

Husband and Wife Team Up

Bennett would make writing a family affair again with the "Trash" novel series begun in 1997. Working with her producer-husband Jeff Gottesfeld and drawing heavily on her daytime drama writing experience, Bennett created series protagonist Chelsea Jennings, the teen-age daughter of a convicted mass murderer. Hoping to conceal her past, Chelsea finds herself with a new boyfriend and a fashionable summer job in New York City, working behind the scenes on a scandalous TV talk show. The author "pulls out all the stops to snare female young adults looking for a read that's, well, just a trifle trashy," according to a *Publishers Weekly* critic in a review of the series' first installment, *Trash*.

Published in 1998, *Life in the Fat Lane* features a sixteen-year-old homecoming queen who lives the life many teens dream about: popularity in school, a perfect boyfriend, and excellent school marks. However, Lara Ardeche's ideal world slowly disintegrates as she begins to add pounds to her beauty pageant figure. Frustrated at her inexplicable weight gain, Lara tries fad diets, intense exercise sessions, and even fasting to shed the added pounds but nothing works. Only after coming to terms with her new size, and the incurable metabolic disorder behind it, is she able to

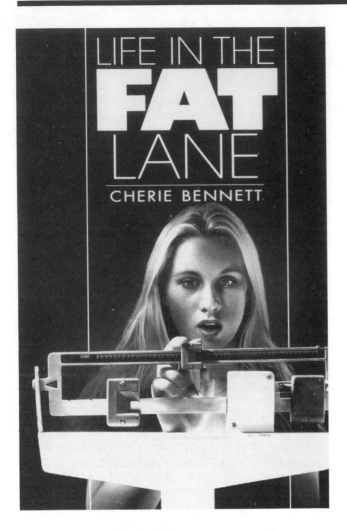

Life changes abruptly for a sixteen-year-old-homecoming queen after she discovers she has an incurable metabolic disorder.

regain her self-confidence and appreciate the few true friends that remain with her. While talking about the damaging effects "unrealistic standards of beauty" have on teenagers, a *Kirkus Reviews* critic claimed that Bennett "lays out the issues with unusual clarity, sharp insight, and cutting irony." Calling the novel an "addicting experience," a contributor to *Publisher's Weekly* insists that Bennett's story about Lara's experience "is sure to hit a nerve" with readers.

In addition to her popular novel series, Bennett has written a number of stand-alone novels, and she continues to put her knowledge of the theater to good use in plays written for both adult and teen audiences. *John Lennon and Me*, a drama about a girl with cystic fibrosis based on her 1993

novel *Good-Bye, Best Friend*, received several awards after it was produced for the stage in 1992. Her play *Anne Frank and Me* about modern American teens, denial of the Holocaust, and the Nazi-occupation of Paris, was produced Off-Broadway by the American Jewish Theater in 1996. In a review for the *New York Times*, Lawrence Van Gelder hailed Bennett's reflection of Anne Frank's story through the eyes of modern—and skeptical—middle-schoolers assigned to perform a play based on Frank's diaries. The critic called the work "an eloquent and poignant play" that "deserves to be seen."

Receiving more than one hundred letters from fans of her columns and books each week, the prolific writer responds personally to each letter. "Garth Brooks taught me," Bennett explained, citing the country music superstar. "He told me early on that you must always respect the people who support you. And that's why anyone who sends me a fan letter gets my personal response. If a girl cares enough to read one of my books or my column, I owe it to her trust in me to write back."

■ Works Cited

Anderson, Beth, review of *The Fall of the Perfect Girl*, *Voice of Youth Advocates*, February, 1994, p. 364.

Bennett, Cherie, *Heaven Can't Wait*, Avon, 1996.

Review of *Life in the Fat Lane*, *Kirkus Reviews*, December 8, 1997, p. 73.

Review of *Life in the Fat Lane*, *Publishers Weekly*, December 15, 1997, p. 1832.

Makowski, Silvia, review of *Wild Hearts*, *Voice of Youth Advocates*, June, 1994, p. 80.

Matter, Laura, "Cherie Bennett Unplugged," *Blast! Magazine* (Nashville), April, 1993, pp. 18-19.

Patterson, Elaine S., review of *The Fall of the Perfect Girl*, *Kliatt*, November, 1993, p. 4.

Pritzker, Karen, "The Ultimate Pen Pal," *React for Teens*, January, 15-21, 1996, p. 13.

Review of *Trash*, *Publishers Weekly*, May 26, 1997, p. 86.

Van Gelder, Lawrence, review of *Anne Frank and Me*, *New York Times*, December 11, 1996.

Ward, Holly M., review of *Heaven Can't Wait* and *Love Never Dies*, *Voice of Youth Advocates*, June, 1996, p. 92.

Review of *Wild Hearts*, *Publishers Weekly*, January 17, 1994, p. 440.

■ For More Information See

PERIODICALS

Bulletin of the Center for Children's Books, February, 1998, pp. 194-95.

Horn Book, January-February, 1998, p. 69.

Kliatt, May, 1996, p. 12.

Publishers Weekly, June 14, 1993, p. 73; January 8, 1996, p. 20; August 3, 1998, pp. 21-22.

Voice of Youth Advocates, December, 1993, pp. 286-87; April, 1996, p. 21.

—Sketch by Pamela L. Shelton

Robert Bloch

■ Personal

Born April 5, 1917, in Chicago, IL; died of cancer, September 23, 1994, in Los Angeles, CA; son of Raphael A. (a bank cashier) and Stella (a teacher and social worker; maiden name Loeb) Bloch; married Marion Holcombe, October 2, 1940 (divorced, 1963); married Eleanor Alexander, October 16, 1964; children: Sally Ann. *Education:* Attended public schools in Maywood, IL, and Milwaukee, WI. *Religion:* Jewish.

■ Addresses

Home—2111 Sunset Crest Dr., Los Angeles, CA 90046. *Agent*—Shapiro-Lichtman Talent Agency, 8827 Beverly Blvd., Los Angeles, CA 90067.

■ Career

Author, editor, scriptwriter, journalist. Gustav Marx Advertising, Milwaukee, WI., copywriter, 1942-53; editor, *Science-Fiction World* magazine, 1956; freelance writer, 1953-94. Conducted workshops and seminars on writing literature and works for the screen, and appeared in the 1985 movie *The*

Fantasy Film Worlds of George Pal. Member: Writers Guild of America, Mystery Writers of America (president, 1970-71), Science Fiction Writers of America, National Fantasy Association.

■ Awards, Honors

E. E. Evans Memorial Award, 1959; Hugo Award, World Science Fiction Convention, 1959, for short story "The Hellbound Train"; Screen Guild Award, 1960; Ann Radcliffe Award for literature, 1960, and for television, 1966; Edgar Allan Poe Award and Special Scroll, Mystery Writers of America, 1960; Trieste Film Festival Award, 1965, for *The Skull;* Convention du Cinema Fantastique de Paris Prize, 1973; Los Angeles Science Fiction Society Award, 1974; Comicon Inkpot Award, 1975; World Fantasy Convention Life Achievement Award, 1975; Cannes Fantasy Film Festival First Prize, for *Asylum.* Guest of Honor, World Science Fiction Convention, 1948 and 1973, Boucheron I, 1971, Dallascon, 1972, Comicon, 1975, First World Fantasy Convention, 1975, premier Festival du roman et cinema policiers, 1979, and at Cinecon One, 1981.

■ Writings

SHORT STORY COLLECTIONS, EXCEPT AS NOTED

Sea-Kissed (booklet), Utopian Publications (London), 1945.
The Opener of the Way, Arkham House (Sauk City, WI), 1945.

Terror in the Night and Other Stories, Ace Books (New York City), 1958, published in England as *House of the Hatchet*, Panther (London), 1976.

Pleasant Dreams—Nightmares, Arkham, 1959, as *Nightmares*, Belmont (New York City), 1961.

Nightmares, Belmont-Tower (New York City), 1961.

More Nightmares, Belmont-Tower, 1961.

Blood Runs Cold, Simon and Schuster, 1961.

Yours Truly, Jack the Ripper: Tales of Horror, Belmont-Tower, 1962, published in England as *The House of the Hatchet and Other Tales of Horror*, Tandem Publishing (London), 1965.

Atoms and Evil, Fawcett (Greenwich, CT), 1962.

Horror-7, Belmont-Tower, 1963, published in England as *Torture Garden*, New English Library (London), 1965.

Bogey Men: Ten Tales, Pyramid Publications (New York City), 1963.

The Skull of the Marquis de Sade and Other Stories, Pyramid Publications, 1965.

Tales in a Jugular Vein, Pyramid Publications, 1965.

Chamber of Horrors, Award Books (New York City), 1966.

The Living Demons, Belmont-Tower, 1967.

Ladies Day/This Crowded Earth, Belmont-Tower, 1967.

Dragons and Nightmares, Mirage Press (Baltimore), 1969.

(With Ray Bradbury) *Bloch and Bradbury*, Belmont-Tower, 1969, published in England as *Fever Dream, and Other Fantasies*, Sphere Books (London), 1970.

Fear Today, Gone Tomorrow, Award Books, 1971.

Cold Chills, Doubleday, 1977.

The King of Terrors: Tales of Murder and Death, Mysterious Press (Yonkers, NY), 1977.

The Best of Robert Bloch, Ballantine (New York City), 1977.

Out of the Mouths of Graves, Mysterious Press, 1978.

Such Stuff as Screams Are Made Of, Ballantine, 1979.

Mysteries of the Worm: All the Othulhu Mythos Stories of Robert Bloch, Zebra Books (New York), 1981, revised edition, Chaosium (Oakland, CA), 1993.

The Twilight Zone: The Movie (fictionalization of screenplay), Warner (New York City), 1983.

Midnight Pleasures, Doubleday, 1987.

Lost in Time and Space with Lefty Feep, edited by John Stanley, cover and sketches by Kenn Davis, Creatures at Large (Pacifica, CA), 1987.

Bitter Ends, Underwood-Miller (Los Angeles), 1987.

Final Reckonings, Underwood-Miller, 1987.

Last Rites, Underwood-Miller, 1987.

The Selected Stories of Robert Bloch (includes *Final Reckoning*, *Bitter Ends*, and *Last Rites*), Underwood-Miller, 3 volumes, 1987, as *The Complete Stories of Robert Bloch*, Citadel Press (New York City), 3 volumes, 1989-91.

Fear and Trembling, Tor (New York City), 1989.

Yours Truly, Jack the Ripper (short story), Pulphouse (Eugene, OR), 1991.

The Skull of the Marquis de Sade (short story), Pulphouse, 1991.

The Early Fears (includes *The Opener of the Way* and *Pleasant Nightmares)*, Fedogan & Bremer (Minneapolis), 1994.

Flowers from the Moon and Other Lunacies, Arkham, 1998.

NOVELS

The Scarf, Dial (New York City), 1947, revised edition, Fawcett, 1966, published as *The Scarf of Passion*, Avon, 1948.

The Kidnapper, Lion (New York City), 1954.

Spiderweb, Ace Books (New York City), 1954.

The Will to Kill, Ace Books, 1954.

Shooting Star, Ace Books, 1958.

Psycho, Simon and Schuster, 1959.

The Dead Beat, Simon and Schuster, 1960.

Firebug, Regency Books (Evanston, IL), 1961.

The Couch (based on the screenplay of same title; also see below), Fawcett, 1962.

Terror, Belmont-Tower, 1962.

The Star Stalker, Pyramid Publications, 1968.

(Under pseudonym Collier Young) *The Todd Dossier*, Delacorte, 1969.

It's All in Your Mind, Curtis Books (New York City), 1971.

Sneak Preview, Paperback Library (New York City), 1971.

Night-World, Simon and Schuster, 1972.

American Gothic, Simon and Schuster, 1974.

The Laughter of a Ghoul/What Every Young Ghoul Should Know, Necronomicon Press (West Warwick, RI), 1977.

There Is a Serpent in Eden, Zebra Books, 1979, as *The Cunning*, Zebra Books, 1981.

Strange Eons, Whispers Press (Browns Mills, NJ), 1979.

Psycho II, Warner, 1982.

The Night of the Ripper, Doubleday, 1984.

Unholy Trinity: Three Novels of Suspense (includes *The Scarf*, *The Dead Beat*, and *The Cover*), illustrated by Harris O. Morris, Scream Press (Santa Cruz, CA), 1986.

Out of My Head, NESFA Press (Cambridge, MA), 1986.

Screams (includes *The Will to Kill, Firebug,* and *The Star Stalker*), Underwood-Miller, 1989.
Lori, Tor, 1989.
Psycho House, Tor, 1990.
(With Andre Norton) *The Jekyll Legacy,* Tor, 1990.
Robert Bloch: Three Complete Novels (includes *Psycho, Psycho II,* and *Psycho House*), Wing Books (New York City), 1993.
Robert Bloch's Psychos, Pocket Books, 1998.

NONFICTION

The Eighth Stage of Fandom: Selections from 25 Years of Fan Writing, edited by Earl Kemp, Advent, 1962.
(With T. E. D. Klein and Fritz Leiber) *The First World Fantasy Convention: Three Authors Remember,* Necronomicon Press, 1980.
The Robert Bloch Companion: Collected Interviews, 1969-1986, compiled and edited by Randall D. Larson, Starmont House (Mercer Island, WA), 1989.
Once around the Bloch: An Unauthorized Autobiography, Tor, 1993.

EDITOR

The Best of Fredric Brown, Ballantine, 1977.
(With Martin Harry Greenberg) *Psycho-Paths,* Tor, 1991.
(With Martin Harry Greenberg) *Monsters in Our Midst,* Tor, 1993.

SCREENPLAYS

(With Owen Cump and Blake Edwards) *The Couch,* Warner Bros., 1962.
The Cabinet of Caligari, Twentieth Century-Fox, 1962.
Strait-Jacket, Columbia, 1964.
The Night Walker (also known as *The Dream Killer*), Universal, 1964.
The Skull, Paramount, 1965.
The Psychopath, Paramount, 1966.
(With Anthony Marriott) *The Deadly Bees,* Paramount, 1967.
Torture Garden, Columbia, 1967.
The House that Dripped Blood, Cinerama Releasing, 1970.
Asylum (also known as *The House of Crazies*), Cinerama Releasing, 1972.
(With others) *The Amazing Captain Nemo,* 1979.

RECORDINGS

Gravely, Robert Bloch, Alternate World Recordings, 1976.
(With Harlan Ellison) *Blood! The Life and Future Times of Jack the Ripper,* Alternate World Recordings, 1977.

OTHER

Also author of *Hell on Earth* and *Ghost Movies.* Author of sixty scripts for television series, including *Alfred Hitchcock Presents, Lock-Up, Thriller, I Spy, Run for Your Life, Star Trek, Journey to the Unknown,* and *Night Gallery.* Author of thirty-nine scripts for the radio series *Stay Tuned for Terror.* Work appears in over 350 anthologies and has been translated into twenty-five languages. Contributor to *The Science Fiction Novel: Imagination and Social Criticism,* edited by Basil Davenport, Advent (Chicago), 1959. Author of introduction to *The Night Walker* by Sidney Stuart (based on a screenplay by Bloch), Award Books, 1964. Former columnist for *Rogue* magazine. Contributor of over 500 short stories and articles, some under pseudonyms, to *Weird Tales, Playboy, Magazine of Fantasy and Science Fiction, Fantastic Adventures,* and other publications. Bloch's papers are housed in a permanent collection at the University of Wyoming American Heritage Centre, Laramie.

■ Adaptations

Bloch's fiction has been adapted into motion pictures, including *Psycho,* directed by Alfred Hitchcock, Paramount, 1960, and the remake of the same name directed by Gus Van Sant, Universal, 1998, and *The Skull* (adaptation of the story "The Skull of the Marquis de Sade"), Paramount, 1965. Bloch's characters from *Psycho* were used in the films *Psycho II,* 1983, *Psycho III,* 1986, and *Psycho IV: The Beginning,* 1990, works unrelated to Bloch's books.

■ Sidelights

An American novelist, short story writer, nonfiction writer, screenwriter, and journalist, Robert Bloch is respected for his contributions to the literary genres of horror fiction, crime fiction, and science fiction as well as to film, television, and radio. A prolific writer whose career spanned nearly sixty years, Bloch specialized in psychological horror. Claiming that he had no formal knowledge of psychology, he explored human psychopathology in works that are noted for combining humor and social consciousness with archetypal scenes of terror. Bloch is best known as the author of *Psycho*, a novel published in 1959 that was turned into a classic movie directed by Alfred Hitchcock and prompted several sequels by other directors. The book and films feature Norman Bates, a schizophrenic killer with extremely strong Oedipal tendencies who preys on the visitors to his family's hotel; Bloch followed *Psycho* with two sequels, *Psycho II* and *Psycho House.*

Throughout his works, Bloch attempted to get into the minds of pyromaniacs, rapists, kidnappers, madmen, and other sociopaths. Fascinated with Jack the Ripper, the notorious criminal who terrorized London during the latter part of the 1880s, he wrote a historically accurate novel, *The Night of the Ripper,* as well as a short story, "Yours Truly, Jack the Ripper" that is considered a classic of its genre. Bloch also created *The Jekyll Legacy,* a sequel to Robert Louis Stevenson's book *The Strange Case of Dr. Jekyll and Mr. Hyde* that he wrote with noted fantasist Andre Norton. Credited with helping to integrate the horror and crime genres with his works, Bloch also wrote well-received supernatural and science fiction in both novel and short story form; his science fiction ranged from witty parodies to longer books with themes regarding overpopulation and the future of humanity.

As a writer, Bloch characteristically blended horror and humor; written in an economic style, his novels, stories, and scripts are filled with suspense as well as irony, wordplay, and trick endings designed to catch his readers unaware. Although he is often playful, Bloch is ultimately considered a serious writer: praised for his understanding of human nature as well as his insight as a social critic, the author often used his characterizations of psychopaths to represent the deterioration of contemporary society and its values. As Stefan Dziemianowicz wrote in *St. James Guide to Horror, Ghost, & Gothic Writers,* in Bloch's works "it is the world outside the asylum that has become dangerously psychotic."

Reviewers generally acclaim Bloch's writings and have called several of his novels and short stories groundbreaking in their approaches; much of his genre fiction, especially his horror stories and science fiction tales, is considered classic in status. Writing in *Twentieth-Century Science-Fiction Writers,* Don D'Ammassa commented, "It is an unfortunate fact that Robert Bloch will probably always be identified as the man who wrote *Psycho.* Unfortunate, not because this wasn't a significant achievement, but because he has written so much other excellent fiction that seems doomed to exist forever in that very long shadow. . . . [Bloch had] an intuitive insight into the darkest recesses of the human psyche, and an inordinately effective flair for storytelling." Dziemianowicz of *St. James Guide to Horror* concluded, "Few weird-fiction writers have had careers as long or as significant as Robert Bloch's. Bloch's writing spanned seven decades of the 20th century, and his fiction helped to shape most of the trends in weird fiction that occurred during this interval. . . . Bloch was not a moralist so much as an ironist who must have found it intriguing that of all the horrors he explored in his life, the one that earned him his biggest audience was the one whose features most closely resembled theirs."

Born in Chicago to a father who worked as a bank cashier and a mother who was both a teacher and a social worker, Bloch grew up in the city and in the nearby suburb of Maywood; it was there, he wrote in *Contemporary Authors Autobiography Series (CAAS),* "society—and contemporary culture—began my informal education." He added, "What we learn in youth we often retain in age—and it certainly is a factor in fashioning what we may come to create." The science fiction writer and publisher Lester del Rey once described Bloch as a lonely youngster who turned to books and magazines for companionship. Queried about this portrayal in an interview in *Contemporary Authors New Revision Series (CANR),* Bloch responded, "I was something of an inaugurator in our neighborhood in all kinds of group activities. . . . I was always the one who fabricated these activities. But at the same time, I was more interested in things that didn't appeal to the others—books and history and art and that sort of thing. I couldn't discuss those things with them and I did a lot more reading. But I was neither sickly nor deprived of companionship nor out of sync with my own age group."

Bloch was allowed to skip ahead in school, beginning with second grade. A voracious reader—

An eerie scene from Alfred Hitchcock's 1960 adaptation of *Psycho*, which starred Anthony Perkins as the infamous Norman Bates.

he described himself in *CAAS* as "a victim of acute bibliophilia"—he read *Robinson Crusoe, Gulliver's Travels,* and *Don Quixote* by the age of ten and also devoured the historical romances of Erkmann-Chatrain; the sentimental stories of Ouida; and the humorous writings of Mark Twain, Ring Lardner, and Robert Benchley while developing, as he called it, "a morbid appetite for fantasy and the supernatural." Exploring the classics of the horror genre, Bloch was led to the monthly magazine *Weird Tales* and through it, as he stated in *CAAS,* to "its most illustrious and erudite contributor, H. P. Lovecraft." After moving to Milwaukee with his family, Bloch attended Lincoln High, a multicultural school; he wrote in *CAAS,* "Both my concern with comedy and fascination with the fantastic helped me through high school. To compensate for introversion I became an onstage extrovert, often using my own immaterial material. Self-conscious about such childish capers, I found

confidence through a continuing correspondence with Mr. Lovecraft, who encouraged me to believe I might develop writing skills of my own." In order to develop his writing talent, Bloch read classic authors such as Charles Dickens and Victor Hugo as well as such novels as *Crime and Punishment* and *War and Peace* and the works of contemporary American and British writers.

First Sales of Weird Tales

At sixteen, Bloch entered his senior year of high school and discovered that he had an IQ of 156. This fact, he noted in his autobiographical essay, "came as a cruel blow to some faculty members who believed the class comic deserved to be detested rather than tested." The principal of Lincoln High offered Bloch a college scholarship that was supplemented by the personal contribution of a family friend. However, he declined the offers; encouraged by H. P. Lovecraft, Bloch had decided to become a professional writer. Although he was a bit unsure of his decision—"I'd declined an education, but I didn't even know how to decline a sentence," Bloch wrote in *CAAS*—he sold a story to *Weird Tales* the month after graduation, and by the end of the year had sold four more. In his interview in *CANR*, Bloch recalled, "I had written and completed perhaps half a dozen stories before that first sale, plus two or three that appeared in amateur magazines, but that was all. I had been encouraged to write and to submit material by H. P. Lovecraft. It didn't take all that long. I lucked out."

In order to supplement his income, Bloch began writing campaign literature, advertising, speeches, and magazine articles in addition to genre fiction. In January 1935, Bloch published his short story "The Feast in the Abbey" in *Weird Tales;* a Gothic thriller influenced by Lovecraft and Edgar Allan Poe that contained a much-imitated surprise ending, the story was called "[o]ne of the most auspicious debuts in modern weird fiction" and "the consummate pulp horror tale" by Stefan Dziemianowicz in *St. James Guide to Horror, Ghost, & Gothic Writers.* Bloch became a member of the "Weird Tales Group," a band of writers including Ray Bradbury, August Derleth, Clark Ashton Smith, and Donald Wandrej who modeled their works after Lovecraft's fiction. In his story "The Slumber from the Stars," Bloch featured a character he called "a mystic dreamer of New England," an obvious homage to H. P. Lovecraft; the fantasist returned the favor in his story "The Haunter in the Dark" by disposing of a writer he called Robert Blake.

Before Lovecraft's death in 1937, Bloch had written several stories in the tradition of the author's cosmic mythology the Othulhu Mythos that introduced a more streamlined, character-driven approach. In 1938, Bloch wrote "Slave of the Flames," his first attempt at examining the inner workings of a pyromaniac; he would later publish a novel, *Firebug,* with a similar theme. In 1939, the author published what is considered one of his most important early stories, "The Cloak," the tale of a man whose rented Halloween costume empowers him with vampiric abilities. Over the next several years, he sold over a hundred stories, most of them horror tales, to a variety of magazines.

Among Bloch's most well-received early stories are his futuristic comic tales about Lefty Feep, a Runyonesque character whose adventures with the supernatural combine horror and slapstick. In 1943, Bloch wrote what is often considered his most popular story, "Yours Truly, Jack the Ripper." Set in modern Chicago, the tale—called "one of the finest horror stories ever written" by Don D'Ammassa in *Twentieth-Century Science-Fiction Writers*—suggests that Jack the Ripper has gained immortality by committing a series of ritual killings. Bloch wrote a series of radio plays for the program *Stay Tuned for Terror* in 1944 and 1945. His first novel, *The Scarf,* was published in 1947. The story of a psychotic strangler told in his own words, the book ends sympathetically with the narrator, novelist Daniel Morley, coming to a re-

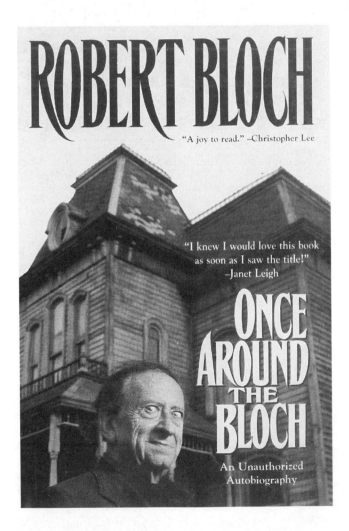

This 1993 autobiography appeared in bookstores shortly before Bloch's death in 1994.

alization of his condition; however, a revised edition published in 1966 places the character's obsession, in the words of R. E. Briney of *Twentieth-Century Crime and Mystery Writers,* in "an altogether more chilling perspective." When *The Scarf* first appeared in hardcover, Bloch included an autobiographical quote on the dust-jacket—"I have the heart of a small boy. I keep it in a jar on my desk."—that became a notorious quotation. During the remainder of the 1940s and 1950s, Bloch continued to publish novels and stories in the horror, crime, and science fiction genres. *The Kidnapper,* a novel about a psychopath published in 1954 that Briney called "cold, clinical, and unsparingly honest in treatment," was one of the author's favorites among his own works. In 1958, he commented in *CAAS,* "I wrote a novel called *Psycho* and sold it to the movies, where it was subsequently filmed by some director whose name I don't recall at the moment. . . ."

The Story of a Strange Hotel Clerk

Based on the case of Ed Gein, a mass murderer who terrorized Wisconsin in 1957, *Psycho* features Norman Bates, a schizoid, middle-aged mama's boy who commits a series of murders at an isolated hotel in western Kansas. Like Gein, he is a transvestite and taxidermist; in addition, Bates is obsessed, in the words of Walter Kendrick of the *Village Voice,* with "sex, death, embalming, [and] Mom." Among his victims is Mary Crane (called Marion in the film versions), a young woman carrying forty thousand stolen dollars who is knifed to death in the shower of her hotel room. Kendrick reported, "A whole generation has grown up with an irrational fear of cleanliness—and Robert Bloch started it all." Most reviewers of the time praised the novel both for its fright-inducing quality and its psychology. Writing in the *New York Times,* Anthony Boucher said that in *Psycho,* Bloch "is more chillingly effective than any writer might reasonably be expected to be. . . . Here Mr. Bloch demonstrates . . . that a believable history of mental illness can be more icily terrifying than all the arcane horrors summoned up by a collaboration of Poe and Lovecraft." James Sandoe of the *New York Herald Tribune Book Review* claimed that Bloch "manages as splendid a set of creeps as we've enjoyed in some time," while a reviewer in the *New Yorker* called *Psycho* a "thoroughly creepy tale" that contains "a series of absolutely jaw-dropping curtains." R. C. Briney

If you enjoy the works of Robert Bloch, you may also want to check out the following books and films:

The works of H. P. Lovecraft, including the stories "The Shadow over Innsmouth," "Cool Air," and "At the Mountains of Madness."
The tales of Edgar Allan Poe, including "William Wilson," "Ligeia," and "The Fall of the House of Usher."
The Haunting, a 1963 film based on Shirley Jackson's *The Haunting of Hill House.*

of *Twentieth-Century Crime and Mystery Writers* called the novel "the watershed of Bloch's career," while Tanita C. Kelly of the *Dictionary of Literary Biography* noted that *Psycho* "has remained the cornerstone of his reputation." Briney also noted that the story "has had a profound effect on both written and filmed suspense stories ever since."

When Alfred Hitchcock purchased *Psycho* for filming, he was mistakenly informed that Bloch was unavailable to write the screenplay. However, the success of Hitchcock's movie established Bloch as a writer of psychological suspense thrillers, and he began to receive a number of offers to write scripts for both film and television. In his autobiographical essay, the author noted that he was already in Hollywood before the film's production had begun, but the success of *Psycho*—which made Norman Bates a household name and spawned rubber knives, shower curtains, bath towels and other items as well as cartoons, jokes, and parodies—contributed to his visibility. Bloch's first teleplays were written for *Alfred Hitchcock Presents* and *The Alfred Hitchcock Hour;* he also wrote for *Thriller, I Spy, Star Trek,* and *Night Gallery,* among many others. Bloch also began writing screenplays for films, among which *The Couch,* a 1962 title about a rapist; *Strait-Jacket* and *The Night Walker,* two 1964 films directed by William Castle; *Torture Garden,* a 1968 anthology produced by the British studio Amicus Films; and *Asylum,* a movie released in 1972 in which an inmate takes control of an insane asylum, are considered his best.

After the publication of *Psycho,* Bloch continued to write novels and stories exploring the world of psychotics and the society that enables them. For example, *The Dead Beat,* a novel published in 1960, features a dangerous young con artist/musician; James Sandoe of *New York Herald Tribune Books* noted, "Mr. Bloch manipulates his narrative with speed, economy, bite, and with appropriately less ruthlessness than he needed last year for the compulsive *Psycho.* But then this is a different book, not by any means a lesser one." In 1974, he published *American Gothic,* a novel based on Herman W. Mudgett, a murderer who operated during the Chicago Exposition of 1893. In this book, wrote Newgate Callendar of the *New York Times Book Review,* Bloch "really has created an American gothic, complete with castles, hidden passageways, and terrified inmates." In 1979, he published *Strange Eons,* a science fiction novel set in the future during an international disaster that is considered both an homage to Lovecraft and a work among Bloch's finest contributions to the genre.

Beyond *Psycho*

The author returned to the world of Norman Bates in two subsequent novels, *Psycho II,* published in 1982, and *Psycho House,* published in 1990. *Psycho II* picks up where the first novel left off, with Bates in a state hospital for the criminally insane. After he escapes by killing a nun and donning her habit, Norman makes his way to Hollywood—murdering all the way—where the movie about his life is about to be filmed. Writing in *Booklist,* Connie Fletcher commented that Bloch "tries so hard to equal the suspense of *Psycho* that he subverts its sequel in the process; this reads more like a teenage monster movie than a sophisticated psychological shocker." Walter Kendrick of the *Village Voice* called *Psycho II* "a haunted book," adding, "Hitchcock made *Psycho* immortal in spite of itself and allowed *Psycho II* to come into being, but the fate of the sequel is in its own hands. Read it quickly, before the paper-shredders arrive." However, Michael E. Stamm of *Science Fiction & Fantasy Book Review,* calling the book "pure-quill Bloch," noted that *Psycho II* "can't have the impact of the original. It isn't as much an exercise in sustained terror as it is a *tour de force,* for it takes place in a world wherein Norman Bates find himself to be an institution, something beyond himself. And if he wasn't sane before. . . ." In an interview in *CANR,* Bloch commented that "*Psycho II* deals with the whole phe-

nomenon of what's coming down today in mystery and suspense and fantasy, and the effect it has on us all."

According to R. E. Briney, the final book in Bloch's trilogy, *Psycho House,* deals with "the exploitation of violence." Set ten years after Bates's death, the novel describes how crime writer Amy Haines, who has traveled to Fairvale, Kansas, to research a book about Norman, becomes involved in solving—at her own peril—a murder that has just been committed at a tourist trap recreation of Bates House and Motel. Sybil Steinberg of *Publishers Weekly* called *Psycho House* "a disappointing effort," concluding that though Bloch "provides all the elements of a horror story, they fail to coalesce into a truly frightening yarn." John Lawson of *School Library Journal* praised Bloch's fine "storytelling skills," and "his masterful use of tension and suspense." Lawson also predicted that the subject matter and Bloch's name alone would win the favor of its young adult readers. Writing in *Wilson Library Bulletin,* Gene LaFaille commented that the first chapter of *Psycho House* "grips your subconscious" before calling the novel "an enjoyable, light reading experience that mystery fans, as well as horror readers, will find entertaining." Assessing the *Psycho* trilogy, Stefan Dziemianowicz concluded that it is Bloch's "most powerful examination of the social ills and evils that inculcate sociopathic behaviour."

Before his death in 1994, Bloch attended many seminars, workshops, and fan conventions on fantasy, science fiction, horror, mystery writing, and film, usually as guest of honor or toastmaster; he also conducted workshops and seminars in these areas. Throughout his career, Bloch was given several awards by fans, including the World Fantasy Life Achievement Award in 1975. Writing in *CAAS* about the state of contemporary horror films, Bloch noted, "I still believe it takes a certain amount of artistry to induce goose-pimples, and that the most eerie effects depend upon stimulating an audience's imagination to become a partner in peril. But the gross-out is a cop-out. Any ape can shove a finger down your throat and make you vomit. The same, of course, holds true in writing for the printed media. A good page-turner is not just a stomach-turner. Again, I think working on a reader's imagination is equivalent to working on the imagination of an audience; in both cases an ounce of suggestion, properly employed, is worth a gallon of gore. Yes, I wrote a book called *Psycho*—but its murder scene in a shower is a far cry from the bloodbaths of today."

In evaluating his career, Bloch concluded, "I cannot assess my own work objectively. No writer can, for all writers are mothers. Our stories are our children—we created them, our minds were their wombs. . . . After giving birth we nursed them, fussed over them until they were ready to be sent out into the world. Some failed, some succeeded, but even when they were established in print with a life of their own we continued to fret about their fate. For better or worse, they bore our names and each inherited a small portion of our identity. Over the long years I have borne many offspring—some big, some small, some weak, some strong, some grave and earnest, some frivolous and dedicated solely to pleasure. My children are ugly and attractive, kindly and cruel, realistic and hyper-imaginative. Some, perhaps, are a trifle mad. Their fate is mine to share, and, like all parents I am frequently surprised at just how they turned out after they went on their own. But whatever life in print may be, I look upon them with tolerance—and, sometimes, love."

■ Works Cited

Bloch, Robert, interview with Jean W. Ross in *Contemporary Authors New Revision Series,* Volume 5, 1984, pp. 62-66.

Bloch, Robert, essay in *Contemporary Authors Autobiography Series,* Volume 20, Gale, 1994, pp. 35-54.

Boucher, Anthony, review of *Psycho, New York Times,* April 19, 1959, p. 25.

Briney, R. E., entry in *Twentieth-Century Crime and Mystery Writers,* edited by Lesley Henderson, 3rd edition, St. James Press, 1991, pp. 103-5.

Callendar, Newgate, review of *American Gothic, New York Times Book Review,* June 30, 1974, pp. 32-33.

D'Ammassa, Don, entry in *Twentieth-Century Science-Fiction Writers,* edited by Noelle Watson and Paul E. Schellinger, 3rd edition, St. James Press, 1991, pp. 58-61,

Dziemianowicz, Stefan, entry in *St. James Guide to Horror, Ghost, & Gothic Writers,* edited by David Pringle, 1st edition, St. James Press, 1998, pp. 66-69.

Fletcher, Connie, review of *Psycho II, Booklist,* July, 1982, p. 1393.

Kelly, Tanita C., "Robert Bloch," *Dictionary of Literary Biography,* Volume 44: *American Screenwriters,* Gale, 1986, pp. 41-47.

Kendrick, Walter, "The Real Norman Bates," *Village Voice,* September 28, 1982, pp. 1, 46, 48.

LaFaille, Gene, review of *Psycho House, Wilson Library Journal,* October, 1990, p. 111.

Lawson, John, review of *Psycho House, School Library Journal,* August, 1998, p. 174.

Review of *Psycho, New Yorker,* June 6, 1959, pp. 159-60.

Sandoe, James, review of *Psycho, New York Herald Tribune Book Review,* April 26, 1959, p. 11.

Sandoe, James, review of *The Dead Beat, New York Herald Tribune Book Review,* May 26, 1960, p. 12.

Stamm, Michael E., review of *Psycho II, Science Fiction & Fantasy Book Review,* December, 1982, pp. 17-18.

Steinberg, Sybil, review of *Psycho House, Publishers Weekly,* January 12, 1990, p. 48.

■ For More Information See

BOOKS

Contemporary Literary Criticism, Volume 33, Gale, 1985, pp. 82-86.

Daniels, Les, *Living in Fear: A History of Horror in the Mass Media,* Scribners, 1975.

Flanagan, Graeme, editor, *Robert Bloch: A Bio-Bibliography,* Graeme Flanagan, 1979.

Hall, Graham M., *Robert Bloch Bibliography,* Graham M. Hall, 1965.

Larson, Randall D., *Robert Bloch,* Starmount House and Borgo Press, 1986.

Larson, Randall D., compiler and editor, *The Complete Robert Bloch: An Illustrated Bibliography,* Farday, 1986, Borgo Press, 1987.

Larson, Randall D., compiler and editor, *The Robert Bloch Companion: Collected Interviews, 1969-1986,* Starmont House, 1989.

Lovecraft, H. P., *Selected Letters V, 1934-1937,* edited by August Derleth and James Turner, Arkham, 1976.

Matheson, Richard, and Ricia Mainhardt, editors, *Robert Bloch: Appreciations of the Master,* Tor, 1995.

Moskowitz, Sam, *Seekers of Tomorrow,* World Publishing, 1966.

Naremore, James, *Filmguide to Psycho,* Indiana University Press, 1973.

Prosser, Harold Lee, *The Man Who Walked through Mirrors: Robert Bloch as Social Critic,* Borgo Press, 1989.

Weinberg, Robert, *The 'Weird Tales' Story*, FAX Collector's Editions, 1977.

PERIODICALS

Algol, spring, 1978.
Analog, December, 1993.
Armchair Detective, fall, 1994.
Booklist, June 1, 1974; June 1, 1977, p. 1484-85; February 1, 1978; March 1, 1979, p. 1042; June 15, 1979.
Books West, October, 1977.
Chicago Tribune, September 25, 1994, section 2, p. 6.
Fantasy Newsletter, January, 1981.
Films and Filming, February, 1972, pp. 26-30.
Films in Review, August-September, 1968.
Harper's Magazine, October, 1989, pp. 45-53.
Kirkus, March 1, 1960.
Library Journal, August, 1972.

Locus, October 27, 1975; June 30, 1976; July, 1993; February, 1994.
Los Angeles Times, March 12, 1980.
New Worlds, May, 1963; July, 1967.
New Yorker, September 10, 1960.
New York Times, December 9, 1945; September 28, 1947; September 25, 1994, p. 48.
New York Times Book Review, June 5, 1960; August 6, 1972, p. 24.
Robert Bloch Fanzine (Los Altos, CA), 1973.
San Francisco Chronicle, May 10, 1959; June 19, 1960.
Saturday Review, November 24, 1945; August 26, 1972, pp. 61-62.
Science Fiction Review, May, 1977; February, 1978.
Starship, summer, 1979.
Thrust, fall, 1979.
Times (London), September 26, 1994, p. 21.
Washington Post, September 25, 1994, p. B6.
Washington Post Book World, October 8, 1995.

—Sketch by Gerard J. Senick

Lilian Jackson Braun

■ Personal

Born c. 1916, in Massachusetts; married first husband (an accountant); married Earl Bettinger (an actor), 1979.

■ Addresses

Agent—Blanche C. Gregory, Inc., 2 Tudor Place, New York, NY 10017. *Office*—Putnam Berkley Group, 200 Madison Avenue, New York, NY 10016.

■ Career

Mystery writer. Crowley Knower Company, Detroit, MI, freelance advertising copywriter; Ernst Kern Department Store, Detroit, began as advertising copywriter, became public relations director; *Detroit Free Press*, Detroit, editor, 1948-78.

■ Awards, Honors

Edgar Award nomination, Mystery Writers of America, 1986, for *The Cat Who Saw Red*.

■ Writings

"THE CAT WHO . . ." MYSTERY SERIES

The Cat Who Could Read Backwards, Dutton, 1966.
The Cat Who Ate Danish Modern, Dutton, 1967.
The Cat Who Turned On and Off, Dutton, 1968.
The Cat Who Saw Red, Jove, 1986.
The Cat Who Played Brahms, Jove, 1987.
The Cat Who Played Post Office, Jove, 1987.
The Cat Who Knew Shakespeare, Jove, 1988.
The Cat Who Had Fourteen Tales (short stories), Jove, 1988.
The Cat Who Sniffed Glue, Putnam, 1988.
The Cat Who Went Underground, Putnam, 1989.
The Cat Who Talked to Ghosts, Putnam, 1990.
The Cat Who Lived High, Putnam, 1990.
The Cat Who Knew a Cardinal, Putnam, 1991.
The Cat Who Wasn't There, Putnam, 1992.
The Cat Who Moved a Mountain, Putnam, 1992.
The Cat Who Went into the Closet, Putnam, 1993.
The Cat Who Came to Breakfast, Putnam, 1994.
Lilian Braun: Three Complete Novels (contains *The Cat Who Knew Shakespeare, The Cat Who Sniffed Glue,* and *The Cat Who Went Underground*), Putnam, 1994.
The Cat Who Blew the Whistle, Putnam, 1995.
The Cat Who Said Cheese, Putnam, 1996.
Three Complete Novels (contains *The Cat Who Wasn't There, The Cat Who Went into the Closet,* and *The Cat Who Came to Breakfast*), Putnam, 1996.
The Cat Who Sang for the Birds, Putnam, 1998.
The Cat Who Tailed a Thief, Putnam, 1998.
The Cat Who Saw Stars, Putnam, 1998.

OTHER

Work represented in anthologies, including *Mystery Cats: Feline Felonies by Modern Masters of Mystery*, Dutton, 1991, and *More Mystery Cats*, Dutton, 1993. Regular columnist, *Lilian Jackson Braun Newsletter*; contributor to *Ellery Queen's Mystery Magazine*.

■ Work In Progress

The Cat Who Robbed the Bank, expected in 2000.

■ Adaptations

The Cat Who . . . Companion: The Complete Guide to Lilian Jackson Braun's Beloved Cat Who . . . *Mysteries—with Plot Summaries, Character Lists, a Moose County Map, and More!*, was written by Sharon A. Feaster, an avid fan of the series, for Berkley, 1998.

■ Sidelights

Former advertising copywriter and newspaper editor-turned-novelist Lilian Jackson Braun has made a name for herself and won a large and loyal audience with her carefully crafted, witty, and highly entertaining "The Cat Who . . ." mystery series. Since her debut, *The Cat Who Could Read Backwards*, the author has completed more than twenty novels in the popular series. While that in itself is impressive, what is even more striking is the fact that the prolific Braun is a spry octogenarian who wrote her first three books in the mid-1960s only to abandon her literary career until 1986—a hiatus of eighteen years. Since then, she has made up for lost time, turning out a number of novels and giving no indications that she is ready to slow down. Reviewing Braun's 1994 novel, *The Cat Who Came to Breakfast,* a critic for *Kirkus Reviews* commented that, "Like Agatha Christie resolutely keeping up British standards in the face of a shrinking Empire, Braun maintains the forms of the American cozy [mystery story]." When Catherine Nelson of *Armchair Detective* asked Braun in a 1991 interview how long she intended to keep writing her trademark series, the author responded with characteristic verve. "Psychologically I'm 39, and physically I'm about 50. I don't think about it," she said.

Braun was born around 1916 in Massachusetts, where she spent her early years. Her family moved to Detroit in the late 1920s, when she was in her early teens. The eldest of three children, Braun came from a creative family; both her parents were imaginative, resourceful people who encouraged their children to think for themselves. Braun's father was an inventor, her mother a born raconteur. The latter, in particular, sparked her daughter's passion for storytelling at an early age. Braun recalled in her 1991 interview with Nelson how, each day at the family dinner table, her mother would recount the events of her day and then ask her two daughters and their younger brother to exercise their own imaginations to do the same thing. "I really think I learned how to describe situations, events, people, and scenery through that early custom in our family," Braun explained to Nelson.

Great Depression Charts Course as Writer

Young Braun was precocious, and she was just three years old when her mother taught her to write so that she could correspond with her grandmother. This early interest in words stayed with Braun. She was fifteen when she began selling "poems" about baseball—written in prose and under a pen name—to the *Detroit News* and other publications. Surprisingly, Braun did not dream of becoming a writer, but rather a school teacher. She might well have done so, had the Great Depression not hit Detroit hard, ending Braun's plans to attend college. Instead, she began writing baseball poems for the *News* on a daily basis, earning $12 per week for doing so. When the baseball season ended she went knocking on the doors of Detroit retail stores, trying to sell them advertising poems. She was eventually hired by the Crowley Knower Company in 1929 to work as an advertising copywriter for a local department store. Braun did so well that a year later she was offered a better job by the Ernst Kern Company, which ran one of the other stores in town. There she settled in for the next eighteen years, working her way up to become public relations director at Ernst Kern. In 1948 Braun decided it was time for a career change. She took an editing job at the *Detroit Free Press*, remaining with the newspaper until she retired in 1978.

Throughout her early life Braun had written short stories as a hobby, although few were ever published. An incident that occurred in the early 1950s prompted her to begin writing about cats; it would also change the course of her life. Braun adored a porcelain figurine of a Siamese cat that someone had given her, and so her husband gave her a real flesh-and-blood feline as a fortieth birthday gift. She adored the animal, which she named Koko after a character in the well-known Gilbert and Sullivan operetta *The Mikado.* Unfortunately, Koko was killed when it fell from the balcony of Braun's tenth floor apartment; neighbors speculated that the cat had been pushed. Braun, feeling angry and sad, began having nightmares about the incident. As a kind of self-help therapy, she wrote a short story called "The Sin of Madama Phloi." "It was not a re-enactment of the incident, but it was inspired by what happened," Braun explained to Nelson. "In it, [a] murdered cat was avenged—which seemed to help me cope with [Koko's senseless death]."

Feline Adventures Prove Popular with Readers

Braun's literary agent sent the story to *Ellery Queen's Mystery Magazine,* where it was published. When the editor asked for another, Braun responded by penning "Phut Phat Concentrates." When that story also proved successful, Braun began sending the magazine one cat mystery story per year for each of the next five years. After two of the stories were included in an anthology published by E. P. Dutton, an editor at the Manhattan-based publishing house asked Braun to write a mystery novel with a cat in it. Although she was busy with her job and married life, Braun felt "one doesn't turn down a request from a publisher," as she later told Nelson.

The Cat Who Could Read Backwards, Braun's first novel, was published in 1966. That book featured a Siamese tom cat named K'o-Kung (Koko, for short) and his amateur detective owner Jim Qwilleran ("Qwill" to his friends), a middle-aged, former big city crime reporter. Qwilleran has just gone through a messy divorce and is drinking too much, so he tries to start over in a small midwestern town, where he lands a job on a newspaper called the *Daily Fluxion.* Qwilleran is hired by an old friend who edits the paper, and is assigned to the local art beat, although he knows little about the subject. Once on the job, Qwilleran soon discovers the petty jealousies and rivalries among the characters in the local art com-

In this 1967 novel reporter Jim Qwilleran, along with his extraordinary felines Koko and Yum-Yum, must solve the murder of a woman whose exclusive home was featured in Qwilleran's magazine.

munity, which also involve the *Fluxion'*s own critic, George Bonifield Mountclemens III. When an artist is murdered, Qwilleran's crime reporter background and his own innate curiosity inevitably draw him and Koko into the mystery. Critical reception to *The Cat Who Could Read Backwards* was mixed. A *Library Journal* critic dismissed the novel as "weak on plot and strong on K'o-Kung," while Anthony Boucher of the *New York Times Book Review* described it as "a highly rewarding first novel," even if its author did have "a great deal to learn."

Despite such lukewarm assessments, Braun's debut novel sold well enough that Dutton asked for two sequels. Braun responded by writing *The Cat Who Ate Danish Modern* and *The Cat Who Turned On and Off*, both of which featured Koko, Qwilleran, and a young female Siamese cat named Yum-Yum, who have become the three most prominent recurring characters in Braun's "The Cat Who . . ." mysteries. *The Cat Who Ate Danish Modern* takes Qwilleran and his feline friends into the world of interior decorating; *The Cat Who Turned On and Off* involves antique dealers. Reviews for both books were varied. "A ton of cat drool to only a peck of proper murder mystery," a British reviewer quipped about *The Cat Who Ate Danish Modern* in the *Times Literary Supplement*, but a *Publishers Weekly* critic praised *The Cat Who Turned On and Off* as a "witty treatment of a curious animal whose curiosity helps to catch a killer."

Lull in Novels Followed by More Cat Tales

By now, Braun was beginning to enjoy writing her cat mystery novels. She had already written a fourth book, *The Cat Who Ordered Caviar*, when Dutton informed her that the company was no longer interested in publishing her work. Around this same time, in 1967, Braun's husband of twenty-four years died. Although Braun continued to create short stories, she abandoned novels and concentrated, until her 1978 retirement, on her job at the *Detroit Free Press*. She remarried the following year, her second husband being actor Earl Bettinger.

One day Bettinger read *The Cat Who Ordered Caviar*, and he encouraged his wife to clean it up and resubmit it to publishers under a new title: *The Cat Who Saw Red*. To Braun's surprise, Berkley bought it and the book appeared in 1986, eighteen years after publication of her previous novel. The reappearance of Qwilleran—now a restaurant critic in a small town called Mooseville—Koko, and Yum-Yum after so many years did not attract a lot of media attention, but those critics who did read the book reacted favorably; for example, a *Publishers Weekly* reviewer commented that "Although Braun . . . occasionally verges on the cutesy, she offers here a delightful tale." Even more important to Braun than any reviews was the fact that *The Cat Who Saw Red* sold strongly and was nominated for an Edgar, an award given

annually by the Mystery Writers of America. As a result, Berkley offered Braun a contract to write ten more mystery novels.

In the years since, Braun has written eighteen more "The Cat Who . . ." mysteries and a book of cat stories, the latter being the only book she has done outside the series. Braun generally starts each new book by coming up with a catchy title; from there, she invents a good mystery to go with it. Oddly enough, Braun commented, the series title, "The Cat Who . . ." just came to her "out of the blue" one day. Each of the works involves

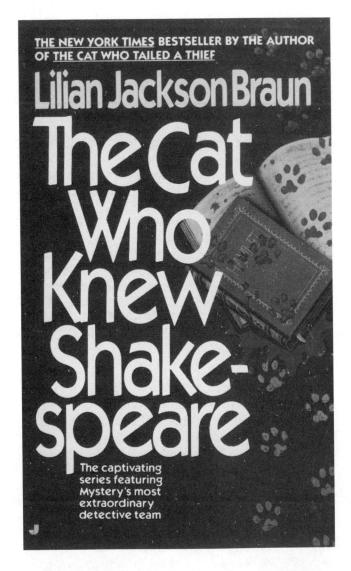

An unusual edition of Shakespeare may be the key to solving a murder in the small town of Pickax in this 1978 work.

Qwilleran, Koko, Yum Yum, and a variety of other characters who turn up from time to time, in intriguing mysteries that play out against different backdrops. "Being a Gemini, I like variety," Braun admitted to Nelson.

If you enjoy the works of Lilian Jackson Braun, you may also want to check out the following books and films:

Bruce Alexander, *Blind Justice*, 1994.
Rita Mae Brown, *Wish You Were Here*, 1990.
Sheila Rousseau Murphy, *Cat on the Edge*, 1996.
Call Northside 777, a film starring Jimmy Stewart, 1948.

Variety is reflected in the series through such things as plot. *The Cat Who Talked to Ghosts* (1990), for example, deals with strange goings-on at a historical museum in Qwilleran's hometown; *The Cat Who Knew a Cardinal*, (1991) with the theatre; *The Cat Who Came to Breakfast* (1994) with a redevelopment scheme at a resort hotel; and *The Cat Who Blew the Whistle* (1995) with railroading. Murder just seems to follow Qwilleran and his cats wherever they go. "The most difficult part of any of my books is figuring out what a cat can do to alert Qwilleran to solve the mystery," Braun told Nelson. "That's the crux of the whole thing. When I know that, I'm all set."

Braun, her husband, and their four Siamese cats—Koko III, Yum-Yum, Pitti-Sing, and Pooh-Bah—spend summers in Michigan and winters at their home in the foothills of the Blue Ridge Mountains in western North Carolina. Braun's husband tends to the house and does the cooking, leaving Braun free to concentrate on writing, when she feels like it. "I'm very casual about the whole thing," Braun admitted to Nelson. Writing can "be a very selfish and demanding occupation. Particularly if you have a deadline to meet." Now in her eighties, Braun is "officially retired" and has had cataract surgery to correct eyesight problems, yet she continues to meet those deadlines, and to write mysteries that satisfy her legions of loyal readers. "Braun's plots are always original. The murder victims are the rich and famous as well as the poor," Carol Barry noted in *Twentieth-Century Crime and Mystery Writers*. "The murders are both surprising and shocking, but the dialogue, the local color, and the characters make up more of the story than the act of murder itself."

■ Works Cited

Barry, Carol, "Lilian Braun," *Twentieth-Century Crime and Mystery Writers*, St. James Press, 1991.

Boucher, Anthony, review of *The Cat Who Could Read Backwards*, *New York Times Book Review*, March 6, 1966, p. 38.

Review of *The Cat Who Ate Danish Modern*, *Times Literary Supplement*, June 6, 1968, p. 603.

Review of *The Cat Who Came to Breakfast*, *Kirkus Reviews*, January 1, 1994, p. 18.

Review of *The Cat Who Could Read Backwards*, *Library Journal*, May 1, 1966, p. 2368.

Review of *The Cat Who Saw Red*, *Publishers Weekly*, March 28, 1986, p. 55.

Review of *The Cat Who Turned On and Off*, *Publishers Weekly*, September 30, 1968, pp. 60-61.

Nelson, Catherine, "The Lady Who . . .," *Armchair Detective*, fall, 1991, pp. 388-98.

■ For More Information See

BOOKS

St. James Guide to Crime and Mystery Writers, St. James Press, 1996.

PERIODICALS

Armchair Detective, spring, 1996, p. 233.

Booklist, August, 1992, p. 1997; February 15, 1993, p. 1038; May 15, 1993, p. 1716; December 1, 1994, p. 635.

Cat Fancy, November, 1994, pp. 40-43; December 1, 1994, p. 635.

Globe & Mail (Toronto), December 17, 1988.

Library Journal, May 1, 1991, p. 123; November 15, 1992, p. 120; March 1, 1993, p. 112; May 1, 1993, p. 130; December, 1994, p. 138.

New York Times Book Review, June 18, 1967, p. 37; January 12, 1969, p. 43; April 2, 1989, p. 33; May 19, 1991, p. 45.

Observer, July 16, 1967, p. 21; March 16, 1968, p. 29; March 24, 1968, p. 29; July 27, 1969, p. 25.

Publishers Weekly, July 8, 1988, p. 29; March 22, 1991, p. 73; October 11, 1991, p. 52; January 25, 1993, p. 80; January 17, 1994, p. 412; January 16, 1995, p. 40; October 19, 1998, p. 42; November 16, 1998, p. 57.

Saturday Review, March 26, 1966, p. 35.

School Library Journal, August, 1988, p. 196.

Times Literary Supplement, September 21, 1967, p. 844; September 18, 1969, p. 1018.

Tribune Books (Chicago), October 19, 1986, p. 5; January 7, 1990, p. 6.*

—Sketch by Ken Cuthbertson

Edwidge Danticat

■ Personal

Name pronounced "Ed-*weedj* Dan-ti-*cah*"; born January 19, 1969, in Port-au-Prince, Haiti; immigrated to the United States, 1981; daughter of Andre (a cab driver) and Rose (a textile worker; maiden name, Napoleon) Danticat. *Education:* Barnard College, 1990; Brown University, M.F.A., 1993.

■ Addresses

Office—c/o Soho Press, 853 Broadway, No. 1903, New York, NY 10003.

■ Career

Freelance writer, 1994—. *Member:* Alpha Kappa Alpha.

■ Awards, Honors

National Book Award finalist, 1995, for *Krik? Krak!*; named one of *Granta*'s Best of American Novelists, 1996; Pushcart Prize for short fiction.

■ Writings

FICTION

Breath, Eyes, Memory, Soho Press (New York City), 1994.
Krik? Krak! (short stories), Soho Press, 1995.
The Farming of Bones, Soho Press, 1998.

■ Sidelights

Fiction writer Edwidge Danticat had accomplished the twin literary feats of winning a Pushcart Prize for short fiction and being nominated for the prestigious National Book Award before she reached the age of thirty. Concentrating her focus on the life that she left behind in Haiti and her personal experiences as an immigrant to the United States, Danticat writes from the point of view of a young woman of color who realizes all to quickly that the attributes she possesses are of little value in either culture. Her novels include *Breath, Eyes, Memory* and *The Farming of Bones,* and her short fiction has been collected in the highly acclaimed *Krik? Krak!* As *Boston Globe* contributor Jordana Hart commented, Danticat "has given the world honest and loving portraits of Haitian people, both on the island and in the United States. She has smashed the numbing stereotypes created by a barrage of media accounts of Haitian poverty, misery and death."

Born in Haiti's capital city of Port-au-Prince, in 1969, Danticat lived in the West Indies until the age of twelve. In 1973, she moved in with her aunt when her parents emigrated to New York City. Danticat joined them there in 1981, but found it difficult to fit in at the Brooklyn junior high school she attended; raised with the French Creole language spoken in Haiti, she had a strong accent, and her clothing and hairstyle were much different than that of her New York classmates, who had been raised on American television and grooved to the sound of rap music. She also encountered prejudice among New York's ethnic

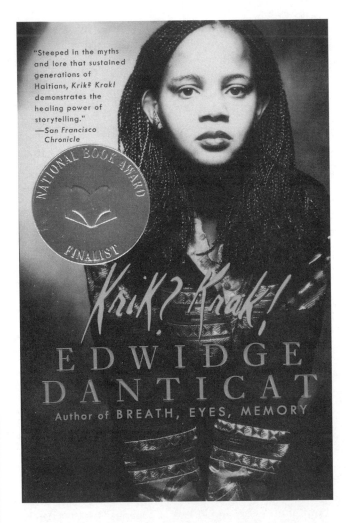

"Steeped in the myths and lore that sustained generations of Haitians, *Krik? Krak!* demonstrates the healing power of storytelling."
—San Francisco Chronicle

NATIONAL BOOK AWARD FINALIST

Krik? Krak!

EDWIDGE DANTICAT

Author of BREATH, EYES, MEMORY

This 1995 collection of short stories is rooted in Danticat's homeland of Haiti.

immigrant community, since by the early 1980s Haitian boat people had become a problem for the U.S. government, which was trying to control their entry into the country. As Danticat explained to *New York Times* contributor Garry Pierre-Pierre, "'Haitian' was like a curse. People were calling you, 'Frenchy, go back to the banana boat,' and a lot of the kids would lie about where they came from. They would say anything but Haitian." Fortunately for Danticat, she found an outlet for her loneliness in her writing; by creating stories she was able to return to her native land, at least in her own imagination.

Finds Solace through Fiction

Although she began to assimilate more into U.S. teen culture, Danticat continued to write during her high school years. This early work evolved into her first novel, *Breath, Eyes, Memory*. Encouraged by her father to pursue a career in health care, Danticat enrolled at one of New York City's many specialized high schools, intending to become a nurse. But writing proved far more seductive, and she eventually abandoned her nursing studies to concentrate on developing her writer's voice. During her undergraduate studies at Barnard College, Danticat earned her bachelor's degree in English, and then an early version of *Breath, Eyes, Memory* served as her thesis at Brown University, where she received her master's degree in 1993. The book was picked up by a New York publisher and appeared in bookstores a year later.

Breath, Eyes, Memory is the first novel written entirely in English by a Haitian woman; not surprisingly, like Danticat's other works, it honors the ties between women. Four generations of Caco women—Sophie, her mother, her grandmother Ifee, and Sophie's own daughter, Brigitte—draw strength from each other as well as from themselves in attempting to rise beyond the poverty, racism, and violence they encounter, both in the West Indies and the United States. Their lives reflect those of many Haitians. The birthplace of voodooism and one of the poorest nations in the Western hemisphere, Haiti has long been plagued by political, economic, and social hardship. Those—like Sophie and her mother—who emigrate from its shores have been viewed with suspicion abroad, while those—like Ifee—who have stayed home have suffered through a succession of violent political upheavals.

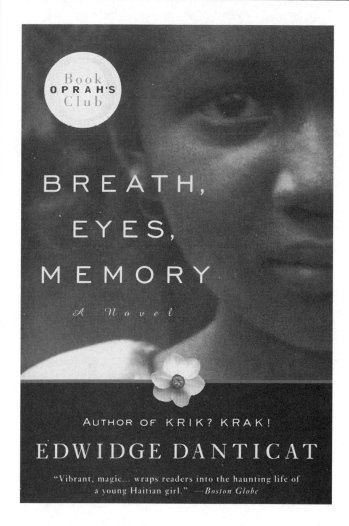

BREATH,
EYES,
MEMORY
A Novel

AUTHOR OF KRIK? KRAK!

EDWIDGE DANTICAT

"Vibrant, magic... wraps readers into the haunting life of
a young Haitian girl." —*Boston Globe*

Danticat chronicles the lives of four Haitian women from four generations struggling to survive poverty, racism, and violence in this 1994 novel.

Focuses on Women's Struggles

Like the author herself, the protagonist of Danticat's *Breath, Eyes, Memory* spent the first twelve years of her life in Haiti. It is when she comes to the United States that Sophie Caco's life and that of Danticat part ways. Responding to her mother Martine's pleas to join her in New York, Sophie travels to the United States. There, she learns an unsettling truth: she was conceived when her mother was raped. She also realizes that the still-traumatized Martine has been unable to come to terms with the violence done to her, even after fleeing from Haiti and attempting to make a new life for herself. While Martine continues a downward spiral toward self-destruction, young Sophie must try to care for both her mother and

herself, and cope with the circumstances of her birth. A return to Haiti after her mother's death brings Sophie an understanding of her mother's life and of the legacy that has been handed down to her through the lives and hardships endured by generations of Haitian women.

But *Breath, Eyes, Memory* does more than document women's struggles. It also covers a broad swath of modern Haitian history, including the twenty-nine hard years—from 1957 to 1986—during which Haiti was ruled by the ruthless dictatorship of the Duvalier family. As grim as Danticat's subject matter sometimes becomes as her characters attempt to survive their oppression, she is able to rise above this darkness through her lyric style and poetic language. *Breath, Eyes, Memory* is "a novel that rewards a reader again and again with small but exquisite and unforgettable epiphanies," reviewer Bob Shacochis commented in *Washington Post Book World*. "You can actually see Danticat grow and mature, come into her own strength as a writer, throughout the course of this quiet, soul-penetrating story about four generations of women trying to hold on to one another in the Haitian diaspora."

Oprah Appearance Brings National Attention

Although Danticat was an unknown writer with just one book to her credit, she found instant fame after popular television talk-show host Oprah Winfrey included *Breath, Eyes, Memory* in an edition of her popular book club. As a means of encouraging women to read, Winfrey regularly profiles new novels and invites authors to come on her show. After Danticat's appearance in June of 1998, the young author became a fledgling media star.

At the same time, Danticat's literary debut sparked controversy in the Haitian-American community. Some of the young novelist's fellow Haitians disapproved of her description of the traditional Haitian practice of "testing," as depicted in *Breath, Eyes, Memory*. Female virginity is prized in Haitian culture, and in the novel Sophie's aunt "tests" to see whether Sophie's hymen is intact by inserting her fingers into the girl's vagina. Most Haitian immigrants to the U.S. have abandoned this primarily rural practice, and many felt that by including this custom in the novel Danticat would cause Haitian-American women to

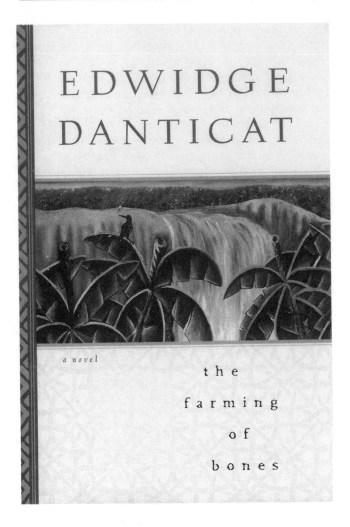

EDWIDGE DANTICAT

a novel

the

farming

of

bones

Danticat describes the 1937 massacre of hundreds of Haitians trying to escape poverty and oppression by Dominican Republic dictator Rafael Leonard Trujillo Molina.

be viewed with continued suspicion, as primitive and abusive.

Despite the mixed response from her own people, American critics praised *Breath, Eyes, Memory*, comparing the novel with the works of African American author Alice Walker; *Ms.* contributor Joan Philpott hailed it as being intensely lyrical, while Jim Gladstone wrote in the *New York Times Book Review* that *Breath, Eyes, Memory* "achieves an emotional complexity that lifts it out of the realm of the potboiler and into that of poetry."

Danticat followed her debut with a 1995 collection of short stories called *Krik? Krak!* The book, which was named as a finalist for the annual

National Book Award, takes its quirky title from the practice of Haitian storytellers. As Danticat explained to *Essence* interviewer Deborah Gregory, storytelling is a popular entertainment in Haiti, where the storyteller customarily inquires of his or her audience, "Krik?," meaning, "Are you ready to listen?" Listeners respond with an enthusiastic "Krak!"

Stories Tell the History of Haiti

A sense of Haiti's tragic history pervades the stories in *Krik? Krak!* The island is home to Africans, who were enslaved and brought there to harvest the sugar cane and other crops introduced by French landowners; Haiti occupies the western third of the Caribbean island of Hispaniola, and the country is separated from its neighbor, the Dominican Republic, by an inland mountain chain. As Danticat quotes a Haitian proverb in one of her stories, "Beyond the mountains there are mountains." In *Krik? Krak!* Danticat introduces a wide variety of characters whose personal lives are touched by Haiti's tragedy, including a man who attempts to flee from the country in a leaky boat; a prostitute who tells her son that the reason she dresses up every night is because she is expecting an angel to descend upon their house; and a childless housekeeper trapped in a loveless marriage who finds an abandoned baby in the streets. In the story "A Wall of Fire Rising," a man trying to support his family by doing odd jobs at the local sugar mill steals a balloon from the mill owners in an attempt to flee Haiti and find a way to better himself in a new land. In "Caroline's Wedding," two immigrant sisters living in New York City cope with a mother who longs to preserve Haitian tradition, even as one of the sisters prepares for an American-style wedding to a non-Haitian man.

Like *Breath, Eyes, Memory, Krik? Krak!* focuses on women's lives. As *Washington Post Book World* contributor Joanne Omang noted, "Danticat seems to be overflowing with the strength and insight of generations of Haitian women." In the story "Children of the Sea," for example, a collection of letters between a young woman and her intended, a radio host who flees the secret police by joining thirty-six other Haitians on a refugee boat bound for Miami, interweaves the poignancy of her love for him with the horrors that he is enduring on his flight from certain death. A woman

If you enjoy the works of Edwidge Danticat, you may also want to check out the following books and films:

Elizabeth Laird, *Kiss the Dust*, 1991.
Louise Moeri, *The Forty-Third War*, 1989.
Frances Temple, *Taste of Salt*, 1992, and *Tonight, by Sea*, 1995.
The Official Story, an Argentinian film about political repression, 1985.

who gives birth to a child while on that same boat appears in another story, "Between the Pool and the Gardenias," as the godmother of the lonely maid who finds a small child abandoned on a city street. "Night Women" mirrors the ancient myth of Penelope and her loom as a mother watches her son sleeping, and recalls the many Haitian women hired as weavers who would rise in the night to undo the work they had performed during the day, "so they will always have more to do." As Danticat writes in the book's epilogue: "The women in your family have never lost touch with one another. Death is a path we all take to meet on the other side. What goddesses have joined, let no one cast asunder. With every step you take, there is an army of women watching over you. We are never any farther than the sweat on your brows, the dust on your toes."

Several of the stories in *Krik? Krak!* were written while Danticat was still an undergraduate student at Barnard College; for this reason, some critics commented on the unevenness of the collection. However, Jordana Hart commented in *Ms.* that the author's young voice was actually an asset: the stories in *Krik? Krak!* are "textured and deeply personal, as if the twenty-six year old Haitian American author had spilled her own tears over each." Writing in *Washington Post Book World*, Omang characterized Danticat's stories as "autobiographical portraits of her family" and maintained that reading *Krik? Krak!* would allow one to "understand [Haiti] far more deeply than you ever thought possible." As Richard Eder noted in a *Newsday* review, Danticat's best stories, "using the island tradition of a semi-magical folktale, or the witty, between-two-worlds voices of modern urban immigrants, are pure beguiling transformations."

Danticat's second novel, *The Farming of Bones*, appeared in 1997. The book focuses on the infamous massacre of 1937, when then-Dominican Republic dictator Rafael Leonard Trujillo Molina ordered the murder of hundreds of Haitians attempting to flee back across the river separating the two countries in a bid to escape racial violence and their back-breaking jobs on Dominican sugar plantations. A *Publishers Weekly* reviewer praised Danticat for telling her tale of racial hatred and violence in "lyric measured language that creates a dreamlike atmosphere." The periodical also hailed *The Farming of Bones* as being one of the best books of 1998. Michael Upchurch, writing in the *New York Times Book Review*, stated that the author "capably evokes the shock with which a small personal world is disrupted by military mayhem," adding that the novel "provides an unnerving reminder that the appalling rationale and logistics of 'ethnic cleansing' have been with us for a very long time." According to *New York Times* contributor Garry Pierre-Pierre, Danticat's fiction heralds her as "the voice" of Haitian Americans. But the title is one Danticat is uneasy with; as she told him: "I think I have been assigned that role, but I don't really see myself as the voice for the Haitian-American experience. There are so many. I am just one."

■ Works Cited

Danticat, Edwidge, *Krik? Krak!*, Soho Press, 1995.

Eder, Richard, "A Haitian Fantasy and Exile," *Newsday*, March 30, 1995, pp. B2, B25.

Review of *The Farming of Bones*, *Publishers Weekly*, November 2, 1998, p. 40.

Gladstone, Jim, review of *Breath, Eyes, Memory*, *New York Times Book Review*, July 10, 1994, p. 24.

Gregory, Deborah, interview with Edwidge Danticat, *Essence*, April, 1995, p. 56.

Hart, Jordana, review of *Krik? Krak!*, *Ms.*, March/April, 1995, p. 75.

Hart, Jordana, "Danticat's Stories Pulse with Haitian Heartbeat," *Boston Globe*, July 19, 1995, p. 70.

Omang, Joanne, review of *Krik? Krak!*, *Washington Post Book World*, May 14, 1995, p. 4.

Philpott, Joan, review of *Breath, Eyes, Memory*, *Ms.*, March/April, 1994, pp. 77-78.

Pierre-Pierre, Garry, "Haitian Tales, Flatbush Scenes," *New York Times*, January 26, 1995, pp. C1, C8.

Shacochis, Bob, "Island in the Dark," *Washington Post Book World*, April 3, 1994, p. 6.

Upchurch, Michael, "No Room for the Living," *New York Times Book Review*, September 27, 1998.

■ **For More Information See**

PERIODICALS

Belles Lettres: A Review of Books by Women, fall, 1994, pp. 36, 38; summer, 1995, pp. 12-15.

Bloomsbury Review, September/October, 1994, p. 12.

Callaloo, Volume 18, number 2, 1995, pp. 524-28.

Newsday, May 21, 1995, p. A52.

New York Times, October 23, 1995, p. B3.

New York Times Book Review, April 23, 1995, p. 22.

Publishers Weekly, January 24, 1994, pp. 39-40; August 17, 1998.

Quarterly Black Review, June, 1995, p. 6.

School Library Journal, May, 1995, p. 135.

Village Voice Literary Supplement, July, 1995, p. 11.

Voice of Youth Advocates, December, 1995, p. 299.*

—Sketch by Pamela L. Shelton

Harlan Ellison

■ Personal

Born May 27, 1934, in Cleveland, OH; son of Louis Laverne (a dentist and jeweler) and Serita (Rosenthal) Ellison; married Charlotte B. Stein, February 19, 1956 (divorced, 1960); married Billie Joyce Sanders, November 13, 1960 (divorced, 1963); married Lory Patrick, January 30, 1966 (divorced, 1966); married Lori Horwitz, June 5, 1976 (divorced, 1977); married Susan Toth, 1986. *Education:* Attended Ohio State University, 1953-54.

■ Addresses

Home—Lost Aztec Temple of Mars, CA. *Office*—The Kilimanjaro Corporation, 3484 Coy Dr., Sherman Oaks, CA 91423. *Agent*—Richard Curtis Associates, Inc., 171 East 74th St., New York, NY 10021.

■ Career

Freelance writer, 1954—. Editor, *Rogue* (magazine), 1959-60; founder and editor, Regency Books, 1961-62. Editorial commentator, Canadian Broadcasting Co. (CBC), 1972-78; president of The Kilimanjaro Corp., Sherman Oaks, CA, 1979—. Creator of weekly television series (sometimes under pseudonym Cordwainer Bird), including *The Starlost*, syndicated, 1973, *Brillo* (with Ben Bova), American Broadcasting Companies, Inc. (ABC), 1974, and *The Dark Forces* (with Larry Brody), National Broadcasting Corporation, Inc. (NBC), 1986; creative consultant and director of television series (sometimes under pseudonym Cordwainer Bird), including *The Twilight Zone*, Columbia Broadcasting Systems, Inc. (CBS), 1984-85, and *Cutter's World*, 1987-88; conceptual consultant, *Babylon 5*, syndicated, 1993—; host of cable magazine show, *Sci-Fi Buzz*, the Sci-Fi Channel, 1993; actor and voice-over talent. Has lectured at various universities, including Yale Political Union, Harvard University, Massachusetts Institute of Technology, London School of Economics, Michigan State University, University of California—Los Angeles, Duke University, Ohio State University, and New York University. West Coast spokesman, Chevrolet GEO Imports, 1988-89. Member of board of advisors, Great Expectations (video dating service). *Military service:* U.S. Army, 1957-59. *Member:* PEN, Science Fiction Writers of America (co-founder; vice-president, 1965-66), Writers Guild of America, West (former member of board of directors), Lewis Carroll Society, Cleveland Science Fiction Society (co-founder), Screen Actors Guild.

■ Awards, Honors

Writers Guild of America Awards, 1965, for *Outer Limits* television series episode "Demon with a

Glass Hand," 1967, for original teleplay of *Star Trek* television series episode "The City on the Edge of Forever," 1973, for original teleplay of *Starlost* television pilot episode "Phoenix without Ashes," and 1986, for *Twilight Zone* television series episode "Paladin of the Lost Hour;" Nebula Awards, Science Fiction Writers of America, best short story, 1965, for "'Repent, Harlequin!' Said the Ticktockman," and 1977, for "Jeffty Is Five," best novella, 1969, for "A Boy and His Dog."

Hugo Awards, World Science Fiction Convention, best short fiction, 1965, for "'Repent, Harlequin!' Said the Ticktockman," best short story, 1967, for "I Have No Mouth, and I Must Scream," 1968, for "The Beast That Shouted Love at the Heart of the World," 1977, for "Jeffty Is Five," and 1986, for "Paladin of the Lost Hour," best dramatic presentation, 1967, for *Star Trek* television series episode "The City on the Edge of Forever," and 1976, for film "A Boy and His Dog," best novelette, 1973, for "The Deathbird," 1974, for "Adrift, Just Off the Islets of Langerhans . . .," special plaques from the World Science Fiction Convention, 1968, for *Dangerous Visions: 33 Original Stories*, and 1972, for *Again, Dangerous Visions: 46 Original Stories*; Nova Award, 1968, for most outstanding contribution to the field of science fiction.

Locus Awards, *Locus* magazine, best short fiction, 1970, for "The Region Between," 1972, for "Basilisk," 1973, for "The Deathbird," 1975, for "Croatoan," 1977, for "Jeffty Is Five," 1978, for "Count the Clock That Tells the Time," 1985, for "With Virgil Oddum at the East Pole," and 1988, for "Eidolons," best original anthology, 1972, for *Again, Dangerous Visions: 46 Original Stories*, and 1986, for *Medea: Harlan's World*, best novella, 1993, for *Mefisto in Onyx*, best novelette, 1974, for "Adrift, Just Off the Islets of Langerhans . . .," 1982, for "Djinn, No Chaser," 1985, for "Paladin of the Lost Hour," and 1988, for "The Function of Dream Sleep," best nonfiction, 1984, for *Sleepless Nights in the Procrustean Bed*, best short story collection, 1988, for *Angry Candy*.

Edgar Allan Poe Awards, Mystery Writers of America, 1974, for "The Whimper of Whipped Dogs," and 1988, for "Soft Monkey"; Jupiter Awards, Instructors of Science Fiction in Higher Education, best novelette, 1973, for "The Deathbird," and best short story, 1977, for "Jeffty Is Five"; Bram Stoker Awards, Horror Writers of America, 1988, for *The Essential Ellison: A Thirty-five Year Retrospective*, 1990, for *Harlan Ellison's Watching*, 1994, for novella Mefisto in Onyx, and 1996, for short story "Chatting with Anubis"; PEN International Silver Pen award for journalism, 1988, for column, "An Edge in My Voice"; World Fantasy Awards, best short story collection, 1989, for *Angry Candy*, and 1993, for lifetime achievement; *Angry Candy* was named one of the major works of American literature by Encyclopedia Americana Annual, 1988; honored by PEN for continuing commitment to artistic freedom and battle against censorship, 1990; inducted into Swedish National Encyclopedia, 1992; selection of short story "The Man Who Rowed Christopher Columbus to Freedom" for inclusion in *The Best American Short Stories*, 1993; recipient of Milford Award for lifetime achievement in editing.

■ **Writings**

SHORT STORY COLLECTIONS

The Deadly Streets, Ace Books, 1958.

(Under pseudonym Paul Merchant) *Sex Gang*, Nightstand, 1959.

A Touch of Infinity, Ace Books, 1960.

Children of the Streets (also published as *The Juvies*), Ace Books, 1961.

Gentleman Junkie, and Other Stories of the Hung-Up Generation, Regency Books, 1961.

Ellison Wonderland, Paperback Library, 1962.

Paingod, and Other Delusions (includes "'Repent, Harlequin!' Said the Ticktockman"), Pyramid Books, 1965.

I Have No Mouth and I Must Scream (also see below), Pyramid Books, 1967.

From the Land of Fear, Belmont, 1967.

Love Ain't Nothing But Sex Misspelled, Trident, 1968.

The Beast That Shouted Love at the Heart of the World, Avon, 1969.

Over the Edge: Stories from Somewhere Else, Belmont, 1970.

Alone against Tomorrow: Stories of Alienation in Speculative Fiction, Macmillan, 1971, abridged editions published in England as *All the Sounds of Fear*, Panther, 1973, and *The Time of the Eye*, Panther, 1974.

(With others) *Partners in Wonder: SF Collaborations with Fourteen Other Wild Talents*, Walker & Co., 1971.

Approaching Oblivion: Road Signs on the Treadmill toward Tomorrow, Walker & Co., 1974.

Deathbird Stories: A Pantheon of Modern Gods (includes "The Whimper of Whipped Dogs"; also see below), Harper, 1975.

No Doors, No Windows, Pyramid Books, 1975.

Strange Wine: Fifteen New Stories from the Nightside of the World, Harper, 1978.

The Illustrated Harlan Ellison, edited by Byron Preiss, Baronet, 1978.

The Fantasies of Harlan Ellison, Gregg, 1979.

Shatterday (also see below), Houghton, 1980.

Stalking the Nightmare, Phantasia Press, 1982.

The Essential Ellison: A Thirty-five Year Retrospective, edited by Terry Dowling, with Richard Delap and Gil Lamont, with an introduction by Dowling, Nemo Press, 1986.

Angry Candy, Houghton, 1988.

Dreams with Sharp Teeth (includes revised editions of *I Have No Mouth and I Must Scream, Deathbird Stories*, and *Shatterday*), Book-of-the-Month-Club, 1991.

Mind Fields: The Art of Jacek Yerka, the Fiction of Harlan Ellison, Morpheus International (Beverly Hills), 1994.

Slippage, Houghton, 1994.

Contributor to *Mel Odom, I Have No Mouth, and I Must Scream: The Official Strategy Guide*, Prima (Rocklin, CA), 1995. Also contributor of over eleven hundred short stories, some under pseudonyms, to numerous publications, including *Magazine of Fantasy and Science Fiction, Ariel, Twilight Zone, Cosmopolitan, Datamation, Omni, Ellery Queen's Mystery Magazine, Analog, Heavy Metal*, and *Galaxy*.

NOVELS

Rumble, Pyramid Books, 1958, published as *Web of the City*, 1975.

The Man with Nine Lives (novel; also see below) [and] *A Touch of Infinity* (stories), Ace Books, 1960.

The Sound of a Scythe (originally published as *The Man with Nine Lives*), Ace Books, 1960.

Spider Kiss (also published as *Rockabilly*), Fawcett, 1961.

Doomsman (bound with *Telepower* by Lee Hoffman), Belmont, 1967, reprinted (bound with *The Thief of Thoth* by Lin Carter), 1972.

(With Edward Bryant) *The Starlost #1: Phoenix without Ashes*, Fawcett, 1975.

All the Lies That Are My Life, Underwood-Miller, 1980.

Footsteps, illustrated by Ken Snyder, Footsteps Press, 1989.

Run for the Stars (bound with *Echoes of Thunder* by Jack Dann and Jack C. Haldeman II), Tor Books, 1991.

Mefisto in Onyx, Zeising Books, 1993.

ESSAYS

Memos from Purgatory: Two Journeys of Our Times, Regency Books, 1961.

The Glass Teat: Essays of Opinion on the Subject of Television, Ace Books, 1970.

The Other Glass Teat: Further Essays of Opinion on Television, Pyramid Books, 1975.

The Book of Ellison, edited by Andrew Porter, Algol Press, 1978.

Sleepless Nights in the Procrustean Bed, edited by Marty Clark, Borgo, 1984.

An Edge in My Voice, Donning, 1985.

Harlan Ellison's Watching, Underwood-Miller, 1989.

The Harlan Ellison Hornbook (autobiographical), Penzler, 1990.

EDITOR

Dangerous Visions: 33 Original Stories, Doubleday, 1967.

Nightshade and Damnations: The Finest Stories of Gerald Kersh, Fawcett, 1968.

Again, Dangerous Visions: 46 Original Stories, Doubleday, 1972.

(With others, and contributor) *Medea: Harlan's World* (includes "With Virgil Oddum at the East Pole"), Bantam, 1985.

(With others, and contributor) *Alien Sex*, New American Library, 1996.

EDITOR; "DISCOVERY" SERIES OF FIRST NOVELS

James Sutherland, *Stormtrack*, Pyramid Books, 1974.

Marta Randall, *Islands*, Pyramid Books, 1976.

Terry Carr, *The Light at the End of the Universe*, Pyramid Books, 1976.

Arthur Byron Cones, *Autumn Angels*, Pyramid Books, 1976.

Bruce Sterling, *Involution Ocean*, Pyramid Books, 1977.

SCREENPLAYS

(With Russell Rouse and Clarence Greene) *The Oscar* (based on the novel by Richard Sale), Embassy, 1966.

Harlan Ellison's Movie: An Original Screenplay, Twentieth Century-Fox, Mirage Press, 1990.

(With Isaac Asimov) *I, Robot: The Illustrated Screenplay* (see also below), Warner, 1994.

Also author of screenplays *Would You Do It for a Penny?*, Playboy Productions, *Stranglehold*, Twentieth Century-Fox, *Seven Worlds, Seven Warriors*, De Laurentiis, *I, Robot*, Warner Bros., *Swing Low, Sweet Harriet*, Metro-Goldwyn-Mayer, *The Dream Merchants*, Paramount, *Rumble*, American International, *Khadim*, Paramount, *Bug Jack Barron*, Universal, *None of the Above, Blind Voices, The Whimper of Whipped Dogs, Nick the Greek*, and *Best by Far*.

TELEPLAYS

The Starlost (series), syndicated, 1973.
Brillo (series), ABC, 1974.
The Tigers Are Loose (special), NBC, 1974.
The Dark Forces (series), NBC, 1986.
The Twilight Zone (series), CBS, 1986.
The City on the Edge of Forever (original teleplay, with introduction by Ellison), 1994, expanded paperback edition published as *Harlan Ellison's The City on the Edge of Forever*, White Wolf, 1996.

Also author of telefilms and pilots *A Boy and His Dog, The Spirit, Dark Destroyer, Man without Time, The Other Place, The Tigers Are Loose, Cutter's World, Our Man Flint, Heavy Metal, Tired Old Man, Mystery Show, Astral Man, Astra/Ella, Project 120, Bring 'Em Back Alive, Postmark: Jim Adam, The Contender*, and *The Sniper*.

Author of teleplays for series, including *Star Trek, Outer Limits, Voyage to the Bottom of the Sea, Dark Room, Circle of Fear, Rat Patrol, Amos Burke—Secret Agent, The Great Adventure, Empire, Batman, Ripcord, The Man from UNCLE, Cimarron Strip, Burke's Law, The Young Lawyers, The Name of the Game, Manhunter, The Flying Nun, Route 66, The Alfred Hitchcock Hour, Logan's Run, Twilight Zone*, and *Babylon 5*.

OTHER

(Contributor) Jack Dann and George Zebrowski, editors, *Faster than Light*, Harper, 1976.
The City on the Edge of Forever (play; based on the teleplay by Ellison), published in *Six Science Fiction Plays*, edited by Roger Elwood, Pocket Books, 1976.
Demon With a Glass Hand (graphic novel; illustrated by Marshall Rogers), D.C. Comics, 1986.

Night and the Enemy (graphic novel; illustrated by Ken Steacy), Comico, 1987.
Vic and Blood: The Chronicles of a Boy and His Dog (graphic novel; based on the novella by Ellison), edited by Jan Strand, illustrated by Richard Corben, St. Martin's, 1989.
Mind Fields: Thirty Short Stories Inspired by the Art of Jacek Yerka, art by Yerka, Morpheus, 1994.
"Repent, Harlequin!" Said the Ticktockman: The Classic Story, illustrated by Rick Berry, Underwood, 1997.
Harlan Ellison's Dream Corridor (graphic novel), Dark Horse, 1995.

Also author of "A Boy and His Dog" (novella), 1968. Author of four books on juvenile delinquency. Former author of columns "The Glass Teat" and "Harlan Ellison Hornbook," *Los Angeles Free Press*, and of "An Edge in My Voice," *L. A. Weekly*; author of syndicated film review column "Watching"; publisher of *Dimensions* magazine (originally *Science Fantasy Bulletin*). Narrator of audiobooks, including Jules Verne's *20,000 Leagues under the Sea*, Dove, 1996, and Ben Bova's *City of Darkness*, Dove, 1998.

Ellison has written under the following variant names or pseudonyms: Al(an) Maddern; Bert Parker; Clyde Mitchell; Cordwainer Bird; Derry Tiger; E. K. Jarvis; Ellis Hart; Ellis Robertson; Harlan Ellison; Harlan Jay Ellison; Ivar Jorgensen; Jay Charby; Jay Solo; Landon Ellis; Lee Archer; Nabrah Nosille; Paul Merchant; Phil "Cheech" Beldone; Price Curtis; Robert Courtney; Sley Harson; and Wallace Edmondson.

■ Adaptations

A Boy and His Dog was filmed by LQJaf in 1975; much of Ellison's work has been cited as the inspiration for the motion picture *The Terminator*, Orion, 1984; several of Ellison's short stories have been adapted for television. The film rights to *Mefisto in Onyx* have been optioned by Metro-Goldwyn-Mayer.

■ Sidelights

Described by fellow author J. G. Ballard as "an aggressive and restless extrovert who conducts his life at a shout and his fiction at a scream," Harlan Ellison is a writer who actively resists being labeled. Though he has written or edited sixty books and has authored more than eleven hundred short stories, he dislikes being called prolific; though his works of fiction and nonfiction are often considered iconoclastic, opinionated, and confrontational, he bristles at the label "irrepressible"; and, though he has garnered numerous major awards from science fiction organizations, he adamantly refuses to be categorized as a science fiction writer, preferring the term "magic realism" to define his writing.

Ellison began his writing career in the mid-1950s after being dismissed from college over a disagreement with a writing teacher who told Ellison that he had no talent. Ellison moved to New York City to become a freelance writer and in his first two years there sold some 150 short stories to magazines in every genre from crime fact to science fiction. It was the science fiction genre, however, that most appreciated Ellison's talent—both to Ellison's benefit and chagrin. Reviewers quickly associated him with the New Wave of science fiction writers—a group that included such authors as Brian W. Aldiss, J. G. Ballard, and Robert Silverberg. James Blish, writing under the pseudonym William Atheling, Jr., proclaimed in *More Issues at Hand*, "Harlan Ellison is not only the most audible but possibly the most gifted of the American members of the New Wave." Donald A. Wolheim concurred in *The Universe Makers:* "Harlan Ellison is one of those one-man phenomena who pop up in a field, follow their own rules, and have such a terrific charisma and personal drive that they get away with it. They break all the rules and make the rest like it."

In response to such reviews, Ellison not only denied his role in the New Wave of science fiction but rejected the notion of a New Wave entirely. "For the record, and for those who need to be told bluntly, I do not believe there is such a thing as 'New Wave' in speculative fiction," Ellison announced in the introduction to *The Beast That Shouted Love at the Heart of the World.* "It is a convenient journalese expression for inept critics and voyeur-observers of the passing scene, because they have neither the wit nor the depth to understand that this richness of new voices is many waves: each composed of one writer." Still, Wolheim maintained, the nature of Ellison's fiction places him firmly among the New Wave school of writing: "In the sense that [his] short stories have most certainly charted new paths in

This 1994 work contains Ellison's original version of the award-winning yet controversial episode for the popular television series *Star Trek.*

writing, in that he has indeed found new ultra-modern ways of narration which yet manage to keep comprehension, . . . in that he takes the downbeat view of the far future and therefore, by implication, seems to accept the view that there is no real hope for humanity. . . . In that sense Harlan Ellison is New Wave [and] is the best of them all."

In the more than forty years since the publication of his first book, Ellison has written essays, reviews, screenplays, teleplays, graphic novels, and drama—yet, he is still plagued with the science fiction label. "In the earliest days when I began writing I was a science fiction fan," he once explained, "so I gravitated toward the genre, naturally; but I wrote far more mystery fiction, far more mainstream fiction than ever I wrote science fiction." Ellison also told a *Publishers Weekly* contributor: "I've long ago ceased to write anything even remotely resembling science fiction, if indeed I ever really did write it." His chief reason for not wanting to be lumped among other science fiction writers, Ellison once related, is that "I conceive of the mass of science fiction writers as very bad writers indeed." Some critics, such as Joseph McLellan of the *Washington Post*, have suggested that to call Ellison a science fiction writer is too limiting. McLellan maintained that "the categories are too small to describe Harlan Ellison. Lyric poet, satirist, explorer of odd psychological corners, moralist, one-line comedian, purveyor of pure horror and of black comedy; he is all these and more."

"Dangerous" Works

Ellison employs the term "magic realism" to describe his writing, a term which he says can be applied to the work of many other writers, including Kurt Vonnegut, John Barth, Jorge Luis Borges, and Luisa Valenzuela. In 1967, after reading a short story by Thomas Pynchon, Ellison was inspired to edit a collection of "magic realism" stories as a means of better defining the term and distinguishing it from science fiction. The result was *Dangerous Visions: 33 Original Stories*. Specifically designed to include those stories too controversial, too experimental, or too well written to appear in the popular magazines, *Dangerous Visions* broke new ground in both theme and style. "[*Dangerous Visions*] was intended to shake things up," Ellison wrote in his introduction to the book. "It was conceived out of a need for new horizons, new forms, new styles, new challenges in the literature of our times."

Critical reaction to the book was largely favorable. "You should buy this book immediately," Algis Budrys urged his readers. Damon Knight, writing in the *Saturday Review*, called it "a gigantic, shapeless, exuberant, and startling collection [of] vital, meaningful stories." Of the thirty-three stories in *Dangerous Visions*, seven became winners of either the Hugo or Nebula Award while another thirteen stories were nominees. The collection received a special plaque from the World Science Fiction Convention. *Again, Dangerous Visions: 46 Original Stories*, Ellison's sequel to *Dangerous Visions*, met with the same success as its predecessor: J. B. Post

of *Library Journal* predicted that *Again, Dangerous Visions* "will become a historically important book," and W. E. McNelly of *America* claimed that the collection was "so experimental in design, concept, and execution that this one volume may well place science fiction in the very heart of mainstream literature."

Both *Dangerous Visions* and *Again, Dangerous Visions* employ a unique format. Each story is preceded by a short introduction by Ellison, who speaks about the author and why the story was chosen for the collection, and is followed by an afterword from the author, who describes how the story came to be written. The format serves to personalize each story and to highlight its place in the collection. Theodore Sturgeon, writing in the *National Review*, described Ellison's introductions to the stories as a "one-man isometrics course [that] will stretch your laugh-muscles, your retch-muscles, your indignation-, wonder-, delight-, mad-, appall-, admiration-, and disbelief-muscles, and strongly affect your blood-pressure thing. You may have perceived that I have not used the word 'dull.' [Ellison] might numb you, but you will not be bored."

Infuriates and Inspires

Through his fiction and, in particular, his essays, Ellison has earned a reputation as a polemic. Michael Schrage, writing in the *Washington Post*, identified Ellison as "brash, arrogant, funny and provocative to the point of insulting." Though he noted that the essays in Ellison's collection *An Edge in My Voice* "may reek of ego and self-indulgence . . . they are very, very funny and very, very entertaining." Wolheim called Ellison "a unique sort of genius who can lead where others can never successfully follow, who can hold an audience enthralled yet never gain a convert, [and] who can insult and have only the stupid offended." Schrage warned: "People who don't like smart-mouthed writers with a flair for caustic repartee are advised to steer clear [of Ellison]."

However provocative it may be, Ellison's fiction has been ranked among America's best. Blish noted in *More Issues at Hand* that Ellison is "a born writer, almost entirely without taste or control but with so much fire, originality and drive, as well as compassion, that he makes the conventional virtues of the artist seem almost irrelevant."

Originally published in 1965, the short story "'Repent, Harlequin!' Said the Ticktockman," here illustrated by Rick Berry, garnered both the Hugo and Nebula awards and is considered one of Ellison's best.

In his book-length study, *Harlan Ellison: Unrepentant Harlequin*, George Edgar Slusser called Ellison "a tireless experimenter with forms and techniques" and concludes that he "has produced some of the finest, most provocative fantasy in America today." And legendary author Isaac Asimov once called Ellison "the best damned writer in the world."

Classic Works

Of all his short stories, the one most often singled out by critics and fans alike as Ellison's best is "'Repent, Harlequin!' Said the Ticktockman." It describes a future civilization in which citizens are held responsible for every second of their day; value is determined by productivity, and tardiness is loathed above all things. Promptness is enforced by the tyrannical Master Timekeeper, known colloquially as the Ticktockman. The protagonist is the Harlequin, who dresses in motley, is always late, and who plays pranks on his coworkers simply to make them laugh. Though in the end the Harlequin is brainwashed and subsumed by the system, his actions create ripples in the pond, planting within his coworkers the seeds of civil disobedience. The moral of "'Repent, Harlequin!'" is, according to Slusser, that "the 'real' men in society are not those who abdicate all freedom of judgment to serve the machine, but those who resist dehumanization through acts of conscience, no matter how small. . . . If such a sacrifice brings even the slightest change, it is worth it." "'Repent, Harlequin!' Said the Ticktockman" is one of the ten most reprinted stories in the English language.

Another popular work of Ellison's is the 1968 novella *A Boy and His Dog*, which was made into a movie in 1975. In the year 2024, shortly after the devastating climax of World War IV, Vic and his dog Blood wander the wastes of the American southwest. The relationship between boy and dog is unusual for two reasons: first, Blood is telepathic, allowing him to communicate with Vic; second, the roles of human and animal have been reversed—Vic is little more than a scavenger, while Blood is literate and cultured. Blood teaches his "master" reading, speech, arithmetic, and history; however, he has forgotten his animal instincts, and must rely upon Vic to hunt game and find shelter. John Crow and Richard Erlich, reviewing *A Boy and His Dog* for *Extrapolation*, described the

If you enjoy the works of Harlan Ellison, you may also want to check out the following books and films:

Jorge Luis Borges, *Labyrinths,* 1964.
The works of Robert Silverberg, including the novella *Sailing to Byzantium*, 1985.
The Terminator, 1984, and *Terminator 2: Judgment Day*, 1991, which were inspired by Ellison's writings.

novella as "a cautionary fable" which "demands consideration of just how consciously our own society is proceeding into its technological future."

Ellison continued to produce successful fiction during the 1990s. The novella *Mefisto in Onyx* features Rudy Pairis, a gifted black man whose ability to read minds is employed by Deputy District Attorney Allison Roche to exonerate a convicted serial killer who awaits an impending death sentence. Though Roche prosecuted the convicted murderer herself, days before his execution she doubts his guilt and persuades Pairis to probe his mind for evidence of his innocence. David Gianatasio praises the Pairis character in an *Armchair Detective* review. "Like most Ellison antiheroes, Pairis's inability to fully accept his heightened mental powers—and in a larger sense, to accept himself—makes him an outcast in his own world." Gianatasio adds, "Pairis's ability to accept who and what he is . . . is the key to his final transcendence." Tom Auer concludes in *Bloomsbury Review*, "This story is a page-turner, quick, lively, and entertaining, and very funny in parts, but colored throughout with a deep sense of humankind's insufferable inhumanity."

Ellison also published *I, Robot: The Illustrated Screenplay*, co-authored with Isaac Asimov, after a protracted and ultimately failed attempt to produce a film version of the story. As Michael Rogers notes in *Library Journal*, this unproduced script achieved near legendary status as "the greatest science fiction movie never made." Based on Asimov's *I, Robot* series and elements of Orson Welles' *Citizen Kane*, Ellison grafts various Asimov subplots and his own material into a story about a journalist's persistent effort to interview Susan Calvin, a reclusive octogenarian, upon the death of her reputed lover Stephen Byerly. Though commending Ellison's achievement, *Locus* reviewer Gary K. Wolfe writes, "*I, Robot* was probably never a very good idea for a movie" because "most of the stories were intellectual puzzles based on permutations of the laws of robotics." However, Wolfe adds, "As a potential moviegoer, there's nothing here to convince me that this relatively simple story about a lonely woman in a lost future is impossible to film." An *Analog* reviewer similarly concludes, "Ellison did indeed make a compelling story of Asimov's material, and the script would indeed make a grand movie."

Commenting on Ellison's style and central themes, Auer writes, "Ellison's prose is powerful and ingenious, but often angry, sometimes sinister, occasionally gloomy, and often with an edge that can cut quickly to and through the heart of his subject, or that of his reader for that matter." As Auer observes, "The bloody truth of our violent times, a subject he writes about with regularity and ease, practically drips from some of his finely crafted pages. He also has a sense of humor, but we don't see it often, and it is frequently black as midnight when we do."

Ellison once commented: "Everything I write is concerned with the world of today. . . . I explain the world through which we move by reflecting it through the lens of fantasy turned slightly askew, so that you can see it from a new angle. I talk about the things people have always talked about in stories: pain, hate, truth, courage, destiny, friendship, responsibility, growing old, growing up, falling in love, all of these things. I don't write about far-flung galactic civilizations; I don't write about crazed robots; I don't write gimmick stories. What I try to write about are the darkest things in the soul, the mortal dreads. . . . The closer I get to the burning core of my being, the things which are most painful to me, the better is my work.

"It is a love/hate relationship that I have with the human race," Ellison continued. "I am an elitist, and I feel that my responsibility is to drag the human race along with me—that I will never pander to, or speak down to, or play the safe game. Because my immortal soul will be lost."

■ Works Cited

America, June 10, 1972.

Armchair Detective, spring, 1994, p. 245.
Atheling, Jr., William, *More Issues at Hand*, Advent, 1970.
Auer, Tom, "The Latest Dangerous Visions of Harlan Ellison: The Slayer of Great Beasts Strikes Again (& Again)," *Bloomsbury Review*, May/June, 1994.
Crow, John, and Richard Erlich, *Extrapolation*, May, 1977.
Ellison, Harlan, *Dangerous Visions: 33 Original Stories*, Doubleday, 1967.
Ellison, Harlan, *The Beast That Shouted Love at the Heart of the World*, Avon, 1969.
Library Journal, April 15, 1972.
Library Journal, February 1, 1995, p. 75.
Locus, November, 1994, p. 61.
McLellan, Joseph, *Washington Post*, August 3, 1978.
Publishers Weekly, February 10, 1975.
Saturday Review, December 30, 1967.
Schrage, Michael, *Washington Post*, July 30, 1985.
Slusser, George Edgar, *Harlan Ellison: Unrepentant Harlequin*, Borgo, 1977.
Sturgeon, Theodore, *National Review*, May 7, 1968.
Wolheim, Donald A., *The Universe Makers*, Harper, 1971.

■ For More Information See

BOOKS

Contemporary Literary Criticism, Gale, Volume 1, 1973, Volume 13, 1980, Volume 42, 1987.
Dictionary of Literary Biography, Volume 8: *Twentieth-Century American Science Fiction Writers*, Gale, 1981.
Platt, Charles, *The Dream Makers: The Uncommon People Who Write Science Fiction*, Berkley, 1980.
Porter, Andrew, editor, *The Book of Ellison*, Algol Press, 1978.
Swigart, Leslie Kay, *Harlan Ellison: A Bibliographical Checklist*, Williams Publishing (Dallas), 1973.
Walker, Paul, *Speaking of Science Fiction: The Paul Walker Interviews*, Luna, 1978.

PERIODICALS

Analog, September, 1960; December, 1962; May, 1968; June, 1968; August, 1970; April, 1973; September, 1995, p. 185.
Bloomsbury Review, January, 1985; February, 1985.
Chicago Tribune, September 24, 1961; June 2, 1985; January 17, 1989.

Esquire, January, 1962.

Extrapolation, winter, 1979.

Fantasy Newsletter, April, 1981.

Galaxy, April, 1968; May, 1972.

Los Angeles Times, September 20, 1988.

Los Angeles Times Book Review, October 24, 1982, p. 14; June 30, 1985, p. 7; January 1, 1989, p. 9.

Luna Monthly, May, 1970; July, 1970; May/June, 1971; June, 1972; September, 1972.

Magazine of Fantasy and Science Fiction, January, 1968; November, 1971; September, 1972; October, 1975; July, 1977.

Manchester Guardian, July 4, 1963.

National Review, July 12, 1966.

New Statesman, March 25, 1977.

New York Times Book Review, October 26, 1958; June 30, 1960; August 20, 1961; June 30, 1968; September 3, 1972; March 23, 1975; April 1, 1979; January 8, 1989, p. 31; September 17, 1989, p. 12; March 18, 1990, p. 32.

Renaissance, summer, 1972.

Review of Contemporary Literature, fall, 1994, p. 229.

Science Fiction Review, January, 1971; September/October, 1978.

Spectator, January, 1971.

Times Literary Supplement, April 16, 1971; January 14, 1977; July 9, 1982, p. 739.

Tribune Books (Chicago), June 2, 1985, p. 35.

Variety, July 8, 1970; March 17, 1971.

Washington Post Book World, January 25, 1981; December 26, 1982; June 30, 1985; September 25, 1988, p. 8; October 28, 1990, p. 10; February 2, 1992, p. 12.

Worlds of If, July, 1960; September/October, 1971.*

—Sketch by Brandon Trenz

Laura Esquivel

■ Personal

Born c. 1951, in Mexico; daughter of Julio Caesar Esquivel (a telegraph operator) and Josephina Esquivel; married Alfonso Arau (a film director), divorced; married Javier Valdez (a dentist); children: Sandra. *Education:* Attended Escuela Normal de Maestros, Mexico. *Hobbies and other interests:* Cooking.

■ Addresses

Home—Mexico City, Mexico. *Office*—Doubleday, 666 5th Ave., New York, NY 10103.

■ Career

Novelist and screenwriter; writer and director for children's theater. Worked as a teacher for eight years.

■ Awards, Honors

Ariel Award nomination for best screenplay, Mexican Academy of Motion Pictures, Arts and Sciences, for *Like Water for Chocolate.*

■ Writings

SCREENPLAYS

Like Water for Chocolate, based on her novel of the same title, Miramax, 1992.

Also author of *Chido One,* released in 1985, and *Little Ocean Star,* a children's feature, released in 1994.

NOVELS

Como agua para chocolate: novela de entregas mensuales con recetas, amores, y remedios caseros, Editorial Planeta Mexicana, 1989, translation by Carol Christensen and Thomas Christensen published as *Like Water for Chocolate: A Novel in Monthly Installments, with Recipes, Romances, and Home Remedies,* Doubleday, 1991.
Ley del amor, translation by Margaret Sayers Peden published as *The Law of Love,* Crown Publishers (New York City), 1996.

■ Sidelights

A teacher by trade, Laura Esquivel gained international attention with *Like Water for Chocolate: A Novel in Monthly Installments with Recipes, Romances and Home Remedies* and *The Law of Love.* In both books she manages to incorporate her teaching abilities by giving her readers lessons about life.

An international success, this 1989 book of tales, romance, Mexican recipes, and home remedies, has been translated into more than thirty languages.

During an on-line *Salon* interview with Joan Smith, she said, "As a teacher I realize that what one learns in school doesn't serve for very much at all, that the only thing one can really learn is self understanding and this is something that can't be taught." With the intensity of a committed teacher incorporating glitzy stunts into the curriculum to get the attention of her students, Esquivel took a bold step when she incorporated multimedia in *The Law of Love* by combining her science fiction, new age, and spiritual story with a CD of arias by Puccini and Mexican *danzones,* and forty-eight pages of illustrations by a Spanish artist.

Esquivel was the third of four children born to Julio Caesar Esquivel, a telegraph operator, and his wife, Josephina. Reared in Mexico City, Esquivel grew up across the street from her grandmother. Her grandmother's house had a chapel and the smell of her grandmothers' cooking mingled with the odors of the chapel. Cooking would always remain an important part of Esquivel's life and it was natural for her to blend the art of cooking into her first novel.

Esquivel attended the Escuela Normal de Maestros, the national teachers' college. A few years after graduating, she married Alfonso Arau, a Mexican film director. They had one child, Sandra. During an interview with Smith, Esquivel explained that she wrote "[o]ut of necessity. . . . I am a kindergarten teacher and I worked in a theater workshop for children and there was very little material available so I began to write children's plays." She went on to write for children's public television. Esquivel credited Arau with teaching her how to write film scripts and for inspiring her to work in film. The power of love is ever present in her books and an important theme in her own life. She told Smith that "love is the most important force. It moves the universe." Esquivel explained that she believes people can change their fate through self-understanding and use that wisdom to choose their paths in life. She was raised in a Catholic family, however, without "a very strong religious upbringing." As a teenager she began to explore Eastern religions and became a vegetarian. "I was a love child," she told Smith. "Since then I've meditated, but my spiritual background has been very eclectic." As with cooking, spiritual ideas permeate her complicated and detailed stories.

Boiling Over

Her first book, *Like Water for Chocolate,* was also made into a movie with the screenplay written by Esquivel. The original Spanish title, *Como agua para chocolate,* refers to the boiling water used to prepare hot chocolate in Mexico, and is a Spanish expression that means intense agitation or sexual arousal. In the United States *Like Water for Chocolate* was simultaneously released as a book and a movie, grossing more money than any previous foreign film. (Esquivel was honored with an Ariel Award nomination for for best screenplay.) The book has been translated into thirty languages with more than three million copies in print worldwide.

Esquivel also wrote the screenplay for the film *Like Water for Chocolate,* released in the United States in 1993 starring Marco Leonardi and Lumi Cavazos.

Spiced with a few traditional Mexican recipes, many of which have been in the author's family for years, the story revolves around Tita De la Garza and her lover, Pedro. The work is set in Mexico during the early 1900s, near a northern peasant city, over the border from San Antonio. Tita is born "on a bed of onions, cilantro and spices," and food will forever be an important element in her life. As she grows up she becomes a gourmet and finds comfort in cooking. Each chapter is prefaced with recipes, like Christmas rolls, quail in rose petal sauce, and oxtail soup. The recipes, however, have more to do with romance than food.

Tita becomes a victim of a tradition mandating that as the youngest daughter she is not to marry.

"If your imagination lets you run for the pot of gold at the end of a rainbow, Laura Esquivel's multisensory novel dares you to travel along the a-maze-ing path of *The Law of Love*. It's that much of an adventure." —*Miami Herald*

LAURA ESQUIVEL

Author of

LIKE WATER FOR CHOCOLATE

the Law of Love

INCLUDES A MUSIC CD

Filled with romance, adventure, and comedy, this 1996 novel spans generations—from the days of Montezuma to the twenty-third century.

Instead, her duty is to care for her domineering mother, Mama Elena. Tita and Pedro fall in love, but because of Tita's role caring for her mother, Pedro marries Tita's older sister. Tita is crushed, but finds solace when Pedro reveals at the wedding that he is doing this to be close to her. While making the wedding cake, Tita's tears fall into the batter. In fairy tale fashion, Tita begins to learn the mystical qualities of food preparations when the entire party eats the cake and begins crying over lost love.

"Consequently, *Like Water for Chocolate* emerges as a sensual, one-of-a-kind novel that uses the kitchen as a stage where all womanly affairs shape up—a challenge to Mexico's macho-oriented society," explained Ilan Stavans in *Bloomsbury Review*. "At home and beyond, women are silently responsible for law and order." Andrea Lockett noted in *Belles Lettres* that the story "is boiling over with passion, color, and sensual beauty." "Esquivel never preaches," Lockett explained, but she nudges readers toward understanding the implications for a culture" in which the price of a woman's obedience is self-effacement and misery." Similarly, Laurie Muchnick of *Voice Literary Supplement* noted that while Esquivel "seems to give women tremendous power, . . . their options are limited to following their libidos, making them hostages to their hormones. . . . What kind of power is that?" A reviewer for *Times Literary Supplement* warned readers not to read too much into the story. The book is not an historical account or "a statement about female repression in rural societies," the reviewer said. Nevertheless, it does have a definite Mexican flavor. Kelli Pryor in *Entertainment Weekly* called this "romantic potboiler . . . the most successful Mexican import since salsa and chips." Stavans was equally impressed, stating: "Laura Esquivel is another indispensable part of Mexico's popular literature."

As a film, *Like Water for Chocolate* won similarly high praise. "Through the repressed steaminess and roiling tragedies, Esquivel (who adapted the screenplay) with director Alfonso Arau spare no opportunity to sweeten things with comedy," explained Desson Howe of the *Washington Post*. Esquivel told Pryor that the film was a "labor of love between us, like a child almost." Roger Ebert of the Chicago *Sun-Times* explained that the movie "continues the tradition of magical realism that is central to modern Latin film and literature." Howe added that the movie is "[h]auntingly and exquis-

If you enjoy the works of Laura Esquivel, you may also want to check out the following books and films:

Sandra Benitez, *A Place Where the Sea Remembers*, 1993.

Gabriel Garcia Marquez, *Love in the Time of Cholera*, 1988.

Elizabeth Borton de Treviano, *Leona: A Love Story*, 1994.

Belle Epoque, a film from Spain about love and romance, 1992.

itely prepared . . . garnished with mystery and wonder." "It's the best movie," he added, "to establish the spiritual link between food and the human condition since 'Babette's Feast' or 'Tampopo.'"

Power of Love

Esquivel's second book, *The Law of Love,* combines time travel, love, and reincarnation. Beginning in the time of the conquistadors, the story jumps to the twenty-third century where the heroine, Azucena, an astroanalyst, helps people resolve incomplete tasks from their past lives. After 14,000 lives, Azucena tries to find Rodrigo, her twin soul. Esquivel explains in the book that a twin soul is one that has died and has been reincarnated many times to reach enough understanding to accept a soul mate. Along with Anacreonte, her guardian spirit, Azucena must also do battle with an evil spirit intent on conquering the world.

The reviews for the novel were mixed. Lilian Pizzichini in *Times Literary Supplement* said the story is "a collision of literary styles that confirm her wit and ingenuity." She concluded, however, that "the gadgetry, in-jokes and lengthy tracts of New Age philosophy fail to compensate for the lack of fresh ideas." The novel seems "too anxious to overwhelm, too determined to entertain at any cost," said a *Kirkus Reviews* writer who also observed, "Esquivel can write, and . . . she possesses considerable originality." Donna Seaman of *Booklist* complained of the novel's "rocky start," but praised the "inventive plot twists that keep Azucena and Rodrigo in suspense and danger and her readers in excellent spirits." In a *New York*

Times review, Robert Houston remarked that the novel was "[c]onfusing, tediously plotted, [and] marred by muddy philosophy and dubious verities." *The Law of Love* has the "same jolly, reckless storytelling energy" that has gained enthusiasts for Esquivel, stated a *Publishers Weekly* reviewer, who faulted the author's "skimpy character development and breathlessly byzantine plot."

Esquivel, who lives in Mexico City, ended her twelve-year marriage to Arau after *Like Water for Chocolate* was released. She later married a dentist, Javier Valdez, who she has referred to as her own twin soul. Esquivel continues to nurture her passion for cooking. "The kitchen, to me, is the most important part of the house," she told Smith. "It is a source of knowledge and understanding that generates life and pleasure." Esquivel also maintains a voracious reading habit. "Personally I like to read stories behind which there is some truth, something real and above all, something emotional," she told Smith. Even her harshest critics maintain that Esquivel provides readers with strong, emotional characters and an element of truth about life.

■ Works Cited

Ebert, Roger, review of *Like Water for Chocolate, Sun-Times* (Chicago), April 2, 1993.

Houston, Robert, "Karma Chameleons," review of *The Law of Love, New York Times,* November 17, 1996, p. 11.

Howe, Desson, review of *Like Water for Chocolate, Washington Post,* March 5, 1993.

Review of *The Law of Love, Kirkus Reviews,* July 1, 1996, p. 917.

Review of *The Law of Love, Publishers Weekly,* July 22, 1996, p. 225.

"Like Water for Hot Chocolate," *Times Literary Supplement,* April 16, 1993, p. 22.

Lockett, Andrea, review of *Like Water for Chocolate: A Novel in Monthly Installments with Recipes, Romance and Home Remedies, Belles Lettres,* Spring 1993, pp. 42-43.

Muchnick, Laurie, review of *Like Water for Chocolate: A Novel in Monthly Installments with Recipes, Romance and Home Remedies, Voice Literary Supplement,* November, 1992, pp. 7-8.

Pizzichini, Lilian, review of *The Law of Love, Times Literary Supplement,* October 18, 1996, p. 23.

Pryor, Kelli, "Like Chocolate for the Mind," *Entertainment Weekly,* April 23, 1993, p. 52.

Seaman, Donna, review of *The Law of Love*, *Booklist*, August 19, 1996.

Smith, Joan, interview with Laura Esquivel at *Salon* on-line, http://www.salon1999.com/oct96/interview961104.html.

Stavans, Ilan, review of *Like Water for Chocolate: A Novel in Monthly Installments with Recipes, Romance and Home Remedies*, *Bloomsbury Review*, November/December, 1993, pp. 3, 26.

■ For More Information See

PERIODICALS

Booklist, September 15, 1992, p. 122.

Entertainment Weekly, December 31, 1993, p. 112; January 7, 1994, p. 47.

Hispanic Times, December/January 1996, p. 42.

Library Journal, January, 1996, p. 81; July, 1996, pp. 156-57.

Los Angeles Times Book Review, November 1, 1992, p. 6.

Ms., November/December, 1993, p. 75.

Nation, June 14, 1993, p. 846.

New Republic, March 1, 1993, pp. 24-25.

New Yorker, June 27, 1994, p. 80.

New York Times, March 31, 1993, pp. C1, C8.

New York Times Book Review, November 17, 1996, p. 11.

Publishers Weekly, May 17, 1993, p. 17; August 15, 1994, p. 13; October 3, 1994, p. 40; February 5, 1996, p. 24.

Time, April 5, 1993, pp. 62-63.

Tribune Books (Chicago), October 18, 1992, p. 8.

Washington Post, September 25, 1992, p. B2.

Wilson Library Bulletin, December, 1993, p. 29.

World Press Review, February, 1996, pp. 43-44.*

—Sketch by Diane Andreassi

Peter and Bobby Farrelly

Bobby Farrelly (left) and brother Peter, whose hit films include *Kingpin* and *There's Something about Mary*.

■ Personal

Peter Farrelly: Born December 17, 1956, in Cumberland, RI; son of Robert Leo (a physician) and Mariann (a nurse practitioner; maiden name, Neary) Farrelly; married, children: one son, one daughter. *Education:* Providence College, B.A., 1979; graduate study at University of Massachusetts—Amherst, 1982-83; Columbia University, M.F.A., 1987. *Religion:* Roman Catholic.

Bobby Farrelly: Born in 1957, in Cumberland, RI; son of Robert Leo (a physician) and Mariann (a nurse practitioner; maiden name, Neary) Farrelly; married, wife's name, Nancy; children: two. *Education:* Graduated with bachelor's degree from Rensselaer Polytechnic Institute.

■ Addresses

Peter Farrelly: Duxbury, MA.

Bobby Farrelly: Duxbury, MA.

■ Career

Peter Farrelly: Writer, director, and producer. Walt Disney Studios, Burbank, CA, screenwriter, 1985-87; Paramount, Los Angeles, CA, screenwriter, 1985—. Director of films, including *Dumb and Dumber*, New Line Cinema, 1994, *Kingpin*, MGM/UA, 1996, and *There's Something about Mary*, 20th Century Fox, 1998. Executive producer of *There's Something about Mary*, 20th Century Fox, 1998. Author of scripts for *Seinfeld*, NBC.

Bobby Farrelly: Writer, director, and producer. Director and producer of *Kingpin*, MGM/UA, 1996, and *There's Something about Mary*, 20th Century Fox, 1998. Author of scripts for *Seinfeld*, NBC.

■ Awards, Honors

Co-winners of ShoWest 1998 Screenwriters of the Year.

■ Writings

Peter Farrelly:

NOVELS

Outside Providence, Atlantic Monthly Press, 1988.

The Comedy Writer, Doubleday, 1998.

SCREENPLAYS

Dumb and Dumber, New Line Cinema, 1994.
Bushwhacked (uncredited), 20th Century Fox, 1995.
There's Something about Mary, 20th Century Fox, 1998.

Bobby Farrelly:

SCREENPLAYS

Dumb and Dumber, New Line Cinema, 1994.
Bushwhacked (uncredited), 20th Century Fox, 1995.
There's Something about Mary, 1998.

■ Work in Progress

The brothers Farrelly are co-writing, co-producing, and co-directing the film *Stuck on You*, a film about Siamese twin brothers, expected 1999; co-writing a film version of *Outside Providence*, produced by Peter, expected 1999.

■ Sidelights

USA Today movie critic Susan Wloszczyna has described Peter and Bobby Farrelly as being "best known as sewer dwellers, Ed Norton class, who dragged gross-out humor to new earthworm-level depths in *Dumb and Dumber* and *Kingpin*." Oddly enough, Wloszczyna went on to give the Farrelly's 1998 comedy film *There's Something About Mary* a lofty rating of three-and-a-half out of a possible four stars. That kind of mixed reaction has become common for the brothers' films. The pair have done everything in their brief Hollywood careers, working as writers, directors, and producers. Despite being known for their low-brow humor—with its heavy reliance on toilet and anatomy jokes, as well as tasteless jabs at people with mental and physical disabilities—the Farrellys have succeeded in making audiences and critics alike laugh in spite of themselves. "Writer-directors Robert and Peter Farrelly are the crown princes of the un-PC belly laugh," according to Elizabeth Snead of *USA Today*.

The Farrelly brothers were born one year apart in Cumberland, Rhode Island, to Robert Leo, a physician, and Mariann, a nurse practitioner. Even after lengthy stints living in California, they still

The 1994 slapstick comedy *Dumb and Dumber*, starring Jim Carrey and Jeff Daniels, was the Farrelly brothers' first screenplay that made it to film.

considered the East Coast to be home. Their films also reach back to their own youths, and echoes of their upbringings and of their own favorite childhood movies—comedies such as *Animal House, Blazing Saddles, Caddyshack,* and *Cat Ballou*—are evident in their own work.

Peter and Robert Farrelly's paths have paralleled most of their lives, except for their college years when they went separate ways. Robert earned a bachelor of arts degree in geological engineering at Rensselaer Polytechnic Institute in Troy, New York (attending on a hockey scholarship), while Peter went to Providence College in Rhode Island. After graduating, both worked for a time as salesmen, but Peter, the elder brother, went back to graduate school at Columbia University, where he earned a master's degree in creative writing. He and a friend named Bennett Yellin then began working together on writing screenplays. Explain-

ing how Robert got involved, Peter said in a *Bold Type* on-line interview that "for about two years every time we wrote a screenplay I'd send it off to my brother because I trusted his instincts with comedy and story; he was good at it." Eventually, they asked Robert to work with them on a project. When Bennett moved on to do other things a couple of years later, the brothers were left to work together.

Meanwhile, Peter had written a novel. *Outside Providence* is set in Pawtucket, a blue-collar Rhode Island town. The story, which focuses on the trials and tribulations of a character named Timothy Dunphy—nicknamed "Dildo" by his father—recounts Dunphy's experiences with sex and drugs at a Connecticut prep school. Early in his career, Peter told *Contemporary Authors* that writing novels "is time-consuming, nerve-wracking, and financially unfulfilling. Screenwriting is quick, relatively easy, and the dough is pretty good. I prefer, however, writing novels. I guess some things never change." A *Booklist* reviewer called *Outside Providence* a "hateful yet perceptive novel," adding that the work bears similarities to J.D. Salinger's classic novel *Catcher in the Rye* and Brett Easton Ellis's *Less Than Zero*.

The Success of *Dumb and Dumber*

The Farrelly's worked for a time in television, writing a couple of *Seinfeld* episodes. They also wrote fifteen screenplays and sold six, but none of them made it to film until *Dumb and Dumber*. Ironically, the film is about two dim-witted guys from Providence, Rhode Island. Changing hats, Peter made his directorial debut, while he and Bobby also served as co-producers along with

Brad Krevoy, Steve Stabler, and Bradley Thomas. The movie, with its decidedly low-brow humor, featured such off-color sight gags as Jim Carrey lighting a fart. Even so, *Dumb and Dumber* earned more than $340 million worldwide and marked the Farrelly brothers coming-of-age as big-time comic filmmakers.

In the film, Carrey plays a limousine driver, while his roommate, played by Jeff Daniels, operates a dog-grooming business for which he rides around in a "dog mobile"—a van that looks like a huge shaggy dog. Carrey falls in love with a beautiful woman who he drove to the airport to catch a flight to Aspen, Colorado. He realizes that she left a briefcase behind and while he tries to return it, Carrey inadvertently foils a kidnap ransom payment. Using the dog mobile, Carrey and Daniels then set out for Aspen, with intentions of return-

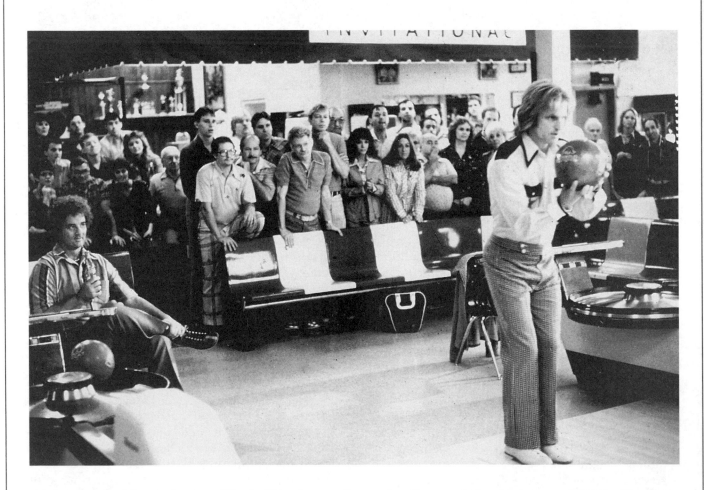

The 1996 film *Kingpin* features Woody Harrelson as former bowling great Roy Munson and Randy Quaid as his Amish protege.

ing the lost briefcase. The reviews for the film were mixed. *Dumb and Dumber* "makes you laugh out loud for almost its entire running time," according to Richard Schickel in *Time*. The film's plot is "lame, but that doesn't matter . . . because the movie is essentially pitched at the level of an *Airplane*-style movie, with rapid-fire sight gags," Roger Ebert wrote in the Chicago *Sun-Times*. He also noted that there was a moment in the movie that "made me laugh so loudly I embarrassed myself . . . I hasten to add that I did not laugh as loudly again, or very often. . . ." Desson Howe of the *Washington Post* was one of those critics who was not amused by *Dumb and Dumber*, dismissing the movie as an "uneven collection of bodily function jokes, facial gyrations, sexual jibes and pedestrian slapstick."

Happily for the Farrellys, the reception for their next movie was more favorable. The brothers joined forces as co-directors for the first time on *Kingpin*. The movie stars Woody Harrelson as Roy Munson, a washed-up bowling pro who befriends an Amish hot-shot bowler named Ishmael Borg, played by Randy Quaid. The story follows the pair's adventures as Harrelson tries to prepare his newfound prodigy for a big money tournament in Las Vegas. According to Bret Watson in *Entertainment Weekly*, the Farrellys—"scraggly" Peter and "cherubically preppy" Bobby—"affably insist that *Kingpin* remains true to their goal—cracking up 16-year-olds of all ages." Peter Farrelly told Watson, "There were opportunities to throw in a few farts and s—— type things. But we thought: 'That was *Dumb and Dumber*.' This is more of a puke movie. We feel we're growing."

Something About *That* Movie

In their own way, the Farrelly brothers proved that with their next movie, which was one of the biggest hits of 1998, taking in more than $175 million at the box office in the U.S. alone. *There's Something About Mary* is a "romantic comedy with its heart in the right place and its mind a little lower," according to Leah Rozen of *People*. The film features a hapless and hopelessly in love character named Ted, played by Ben Stiller, who tries to catch the heart of the brilliant and radiantly gorgeous Mary, played by Cameron Diaz. However, her down-to-earth, carefree personality also attracts a bizarre assortment of weirdos, psychos, and stalkers.

If you enjoy the works of Peter and Bobby Farrelly, you may also want to check out the following:

Blazing Saddles, a film by Mel Brooks, 1974.
National Lampoon's Animal House, a film starring John Belushi, 1978.
Revenge of the Nerds, a film starring Robert Carradine and Anthony Edwards, 1984.
South Park, an animated television show on Comedy Central.

The movie is an offbeat love story that's packed with crude jokes and outrageous sight gags. Ted has not seen Mary since high school, when she asked him to be her date at the senior prom. However, this first and only date ends abruptly when Ted catches part of his anatomy in the zipper of his pants while using the bathroom. Thirteen years later, the still lovestruck Ted tracks down Mary in Miami Beach, only to become the victim of yet another mishap: the private detective whom Ted hires falls in love with Mary, and tells him that his love is obese, wheel-chair bound, has four children by three fathers, and has moved to Japan as a mail-order bride. When asked whether they "once again crossed the delicate line of vulgarity," Peter quipped, "We live on the other side of the line. Do you mean cross it back to normal?"

Robert Ebert in the Chicago *Sun-Times* got caught up in the fun he saw on the screen. "*There's Something About Mary* is an unalloyed exercise in bad taste, and contains five or six explosively funny sequences," Ebert wrote. "I love it when a movie takes control, sweeps away my doubts and objections, and compels me to laugh. I'm having a physical reaction, not an intellectual one. There's such freedom in laughing so loudly. I feel cleansed." Richard Corliss of *Time* magazine agreed; as long as audiences "park their sense and sensibility at the 'plex door, there's plenty to enjoy in the performances," he wrote. Referring to the Farrelly's fondness for jokes about mentally and physically disadvantaged people and people in excruciating and embarrassing pain, Charles Taylor in *Salon* remarked: "Sick yes, but [the brothers] are as good-natured as two shameless gagsters can be."

Ben Stiller and Cameron Diaz pair up in the Farrelly brothers' 1998 often-outrageous romantic comedy *There's Something About Mary.*

The Farrellys can pull off this kind of silliness only because they are known for their ability to relax their actors so much that they feel comfortable doing the most outrageously embarrassing things while the cameras are rolling. "Our feeling is that the most important thing on a set is that actors have enough confidence to try different things," explained Peter in a *Boldtype* on-line interview. He went on to explain that if the atmosphere is not loose, the actors won't extend themselves to pull off the joke because they will be afraid of being embarrassed. "It doesn't always work, but if you're on a comfortable set, you don't mind failing, because you know you're among friends," he went on to say. As Harrelson explained in an interview that appears on the *Kingpin* Web site: "I never had the experience of working with two directors before, but Peter and Bobby are amazing together." The brothers also use another tactic that endears them to actors (in-

cluding their own father), and entices them to appear in successive Farrelly movies. "Our unspoken rule is that if somebody's in one of our movies, and they do a good job, they'll be back," Peter Farrelly said.

Forging Ahead

Between various projects and working on his films, Peter Farrelly somehow also found time to complete a satirical novel about the excesses of Hollywood, *The Comedy Writer*. He explained that he wrote the novel for a few weeks here and a few weeks there over a ten-year period. Finally, he took the summer of 1992 off to complete it, although it was not published until 1998. In this, his second novel, the protagonist is Henry Halloran, an earnest screenwriter. He works in a dead-end salesman job and packs up his car to move West after his girlfriend breaks up with him. "A must-read for any Hollywood newcomers experiencing career frustration," according to R. Hunter Garcia in *USA Today*. With some of the same hapless tendencies as Ted in *There's Something About Mary*, Henry fumbles his way through trying to pick up women and trying to put some order in his chaotic life.

Meanwhile, Peter and Bobby Farrelly were working on their next film, *Stuck on You*, which is a comedy about Siamese twins joined at the hip. Aside from the obvious similarities in their own lives, the movie focuses on the Siamese brothers' dilemma of whether or not to have an operation to separate themselves. The problem lies in the fact that one of the brothers is sure to come through the operation just fine, while the other brother has a 50-50 chance of surviving. Among the other projects the Farrelly brothers are working is turning Peter's novel, *Outside Providence*, into a movie.

Away from the movie business, the Farrellys spend their spare time getting together with friends and playing golf. While they lived in California for several years, the brothers say that they prefer the East Coast. Bobby explained in a *Providence Phoenix* interview that in his heart he never left. "I always considered Rhode Island my home," he said. "But I have two children now . . . you need a place where you can put them in the yard and let them run around and not worry your brains off every day."

If past performances are any indication, whatever their endeavor and whatever their roles, it seems likely the brothers are bound to draw attention. "Peter and Bobby Farrelly are among a handful of directors in the world who know how to make audiences laugh out loud. I think they are geniuses at broad-based comedy, the kind that will bring the notion of bellyaches to a whole new generation of moviegoers," Brad Krevoy, one of the coproducers of *Dumb and Dumber* stated. The stars of *There's Something About Mary*, summed up the Farrellys in comments that appeared on that film's Web site. "There was no competitiveness. They worked totally harmoniously, with Peter as sort of the front man and Bobby behind-the-scenes," said Cameron Diaz. Her co-star Ben

Stiller agreed. "They have that perfect relationship as brothers, co-writers and co-directors," he observed.

■ Works Cited

Corliss, Richard, review of *There's Something About Mary*, *Time*, July 20, 1998, p. 62.
Ebert, Roger, review of *Dumb and Dumber*, *Sun-Times* (Chicago), December 16, 1994.
Ebert, Roger, on-line review of *There's Something About Mary*, *Sun-Times* (Chicago), located at http://www.suntimes.com/ebert.
Farrelly, Bobby, on-line interview with *Providence Phoenix*, located at http://www.providence phoenix.com/archive/movies.
Farrelly, Peter, comments in *Contemporary Authors*, Volume 127, Gale, 1989, pp. 137-38.
Farrelly, Peter, on-line interview with *Boldtype*, located at http://www.boldtype.com, June, 1998.
Garcia, R. Hunter, review of *The Comedy Writer*, *USA Today*, September 3, 1998, p. 40.
Howe, Desson, review of *Dumb and Dumber*, *Washington Post*, December 16, 1994.
Kingpin Web site, located at http://mgmua.com/kingpin/main.html.
Rozen, Leah, review of *There's Something About Mary*, *People*, July 20, 1998, p. 33.
Schickel, Richard, review of *Dumb and Dumber*, *Time*, January 9, 1995, p. 66.
Snead, Elizabeth, interview with Robert and Peter Farrelly, *USA Today*, July 15, 1998, p. D1.
There's Something About Mary Web site, located at http://www.aboutmary.com.
Watson, Bret, review of *Kingpin*, *Entertainment Weekly*, August 2, 1996, p. 14.
Wloszczyna, Susan, review of *There's Something About Mary*, *USA Today*, July 15, 1998, p. D1.

■ For More Information See

PERIODICALS

Hollywood Reporter, February 2, 1999.
Newsweek, July 20, 1998, p. 64.
Publishers Weekly, January 13, 1997, p. 24.*

—Sketch by Diane Andreassi

Charles Ferry

Journal, and Best Books for Young Adults, American Library Association (ALA), all 1983, all for *Raspberry One;* Best Book for Young Adults, ALA, 1993, Books for the Teen Age, New York Public Library, 1994, and Best Book for High School Seniors, National Council of Teachers of English, 1995, all for *Binge.*

■ Personal

Born October 8, 1927, in Chicago, IL; son of Ignatius Loyola (a postal clerk) and Madelyn Anne (Bartholemew) Ferry; married Ruth Louise Merz (an executive travel coordinator), September 26, 1958; children: Ronald Edmund Richardson (stepson). *Education:* Attended University of Illinois, 1952. *Politics:* Republican. *Religion:* Episcopalian. *Hobbies and other interests:* "I cook, bake bread, and tutor persons of all ages in writing."

■ Addresses

Home—Rochester Hills, MI. *Office*—Daisy Hill Press, P.O. Box 1681, Rochester, MI 48308.

■ Career

Radio and newspaper journalist, 1949-71; writer, 1971—. *Military service:* U.S. Navy, 1944-49.

■ Awards, Honors

Best Children's Book, Friends of American Writers, Best Books of the Year selection, *School Library*

■ Writings

Up in Sister Bay, Houghton, 1975.
O Zebron Falls!, Houghton, 1977.
Raspberry One, Houghton, 1983.
One More Time!, Houghton, 1985.
Binge, Daisy Hill Press (Rochester, MI), 1992.
A Fresh Start, Proctor Publications (Ann Arbor, MI), 1996.
Love, Proctor Publications, 1998.

■ Adaptations

Binge was optioned for film by Walt Disney Educational Productions.

■ Sidelights

A career as a children's book writer came relatively late in life for Charles Ferry. After working as a journalist and in related fields for several years, Ferry began writing his first book for young readers after he had reached his forties. Prompted by recollections of his own wide-ranging life experiences—from happy childhood vacations in the northern United States to tragic adult years during which his life was controlled by a growing dependence on alcohol—Ferry published the first of several novels that would vividly recreate young peoples' movement toward adulthood. While his early novels take place during the years surrounding World War II, his later fiction deals with contemporary—and controversial—topics, including alcoholism. "I have no interest in writing for adults," Ferry once commented. "In general, I think the best writing is being done in the children's field. Authors have the freedom to give of themselves and to dream a little."

"I began writing vignettes about my boyhood summers in northern Wisconsin," Ferry once explained, describing how he "eased into the role of author." He eventually collected these vignettes into the manuscript of his first novel, *Up in Sister Bay,* which was published in 1975. Set in northern Wisconsin in the year 1939, the story revolves around the challenges facing four teens during wartime. "In *Up in Sister Bay,* Hitler's armies invade Poland," the author noted, "triggering the war and changing the lives of simple people."

Examines World War II Era

Up in Sister Bay would be the first of Ferry's books to illuminate the events of everyday life during the World War II era. 1977's *O Zebron Falls!* portrays a young woman approaching high school graduation, whose efforts to find a direction in her life are complicated by an unresolved conflict with her father and the onset of the Second World War. Sixteen-year-old Lukie Bishop tries to get the most from her last year in school, knowing her future as a woman in a small Midwestern town is limited. At a glance, Lukie's life seems idyllic—she's elected Class Sweetheart, serves as homecoming chairman, and enjoys the company of Billy Butts, football hero and school valedictorian. However, readers soon understand Lukie's sorrows. Her relationship with Billy, an African American, can never become serious because of the townspeople's prejudices; her uncle dies in a munitions factory while contributing to the war effort; and her elders suggest she should limit her goals to teaching or nursing, respectable professions for women. Critics praised Ferry for writing about times long past without sugarcoating or ignoring the difficulties young adults experienced. Marianne M. Rafalko, writing in *Best*

In this 1992 novel, Ferry relates his devastating experiences with alcohol through the character of eighteen-year-old Weldon Yeager.

Sellers, commended Ferry for his perceptive portrayal of a teenage girl of the 1940s, saying "today's young reader may readily identify with her problems and fears: growing up, falling in love, maturing sexually, relating to one's parents, and deciding one's future." In a *Horn Book* review, Ann A. Flowers applauded *O Zebron Falls!,* asserting that it "contains the sweetness of a simpler time but emphasizes that every era has its unsolvable problems."

Ferry's award-winning *Raspberry One,* published in 1983, also focuses on the tensions young Americans felt during the Second World War. The young protagonist, Nick Enright, attempts to deal with the brutalizing effects of combat while serving aboard a U.S. Navy torpedo bomber destined to fight in the bloody battle for control of the island of Iwo Jima. *"O Zebron Falls!* deals with life on the wartime home front, while *Raspberry One,* a hard look at the horrors of war, ends with V-J Day and victory," explained Ferry. "Prior to that war, in 1936, President Franklin Delano Roosevelt had told his countrymen, 'To some generations, much is given. Of some generations, much is expected. This generation of Americans has a rendezvous with destiny.' That generation had an awesome rendezvous, with history's greatest war," Ferry maintained, "and it acquitted itself admirably." Because he had never actually experienced a combat situation, Ferry put an enormous amount of effort into researching the historic backdrop of *Raspberry One.* He once said in a *Horn Book* article, "For two years . . . I relived the war, in all of its theaters. God, what a horror!" . . . *Raspberry One* is my little prayer that it will never happen again." Ferry expects that his first four titles will soon be reissued, in a boxed set, as "The Rendezvous Quartet."

Calling the characters in *Raspberry One* "well-realized," Micki S. Nevett in *Voice of Youth Advocates* remarked on Ferry's ability to dramatize war without glorifying it and suggested the novel will give new readers an idea of "what a generation of young people in the 1940s experienced." In *School Library Journal,* reviewer David A. Lindsey appreciated Ferry's war narrative as a refreshing change of pace and described *Raspberry One* as being "long on action and strong in characterization."

Another of Ferry's historical novels, 1985's *One More Time!,* takes place during the same period, depicting the impact of the Japanese attack on Pearl Harbor on an older group of Americans: the members of a popular Big Band dance orchestra. Ferry details the life of a musician and American culture in general during the Big Band era. Writing in *Booklist,* Stephanie Zvirin complimented Ferry on "capturing the nostalgia and the trepidation of the American people" during the 1940s as they prepared for the "unknown." While admitting *One More Time!* may appeal to a smaller audience because of its subject, *School Library Journal* contributor Lindsey praised the novel's "well-crafted narrative," adding that Ferry presents solidly constructed characters and provides readers "a detailed knowledge of the milieu in which [these characters] live."

"In the writing of my first four titles, I was keenly aware that I was probably creating the most im-

portant body of work on life in America during World War II ever written for young people," Ferry once disclosed. "I knew that because I was drawing heavily from personal experience and was confident of the integrity of my work." While providing his readers with a vivid recreation of life in the United States during wartime, Ferry also accomplished something of a personal nature while writing those first four novels. "I had an ambivalent relationship with my father," he explained. "As a result, when I started my creative writing, I couldn't handle a father as a fictional character, even though my own father had passed away fifteen years earlier.

"And so in *Up in Sister Bay,* I wrote the father out of the story. He is away in Chicago looking for work. We learn about him indirectly through his son, Robbie, who remembers unkind things about him: his meanness, his drinking, things that applied to my own father. Yet it is clear that Robbie loves his father and looks up to him—again reflecting my own situation.

"In my second book, I could handle a father, but he is a gruff man who embarrasses his daughter in front of her friends, which my father often did. Then, in my third book, *Raspberry One,* the character George Enright is a marvelous father. The self-therapy had worked; I had come to terms with my own father. In researching that book, I learned about the horrors he had experienced in World War I. I came to understand him and to realize that I loved him dearly—and still do."

Face-to-Face with Addiction

At this point in his career as an author, all of Ferry's books had focused on the lives of young people during the period of his own adolescence. A change in direction came in the 1990s with the publication of *Binge.* Considering it "the most personally important book" he would ever write, Ferry bravely confronted the reality of the addiction that had diminished his own life, career, and relationships with family and friends for more than two decades. "For much of my life I was plagued by the ravages of alcohol," he remarked. "I could fill a large volume, recounting the horrors it caused in my life. [In the early 1970s], I finally whipped the problem. Still, hardly a night goes by that some bad memory of that period doesn't return to haunt me." In his essay for

If you enjoy the works of Charles Ferry, you may also want to check out the following books and films:

Michael Cadnum, *Calling Home,* 1991.
Bette Greene, *Summer of My German Soldier,* 1973.
Todd Strasser, *The Accident,* 1988.
Clean and Sober, a film starring Michael Keaton, 1988.

Something about the Author Autobiography Series, Ferry shares how alcohol consumed his life for over twenty-five years, leading him to commit crimes and even spend time in prison. "Why was I sent to prison in the first place? Forgery, and uttering, and publishing—three-and-a-half to fourteen years. The sentence . . . may seem rather harsh, but it wasn't. [It] was merely the tip of the iceberg. [It] was the disgraceful culmination of my six-month, nine-state drinking binge. During that time I was a mini crime wave. Two stolen cars, one abandoned, one totaled. Five break-ins, most of them senseless. Bad checks, whenever I got my hands on a blank one. Larceny, whenever there was an opportunity. Anything to keep alcohol flowing through my bloodstream."

Ferry wanted to write these experiences out of his system; he did, publishing *Binge* in 1992. The story of Weldon Yeager, an eighteen-year-old petty criminal with a serious drinking problem, *Binge* follows its dissolute protagonist on a colossal binge that has tragic consequences. Waking up in a hospital ward under police guard—and not remembering how he got there—Weldon must eventually accept responsibility for actions that resulted in not only the loss of his own right foot, but in the deaths of two people struck and killed by the car he was driving. "If the book spares one young person the ravages of alcohol, I will consider it the greatest achievement of my life," Ferry declared. "You see, when I set out to write a young adult novel about how alcohol destroys young lives, my primary target was not young people who already have a drinking problem (although some would surely be influenced by such a book) but those who *don't,*" the author said in his *SAAS* essay. "Hopefully the images in *Binge* would remain fixed in the minds of some of them and

spare them the horrors of alcoholism in future years. I would achieve that effect, I decided, with a short novel that could be read in one sitting and have a stunning impact on the reader."

Since its publication, critical reception has marked *Binge* a success: Mary K. Chelton in a review for *Voice of Youth Advocates* called the novel "an incredibly powerful, mesmerizing, tragic, read-in-one-sitting little book with an authenticity and understanding rare in adolescent literature." In the same publication, critic Carol Otis Hurst termed the work "a brutal book with a strong moral impact. It walks a thin line between being a tract on the evils of alcohol and a novelette and, thanks to the skills of Mr. Ferry, it succeeds."

Binge proved to be pivotal, both in the field of publishing as a whole—it was the first self-published book in the history of the American Library Association to receive an ALA Best Book citation—as well as in its author's personal life. "I had gone public with my troubled background: my twenty-five-year battle against alcohol, which had been a torment in my life: lost jobs, wrecked cars, dirty jail cells, prison. *Binge,* which tells a powerful story about how alcohol destroys young lives, was written as my personal redemption. When sixty-one mainstream publishers rejected it, I published the book myself . . . [and] when the American Library Association chose it as a Best Book for Young Adults, almost overnight I became something of a legend."

Ferry has continued writing in the candid, forthright vein characteristic of *Binge*; he released *A Fresh Start* in 1996. "*A Fresh Start* points the way to recovery from alcoholism [using] my Eight Steps to Sobriety and a Better You," the author explained. "This time, I ignored establishment publishers and went directly to small presses." The novel recounts the efforts of four high school seniors in fighting the demons of alcohol and regaining sobriety through an eight-step program that Ferry devised during his own recovery from alcoholism. After failing courses during their final year in school, these four students struggle to earn their diploma, all the while reflecting on how alcohol abuse has affected their relationships with friends, family, and classmates. In *Voice of Youth Advocates,* C. A. Nichols emphasized that *A Fresh Start*'s message would be lost if it were viewed as "a novel or short story." Instead the reviewer insisted the work be used "to empower teens (or adults) to examine and take control of their own lives."

A more recent novel, *Love*, departs from the topic of alcohol to focus on two terminally ill children—Robbie and Sue Ellen, both age eleven—and the strong bond of love that develops between them in a hospital cancer ward. "I think . . . *Love* is my best work to date," the author explained, although he believes that, like *Binge, Love* will be regarded as controversial for dealing with issues that are not typical of children's literature.

Despite the controversy surrounding his most recent novels, Ferry remains dedicated to his work. "To one degree or another, all good fiction involves truth," he once commented. "As William Faulkner put it, 'Truth is what a person holds to his or her heart.' What do my books offer that young people can hold to their hearts? It's not for me to say, really. My strong suit appears to be evoking mood and atmosphere. I tell stories of young people coming of age. . . . My books come from deep inside of me, and they are slow to develop." After more than two decades as a published author, Ferry continues to live modestly, researching, lecturing, and writing from his home in Rochester Hills, a suburb of Detroit, Michigan. There, he explains, "our gregarious Belgian sheepdog, Emily Anne, rules the household. My wife, Ruth, who is a partner in my work, and I have touched a lot of young lives throughout America. We feel privileged."

■ Works Cited

Chelton, Mary K., review of *Binge, Voice of Youth Advocates*, June, 1993, p. 8.

Ferry, Charles, article in *Horn Book*, December, 1983, p. 651.

Ferry, Charles, essay in *Something about the Author Autobiography Series*, Volume 20, Gale Research, 1995, pp. 201-18.

Flowers, Ann A., review of *O Zebron Falls!, Horn Book*, October, 1977, p. 539.

Hurst, Carol Otis, review of *Binge, Voice of Youth Advocates*, August, 1994.

Lindsey, David A., review of *Raspberry One, School Library Journal*, September, 1983, pp. 132-33.

Lindsey, David A., review of *One More Time!, School Library Journal*, August, 1985, p. 74.

Nevett, Micki S., review of *Raspberry One, Voice of Youth Advocates*, April, 1984, p. 30.

Nichols, C. A., review of *A Fresh Start, Voice of Youth Advocates*, October, 1996, p. 208.

Rafalko, Marianne M., review of *O Zebron Falls!, Best Sellers*, December, 1977, p. 293.

Zvirin, Stephanie, review of *One More Time!, Booklist*, May 15, 1985, p. 1325.

■ For More Information See

PERIODICALS

Booklist, May 15, 1983, p. 1196; March 15, 1993, p. 1342.

Children's Literature in Education, spring, 1985, pp. 15-20.

Detroit Free Press, October 11, 1998, pp. 1G-2G.

Horn Book, December, 1975, p. 601; June, 1983, p. 310; September-October, 1985, p. 563.

Kirkus Reviews, August 15, 1975, p. 924.

New York Times Book Review, November 2, 1975, p. 10; March 5, 1978, p. 26.

Publishers Weekly, March 29, 1985, p. 73.

School Library Journal, December, 1975, p. 59; October, 1977, p. 123; May, 1996, p. 132.

Voice of Youth Advocates, August, 1985, p. 183; October, 1993, pp. 206-8; December, 1994, p. 272.

Daniel Hayes

■ Personal

Born April 17, 1952, in Troy, NY; son of Thomas Robert (a dairy farmer) and Mary (maiden name, Welch) Hayes. *Education:* State University of New York at Plattsburgh, B.S., 1973; State University of New York at Albany, M.S., 1982.

■ Addresses

Home—RD No. 11044, Route 40, Schaghticoke, NY 12154. *Agent*—Hy Cohen Literary Agency, P.O. Box 43770, Upper Montclair, NJ 07043. *E-mail*—hayesdm@aol.com.

■ Career

Waterford Central Catholic School, Waterford, NY, English teacher, 1975-84; Troy High School, Troy, NY, English teacher, 1984—; freelance writer.

■ Awards, Honors

Best Book for Young Adults citation, American Library Association, 1992, for *The Trouble with Lemons*, 1995 for *No Effect*, and 1998 for *Flyers*; Edgar Award nomination for Best Young Adult Novel, 1997, for *Flyers*.

■ Writings

The Trouble with Lemons, David Godine, 1991.
Eye of the Beholder, David Godine, 1992.
No Effect, David Godine, 1993.
Flyers, Simon and Schuster, 1996.

■ Sidelights

Inspiration comes to writers from the most unlikely places. For Daniel Hayes, author of popular young adult fiction such as *The Trouble with Lemons, The Eye of the Beholder,* and *No Effect*, the muse took the form of slapstick comedy. "There was a point in my youth when I discovered the Three Stooges on television," Hayes told *Authors and Artists for Young Adults (AAYA)* in an interview. "Looking back now, I really think they've had an influence on my work, especially in the way many of my male characters interact with each other. I mean, the Stooges call each other names and hit each other over the head, but they are loyal to each other as well. My characters Tyler and Lymie from my first three books have a very Stooge-like friendship. They are always bantering and insulting one another, but there is no question they are friends. It's how lots of adolescent males act with each other."

Adolescent male behavior is the territory that Hayes has set out to chart. In his series novels about Tyler and Lymie, and in his novel *Flyers*, featuring an older protagonist, fifteen-year-old Gabe Riley, Hayes examines the complexity of loyalties, friendships, and dreams that fuel the engine of adolescence. His novels, more picaresque adventures than linear plot-driven works, employ comedy in large doses and hit close to the bone on issues such as adult hypocrisy, single-parenting, male virtues, and even alcoholism—though Hayes rejects the idea of problem novels. "My books start with characters," he told *AAYA*, "and of course if you have real characters you're going to have problems. But I don't write books, like some TV shows, that 'feature' a disease. For me that's putting the cart before the horse." Hayes has managed to make a success out of not following the rules in his fiction, just as many of his protagonists do in their lives. Loosely formed and organic in structure, Hayes's novels are held together more by the energy of characterization and dialogue than by a tightly woven plot.

Life on the Farm

Hayes grew up outside Troy, New York, on a dairy farm. One of three brothers and two sisters, Hayes was never at a loss for things to do on the farm. "We were thirteen miles from school," Hayes told *AAYA*, "and so we siblings, especially the brothers, formed a tight bond with each other. We also helped our father and uncle with the chores. But in ways I used to envy the kids from the nearby town. It was like they were the city kids. When I went to school in the little town of Greenwich, I thought that was really something—that was living." But Hayes was not so seduced by the allure of Greenwich; he still chose to raise calves and show them at the county fair—an experience that he re-created in his novel *Flyers*.

At school he was "a good under-achieving student," who focussed more on sports and social activities than he did on homework. "I liked sports and outdoor things, but I also loved books. When I had nothing else to do, I would pick up a book. I remember riding the bus home from school one day in the second grade and I borrowed the reader of this girl riding the bus with me. Suddenly I discovered how books can work: how they can transport you to another world. It

was amazing to lose yourself in that other world of ideas and stories. They were so real to me. So I came to look at books as a great way to escape being out in the country—a great way to travel and experience difference." A favorite genre for Hayes was mysteries, and the influence of that reading can be seen in his own work, especially in his first novel, *The Trouble with Lemons*.

In high school, Hayes went through the usual agonies of what to be when he grew up—none of these included writing. As a freshman, he dreamed of being a star basketball player, though his height worked against such dreams. Then

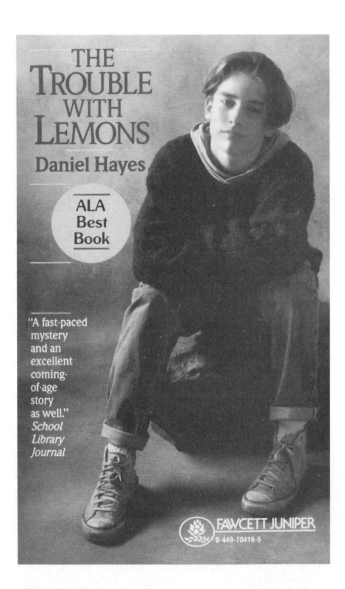

Mystery and adventure abound in this 1991 novel of two teenage boys, Tyler and Lymie, who discover a dead body while swimming in an old quarry.

came a period of wanting to be a rock star. "I got an electric guitar," Hayes told *AAYA*, "but had no talent." It was not until he went to college at SUNY Plattsburgh in upstate New York that he even considered writing as a possible career. He was attracted to English literature as a major "because I kind of liked to read and thought, hey, here's a way I can get a degree just by reading books. I remember specifically re-reading *Huckleberry Finn* in college, but at nineteen it was an entirely different thing—a brilliant satire and brilliant in the way Twain captures the dialects." The same was true for his new reading of Charles Dickens. "I'd read *Great Expectations* in high school, but upon re-reading I suddenly saw the enormous humor in it. I laughed all the way through. Dickens creates these incredibly funny minor characters and gives them all sorts of peculiar ticks and idiosyncracies." Hayes took several writing classes in college and was so eager to get out into the world that he finished his studies in three years.

From Hollywood to Teaching

Upon graduation, Hayes headed west to try his luck in Hollywood as a screenwriter. In the event, he wrote some articles for *Black Belt* magazine; the closest he got to the movie industry was working as an extra in a film that was being shot in the Los Angeles Coliseum. "We liked to call ourselves 'background players'," Hayes commented of this experience. Fed up with the Hollywood scene, Hayes headed back to New York state and began substitute teaching around Troy. This ultimately led to a full-time position in a Catholic school, teaching English. "I went into teaching for all the wrong reasons," Hayes told *AAYA*. "I wanted to be a writer, but knew it wasn't that easy. I needed to earn a living and thought with teaching I would be able to work and have time for writing. Luckily, I enjoyed teaching when I started."

Hayes taught junior high school students for his first eight years. "It's a neat age. The kids all want to tell you stuff they did last night and some of it was pretty goofy. But at first it was difficult for me. I mean I would take it personally if the super lesson I had planned half the night bored the students. Now I'm not phased by that." Earning his masters degree in 1982, Hayes moved on to teaching high school two years later. "The best thing about teaching is that you get to talk about books all day long. But some of the kids—actually a lot of them—have trouble with the pace of books, especially older novels. They have grown up with the fifteen-second news clip and with MTV and computers. Novels, on the other hand, take time to set up. Kids are resistant to them."

Another fringe benefit to Hayes's teaching job was a built-in cast of characters for the stories that he was creating in his spare time. "The books I have liked the most are coming-of-age stories, so when it came time for me to write my own, it was natural that I turned to young adult and juvenile novels," Hayes explained in his *AAYA* interview. Slowly such stories began to coalesce into a novel about an adolescent boy named Tyler and his buddy Lymie. The episodic nature of that book began to hold together when Hayes read a news article. "I was in the faculty room one day and picked up a copy of the *National Enquirer* somebody had left there. I read the story of some kinds partying at an old rock quarry and how they had discovered a body in the water, and I suddenly realized this was what I needed for my book."

Despite his sudden inspiration, Hayes still took six years to write and sell this first novel, *The Trouble with Lemons*. "I was told by editors that kids would never follow a long book like mine. They urged me to keep the mystery aspect front and center; I often left it on the back burner while I had fun with my characters. Other editors urged me to write more of a problem book, but I wanted a palliative to all those sorts of books. I wanted mine to take young readers away, like books did for me when I was a kid and like they still do for me."

The Tyler/Lymie Novels

Persistence paid off for Hayes; ultimately he sold his novel to the publisher David Godine, and that house brought it out as their first YA novel. *The Trouble with Lemons* is the first of what has thus far been three titles following the misadventures of two adolescent boys: asthmatic, insecure Tyler and his best friend, chubby Lymie. *The Trouble with Lemons* is, according to Cathi Dunn MacRae in *Wilson Library Bulletin*, a "mystery imbued with the thoroughly original spirit of its narrator, Tyler." This narrator lets the reader know the score right

The slapstick adventures of Tyler and Lymie continue when the two teens play a prank that goes awry in this 1992 novel.

off: "I'm not even thirteen, and I've already experienced more humiliation than most adults."

Tyler's poor self-image—he sees himself as the family 'lemon' of the title—is the result of childhood asthma that has kept him a steady customer of local doctors and in delicate health, of his inability to navigate the troubled waters of school society and one bully in particular, and of guilt feelings that he is somehow responsible for his parents' separation. Tyler's troubles are compounded by the death of his father in an accident. It doesn't help either that his mother and older brother are movie stars, leaving Tyler's scant achievements far behind in the dust. It is no surprise then when a late-night swim in the local quarry with Lymie ends up badly for Tyler. The pair quite literally bump into a dead body on this forbidden swim and then also witness a car leaving the scene. An anonymous call to the police from them does not solve their problem: is the culprit on to them? Are they in danger of becoming the next victims? As Nancy Vasilakis wrote in a *Horn Book* review of the novel, "Self-acceptance, the vagaries of human nature, finding one's niche . . . make up the elements of this fine first novel by a promising author."

Tyler is forced to come to grips with his own insecurities and—with the aid of kindly Mrs. Saunders, the housekeeper, and Chuckie, a martial arts expert and family gardener—to trust his own instincts. Soon he becomes convinced that the principal's son is involved in the crime and he must force the real culprits to confess before they try to silence him. As Jody McCoy noted in *Voice of Youth Advocates,* Tyler "may not be a talented movie star like his mother and older brother but he can run and can face the truth when justice demands it." McCoy concluded that *The Trouble with Lemons* was a "satisfying mystery with an engaging central character in a tale that bubbles right along." Vasilakis added in *Horn Book* that Hayes's characterizations are good and the protagonist makes readers sympathize with him. She added that the novel was a "believable and appealing story."

Other reviewers also commended the novel. A reviewer for *Five Owls* complimented Hayes on the "best opening chapter in recent memory," and went on to call this debut novel "a first-rate mystery. . . . Instead of solely creating a thriller according to formula, Hayes has taken the time to write a novel with texture and nuance." A *Publishers Weekly* critic also had high praise for this first novel: "Tyler's unique, deftly drawn character highlights this carefully crafted, powerful story. As a mystery it is intriguing, but as a novel about introspection and self-acceptance, it is irresistible." This first novel became an American Library Association Best Book and earned Hayes a large readership eager for more adventures featuring Tyler and Lymie. Hayes proved his own instincts were right about the possibilities of a free-form novel. "I'm perfectly content to have kids banter and react to one another. I have to consciously remind myself to lay in plot. But I figure if you get wrapped up in character, you'll feel that my books are fast-paced. They are, however, definitely not plot-oriented."

Hayes had already started his second novel while he was trying to sell *The Trouble with Lemons,* and again this novel was in part inspired by a magazine article. This time the article spoke not of dead bodies but of phoney Modigliani heads in Italy; about how young architecture students decided to play a trick on the art world by fabricating a work by the famous sculptor that was subse-

quently 'found' and ultimately—to the horror of the pranksters—authenticated by art experts around the world. In *Eye of the Beholder,* Hayes transplanted this story to upstate New York and into the hands of Tyler and Lymie. Wakefield, where they live, is celebrating the work of a famous local sculptor, Badoglio, and the duo decide to have some fun with the serious adults.

As a Halloween prank, they carve stone heads a la Badoglio and causally throw their handiwork away in the river where the sculptor was reputed to have thrown two of his unrecovered creations. But when the heads are discovered and dubbed genuine by art critics, the boys are faced with a dilemma. "By the time the truth is discovered," noted *Horn Book*'s Nancy Vasilakis, "the boys have had a few nervous moments and learned a valuable lesson or two about adult pretensions and weaknesses." Lucinda Snyder Whitehurst commented in *School Library Journal* on Hayes's "episodic and quick pace," noting also Tyler's "fresh, natural voice," and Lymie, Tyler's "comic foil" who has "more heart than brains." A reviewer for *Publishers Weekly* concluded that "Readers will delight in these protagonists' sundry predicaments, all of which are resolved with ingenuity and imagination," while a *Booklist* contributor dubbed this second Tyler/Lymie novel "Downright hilarious." A *Voice Literary Supplement* reviewer described it as a "laugh-out-loud sequel to [Hayes's] excellent first novel."

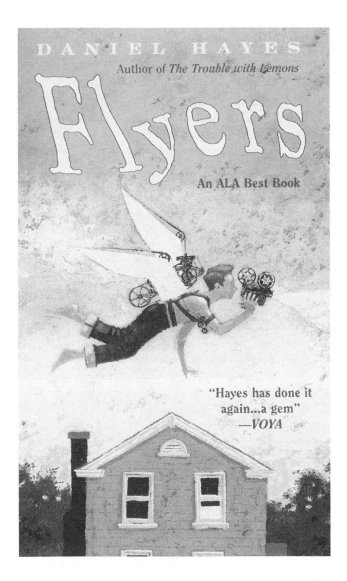

Fifteen-year-old Gabe Riley uses his filmmaking skills to solve a mystery at Blood Red Pond in this 1996 work.

Hayes decided that with his third Tyler/Lymie creation, *No Effect,* he wanted "nothing unusual happening,"' as he explained to *AAYA.* "I wanted this one to be simply a school book with some unrequited love thrown in." Tyler is determined to become a man; in pursuit of this goal he joins the high school wrestling team, though he is only in the eighth grade. He has dreams of grandeur: "I'm being led off the mat. Women are going crazy. Not even girls now. Real women. And not disturbed ones either. Nice, normal women who are beautiful." Tyler falls in love with one such normal woman, but in typical Tyler fashion she is unreachable—the new science teacher, Miss Williams. Complications arise when Tyler finally discovers that the object of Miss Williams's affections is Chuckie, the gardener, who has become something of an older brother figure for Tyler. "The result," noted a reviewer for the *Voice Literary Supplement,* "is excruciating. But funny. . . . In fact, Hayes has such a sure touch that he can make

If you enjoy the works of Daniel Hayes, you may also want to check out the following books and films:

Anne Fine, *My War with Goggle-Eyes,* 1989.
Gordon Korman, *A Semester in the Life of a Garbage Bag,* 1987.
Stand by Me, a film by Rob Reiner, 1986.

13-year-old-boy humor hit your funny bone, even if you're not a 13-year-old boy."

Other reviewers also complimented the novel. Susan R. Farber wrote in *Voice of Youth Advocates* that the events of *No Effect*, told by a "less talented writer" could have been simply "slapstick" or "trite." Farber noted, however, that "Hayes is a master at imitating teenage dialogue and he smoothly integrates more serious themes without disrupting the flow or appearing didactic." A reviewer in *Publishers Weekly* applauded the novel, noting that "Hayes masterfully blends humor and heartache," and dubbing the book "Perceptive, funny, and above all, believable." *Booklist*'s Ilene Cooper concluded that "Certainly young people—and yes, especially boys—will identify with both longing for the unattainable and getting into something physical to work off all that excess energy. This one's a page-turner, but readers may also have some things to think about after they close the book."

Flyers and Beyond

With the 1996 novel, *Flyers*, Hayes departed from the world of junior high for the more troubled waters of high school in a book featuring the fifteen-year-old protagonist, Gabe Riley. "After doing three Tyler books, I felt I was ready to try something different," Hayes told *AAYA*. Vanessa Elder, writing in *School Library Journal*, noted that a "mysterious, supernatural element is always lurking around the corners of this story," and indeed Gabe is a grab-bag of vagaries. He is an ardent filmmaker with a good sense of humor—a must for any Hayes protagonist. He is also the son of a single-father lawyer with a drinking problem. Gabe and his friends are making a movie about ghosts and swamp monsters, but things go awry when the townspeople see these youngsters dressed in costume and take them for the real thing.

Candace Deisley had high praise for *Flyers* in the pages of *Voice of Youth Advocates,* calling it a "gem of a young adult novel" that not only dealt with issues such as "dating, drinking, driving and peer pressures," but that also blended Hayes's "marvelous humor" to create a "terrific" combination. A reviewer in *Publishers Weekly* commented that this tale "goes straight from the funnybone to the heart," and that throughout, "this spry work blends wisecracks with insightful reflections on life, death and relationships."

"I want to write more about Gabe," Hayes told *AAYA* in his interview. "He's a likeable kid, and I also grew to appreciate his father. He's definitely got problems, but I like him, too." This liking of his protagonists is an essential element in Hayes's writing method. "I write when I really have something to say," Hayes noted. "I don't force myself to write to a schedule because then it gets dry, the results aren't good and I throw big chunks of it away. But inspiration is all around. Many of my ideas come from my own childhood, and being around kids all day teaching reminds you that there is really a generic kind of kid-dom that cuts across culture and generations. Fashions may change and language may change, but the elemental kid does not. Kids just blurt it out. They let their feelings out spontaneously. And in the end, kids are amazingly resilient. They are survivors. It's my job as a writer to show this resiliency and to poke some fun at the world in general. I hope my books have an over-riding and underlying optimism. The sort of optimism like at the end of a Chaplin film when Charlie gives that little click of the heels at life. Life springs eternal. That's the sort of optimism I'm aiming for at the end of my books; no matter how hard life is there is some hope there."

■ Works Cited

Cooper, Ilene, review of *No Effect, Booklist,* May 1, 1994, p. 1595.

Deisley, Candace, review of *Flyers, Voice of Youth Advocates,* February, 1997, p. 327.

Elder, Vanessa, review of *Flyers, School Library Journal,* November, 1996, p. 120.

Review of *Eye of the Beholder, Booklist,* February 1, 1993, p. 984.

Review of *Eye of the Beholder, Publishers Weekly,* November 30, 1992, p. 56.

Review of *Eye of the Beholder, Voice Literary Supplement,* December, 1992, p. 21.

Farber, Susan R., review of *No Effect, Voice of Youth Advocates,* February, 1994, p. 368.

Review of *Flyers, Publishers Weekly,* November 4, 1996, p. 177.

Hayes, Daniel, interview with J. Sydney Jones for *Authors and Artists for Young Adults,* conducted December, 1998.

MacRae, Cathi Dunn, "The Young Adult Perplex," *Wilson Library Bulletin,* December, 1991.

McCoy, Jody, review of *The Trouble with Lemons, Voice of Youth Advocates,* August, 1991, p. 171.

Review of *No Effect, Publishers Weekly,* November 22, 1993, p. 64.

Review of *No Effect, Voice Literary Supplement,* December, 1993, pp. 26-27.

Review of *The Trouble with Lemons, Five Owls,* January, 1992, p. 64.

Review of *The Trouble with Lemons, Publishers Weekly,* March 22, 1991, p. 80.

Vasilakis, Nancy, review of *The Trouble with Lemons, Horn Book,* July-August, 1991, pp. 462-63.

Vasilakis, Nancy, review of *Eye of the Beholder, Horn Book,* January-February, 1993, p. 91.

Whitehurst, Lucinda Snyder, review of *Eye of the Beholder, School Library Journal,* December, 1992.

■ For More Information See

ON-LINE

Daniel Hayes's Internet home page is located at http://www.danielhayes.com.

PERIODICALS

Booklist, March 15, 1992, p. 1364; March 15, 1998, p. 1214.

Bulletin of the Center for Children's Books, June, 1991.

Horn Book, March, 1994, p. 205; January, 1997, p. 56.

Kirkus Reviews, March 15, 1991, p. 393; November 15, 1992, p. 1443; September 1, 1996, pp. 1322-23.

Kliatt, March, 1995, p. 6.

School Library Journal, June, 1991, p. 125; January, 1994, p. 132.

Voice of Youth Advocates, April, 1998, p. 42.

—Sketch by J. Sydney Jones

John Hersey

■ Personal

Born June 17, 1914, in Tientsin, China; died of liver and colon cancer, March 24, 1993, in Key West, FL; son of Roscoe Monroe (a Y.M.C.A. secretary in China) and Grace (a missionary; maiden name, Baird) Hersey; married Frances Ann Cannon, April 27, 1940 (divorced, February, 1958); married Barbara Day Addams Kaufman, June 2, 1958; children: (first marriage) Martin, John, Ann, Baird; (second marriage) Brook (daughter). *Education:* Yale University, B.A., 1936; attended Clare College, Cambridge, 1936-37. *Politics:* Democrat. *Hobbies and other interests:* Sailing, gardening, fishing, reading.

■ Career

Writer. Private secretary, driver, and factotum for Sinclair Lewis, summer, 1937; *Time* magazine, writer, editor, and correspondent, 1937-44, correspondent in China and Japan, 1939, covered South Pacific warfare, 1942, correspondent in Mediterranean theater, including Sicilian campaign, 1943, and in Moscow, 1944-45; editor and correspondent for *Life* magazine, 1944-45; writer for *New Yorker* and other magazines, 1945-93; made trip to China and Japan for *Life* and *New Yorker,* 1945-46; fellow, Berkeley College, Yale University, 1950-65; master, Pierson College, Yale University, 1965-70, fellow, 1965-93; writer-in-residence, American Academy in Rome, 1970-71; lecturer, Yale University, 1971-75, professor, 1975-84, professor emeritus, 1984-93. Chairman, Connecticut Volunteers for Stevenson, 1952; member of Adlai Stevenson's campaign staff, 1956. Editor and director of writers' co-operative magazine, '47. Member, Westport (CT) School Study Council, 1945-50, Westport Board of Education, 1950-52, Yale University Council Committee on the Humanities, 1951-56, Fairfield (CT) Citizens School Study Council, 1952-56, National Citizens' Commission for the Public Schools, 1954-56; member of Board of Trustees, Putney School, 1953-56; consultant, Fund for the Advancement of Education, 1954-56; chairman, Connecticut Committee for the Gifted, 1954-57; delegate to White House Conference on Education, 1955; trustee, National Citizens' Council for the Public Schools, 1956-58; member, visiting committee, Harvard Graduate School of Education, 1960-65; Yale University Council Committee on Yale College, member, 1959-61, chairman, 1964-69; trustee, National Committee for Support of the Public Schools, 1962-68; member, Loeb Theater Center, 1980-93. *Member:* National Institute of Arts and Letters, American Academy of Arts and Letters (secretary, 1961-78, chancellor, 1981-84), American Academy of Arts and Sciences, Authors

League of America (member of council, 1946-70, 1975-93, vice-president, 1949-55, president, 1975-80), Authors Guild (member of council, 1946-93), PEN.

■ Awards, Honors

Pulitzer Prize, 1945, for *A Bell for Adano*; Anisfield-Wolf Award, 1950, Daroff Memorial Fiction Award, Jewish Book Council of America, 1950, and Sidney Hillman Foundation Award, 1951, all for *The Wall*; Howland Medal, Yale University, 1952; National Association of Independent Schools Award, 1957, for *A Single Pebble*; Tuition Plan Award, 1961; Sarah Josepha Hale Award, 1963; named honorary fellow of Clare College, Cambridge University, 1967. Honorary degrees: M.A., Yale University, 1947; L.H.D., New School for Social Research, 1950, Syracuse University, 1983; LL.D., Washington and Jefferson College, 1950; D.H.L., Dropsie College, 1950; Litt.D., Wesleyan University, 1954, Bridgeport University, 1959, Clarkson College of Technology, 1972, University of New Haven, 1975, Yale University, 1984, Monmouth College, 1985, William and Mary College, 1987, Albertus Magnus College, 1988.

■ Writings

FICTION

A Bell for Adano, Knopf, 1944, with new foreword by Hersey, Modern Library, 1946.
The Wall, Knopf, 1950.
The Marmot Drive, Knopf, 1953.
A Single Pebble, Knopf, 1956.
The War Lover, Knopf, 1959.
The Child Buyer, Knopf, 1960.
White Lotus, Knopf, 1965.
Too Far to Walk, Knopf, 1966.
Under the Eye of the Storm, Knopf, 1967.
The Conspiracy, Knopf, 1972.
My Petition for More Space, Knopf, 1974.
The Walnut Door, Knopf, 1977.
The Call: An American Missionary in China, Knopf, 1985.
Fling and Other Stories, Knopf, 1990.
Antonietta, Knopf, 1991.
Key West Tales (stories), Knopf, 1994.

OTHER

Men on Bataan, Knopf, 1942.

Into the Valley: A Skirmish of the Marines, Knopf, 1943.
Hiroshima (first published in *New Yorker*, August 31, 1946), Knopf, 1946, new edition published as *Hiroshima: A New Edition with a Final Chapter Written Forty Years after the Explosion*, 1985.
Here to Stay: Studies on Human Tenacity, Hamish Hamilton, 1962, Knopf, 1963, new edition with preface, 1988.
The Algiers Motel Incident, Knopf, 1968, with an introduction by Thomas J. Sprague, Johns Hopkins University Press, 1997.
(With others) *Robert Capa*, Paragraphic, 1969.
A Letter to the Alumni, Knopf, 1970.
(Editor) *Ralph Ellison: A Collection of Critical Essays*, Prentice-Hall, 1973.
(Editor) *The Writer's Craft*, Knopf, 1974.
The President, Knopf, 1975.
Aspects of the Presidency: Truman and Ford in Office, Ticknor & Fields, 1980.
Blues, Knopf, 1987.
(Author of commentary) John Armour and Peter Wright, *Manzanar*, Times, 1988.
Life Sketches, Knopf, 1989.

Author of introduction to *Let Us Now Praise Famous Men*, by Walker Evans, Houghton Mifflin. Contributor to numerous periodicals, including *Atlantic Monthly*, *Fortune*, *Life*, *New Yorker*, *Time*, and *Yale Review*.

■ Adaptations

A Bell for Adano was adapted as a stage play by Paul Osborn and was first produced at the Cort Theater in New York in December, 1944, and was filmed by Twentieth Century-Fox in 1945; *The Wall* was dramatized by Millard Lampell and was first produced at the Billy Rose Theater in New York in December, 1960, and was filmed for television by Columbia Broadcasting System in 1982; *The War Lover* was filmed by Columbia Pictures in 1962; *The Child Buyer* was adapted as a stage play by Paul Shyre and was first produced at the University of Michigan Professional Theater Program in Ann Arbor in 1964.

■ Sidelights

"I feel, often, as if I am making my life sketches not with a fine pen or a sharp pencil but with a thickish piece of charcoal," journalist and novelist

John Hersey wrote in the introduction to *Life Sketches*. "The best I can hope for is that the smudged and blurred lines will lie on the page in such ways as to hint at, even if they cannot really represent, the amazingly clear pictures that I believe I have seen in my mind." Despite these words, over the fifty-plus years of his career Hersey came to be known for his ability to bring important incidents and issues to life for readers through both nonfiction and novels. The author not only recounted pivotal events of the twentieth century—World War II, the bombing of Hiroshima, the Holocaust—he looked at the moral questions that they raised. Unlike many authors of his time, Hersey believed that writers had a responsibility to educate their readers. Writing, the author noted in the *Yale University Library Gazette*, is "the only hope man has of rising above his unmentionably horrible existence, his foul nest of murder, war, greed, madness and cruelty. Only the poets can persuade us to move up out of the slime into a hopeful shore, there by evolution to transform ourselves into higher and more intelligent creatures."

Hersey's unusual childhood may have accounted for his nonconformist views. He was born in Tientsin, China, in 1917 to parents who were missionaries for the Young Men's Christian Association. His first seven years were spent in China, and although he attended American and British schools he saw much of the Chinese people and countryside as his parents travelled around spreading the gospel. He recalled, for instance, the strange feeling it gave him when he was taken to school in a ricksha, a cart pulled by an adult. His father contracted encephalitis while travelling through an area hit by famine, and the family returned to the United States so that he could seek treatment. Despite the change in his surroundings, Hersey still felt like an outsider. "I was born a foreigner," he told *Publishers Weekly* interviewer Tom Spain. "I was born in China, and I think in some ways I have been an outsider in America because of that."

In spite of receiving medical treatment, Hersey's father soon died of his illness and the family settled in New York. The author attended public schools for three years, then won a scholarship to a private school, where he supported himself by cleaning classrooms and working as a waiter. He gained entrance to Yale University in 1932, and played football for coach Gerald Ford, who would

In this 1944 novel, an Italian American major tries to promote good will in an old Sicilian town recovering from Fascist occupation during World War II.

become president of the United States in 1974. He also got his first taste of journalism at college, working for the *Yale Daily News;* at the same time he took odd jobs to finance his way through school. He completed his degree in 1936, and spent the following year at Cambridge University in England, where he studied English literature. When he returned to America the following summer, his first job was as a secretary and general helper to the writer Sinclair Lewis, the celebrated author of *Main Street, Arrowsmith, Babbitt,* and *Elmer Gantry* who won the Nobel Prize in 1930.

In the fall of 1937 Hersey signed on as a staff member of *Time* magazine, America's first and most preeminent news weekly. *Time*'s cofounder and publisher, Henry R. Luce, although a generation older, was also a China-born child of missionaries, and the two hit it off. In 1939 Luce sent the young reporter to Chungking, China, a location from which Hersey saw the beginnings of the war in the Pacific begin to unfold. During World War II Hersey contributed reports on Japanese advances into China, as well as the developing military situation in the Philippines and South Pacific. In 1942 he was cited by the Secretary of the Navy for his role in helping to evacuate wounded soldiers from the battlefield on Guadalcanal Island.

Dispatches from the Front

Hersey returned to *Time*'s offices in New York in 1942 and began research to supplement his understanding of the war on the Pacific front. He interviewed other foreign correspondents, American veterans who served in the Pacific, and the families they had left behind. He combined these first-hand accounts with speeches, letters, memos, and other records of the war to produce his first book, *Men on Bataan*. While this study of America's Pacific troops and their commander, General Douglas MacArthur, openly celebrated their toughness and commitment, it was not a blindly positive portrayal of the military. Hersey deliberately attempted to dispel some of the myths surrounding MacArthur and included some negative details from the general's youth. This account "is well done and something we've needed and wanted," *New Yorker* writer Clifton Fadiman stated, praising how the author "has gone to much trouble to dig up backgrounds and make living men out of these soldiers." *Dictionary of Literary Biography* contributor Dan R. Jones noted that with its "synthesis of personal experience and objective journalism," *Men on Bataan* indicated that "even at this early stage in his career Hersey was exploring the literary potential of combining the techniques of fiction with the substance of fact."

While still working as a correspondent for *Time* and its sister publication *Life*, Hersey published another nonfiction account of the war in 1943. *Into the Valley: A Skirmish of the Marines* related the events of October 8, 1942, when Hersey accompanied a group of American soldiers as they attempted to secure an airbase on Guadalcanal Island. The company encountered sniper fire as they moved toward their objective, and later lost communication with the other American forces on the island. Eventually the order to retreat came, and the battle for position turned into a battle for survival. The work received favorable criticism, being compared to Stephen Crane's classic war novel *The Red Badge of Courage*. "It is simply told, yet it reveals more about war and its weird psychology than many other so-called important volumes," B. T. Williamson commented in the *New York Times Book Review*. Jones remarked that while *Into the Valley* followed *Men on Bataan* by only a few months, it is "a considerably more sophisticated example of literary journalism. Still supportive of the American war effort, it is driven less by patriotic impulse than by the immediacy of human experience." The critic concluded that the work "confirms that Hersey's journalistic gift was his ability to make humans, not events, the basis for journalistic texts."

After his stint in the Pacific, the journalist was sent to the Mediterranean, where he reported on the Allied efforts near Italy. Hersey spent some of his time there studying the Allied occupation of Sicily, an island off the coast of Italy. This experience served as the basis for his first novel, *A Bell for Adano*, which details the experiences of Major Joppolo, an Italian-American who has been appointed senior civil-affairs officer of the fictional Sicilian town of Adano. The ruling Fascists have departed Adano, along with much of its population, and Major Joppolo is responsible for helping the town recover from the destruction of the war. The most symbolic act he performs is the replacement of the town hall's bell, but he also must work against the unfeeling and unrealistic pronouncements of his own superior officers. "It is a typical story of what good will can achieve, and also where it fails," Virgilia Sapieha summarized in the *New York Herald Tribune Weekly Book Review*, as the major is eventually dismissed from his post despite his obvious care and competence. "Beneath the story flows a genuine love of justice, scorn of pettiness, and faith in mankind," the critic concluded, "ideals as implicit in the book as they are fundamental in America."

The novel was published at the height of the war, in 1944, and although it portrayed some members of the military in a negative light, it was still very popular with the public and won the 1945 Pulitzer Prize for fiction. Ben Ray Redman praised the work for its humor and entertaining characters, noting in the *Saturday Review of Literature* that "whatever its seriousness of intention and execution, stressed in a foreword, you will be laughing much of the time you are reading and smiling most of the time. Which is not to say you will miss hearing the message the author would have you hear," the critic explained. "Notwithstanding its self-imposed limitations of time and knowledge, *A Bell for Adano* is an entertaining story, a candid report from behind the lines and an effective tract," *New Republic* writer Malcolm Cowley noted, adding, however, that "to demand that it be a soundly constructed novel as well would be asking too much." While these early reviews stressed the major's individual heroism and the virtues of democracy, "in retrospect, it is evident that there is a basic conflict in the novel between the traditional idea of democracy and the new concept of social control and political organization typified by the American military government," Sam B. Girgus noted in the *Dictionary of Literary Biography*. This concern with greater social issues was to characterize most of Hersey's future work.

Highlighting the Horror of Hiroshima

Although Hersey was still a correspondent for both *Time* and *Life*, by the end of the war in 1945 he was beginning to feel restricted by the simple, news-oriented editorial approach of Luce's magazines. He was looking for chances to produce in-depth articles that would examine not just contemporary events, but the moral, ethical, and human issues they raised. He saw one such opportunity after U.S. forces dropped atomic bombs on the Japanese cities of Hiroshima and Nagasaki in 1945, leading to the Japanese surrender. Hersey convinced *New Yorker* editor William Shawn that a first-person account of the consequences of Hiroshima would make for compelling reading. After researching all he could on the blast, the journalist travelled to the devastated city and interviewed several survivors with the aid of an interpreter. He chose to present the experiences of six of them for his article: Father Wilhelm Kleinsorge, a German Jesuit priest; Miss Toshio Sasaki, a clerk for a tin company; Dr. Masakazu Fujii, a doctor with his own hospital; the Reverend Kiyoshi Tanimoto, a minister of a Methodist church; Dr. Terufumi Sasaki, a surgical resident at a Hiroshima hospital; and Mrs. Hatsuyo Makamura, a war widow with several children. To help his readers overcome differences of language and culture, Hersey "responded in a manner which by now had become characteristic of his literary journalism: focusing on the immediate actualities of human experience as reported to him by the firsthand participants of the event he was chronicling," Jones related in the *Dictionary of Literary Biography*. "The result is an unadorned narrative which draws its considerable power from understatement."

JOHN HERSEY

HIROSHIMA

"EVERYONE ABLE TO READ SHOULD READ IT."
—SATURDAY REVIEW OF LITERATURE

This 1985 edition of what is now considered a World War II classic includes Hersey's final chapter detailing his search for the bombing victims he originally interviewed in 1945.

Hersey's *Hiroshima* was first published in the *New Yorker*, which devoted its entire edition of August 31, 1946, to the story. The magazine quickly sold out, and the piece soon found alternative methods of circulation: full-text readings on national radio stations; free copies distributed by the Book-of-the-Month Club (who said nothing else in print "could be of more importance at this moment to the human race"); and unabridged reprintings in other publications. Prior to *Hiroshima,* all the American public knew of the bombing was statistics—figures about explosive power, numbers of casualties—and that it had finally led to the end of the war. In addition, some postwar propaganda claimed that the atomic bomb was no more destructive to modern construction than ordinary explosives, and that the unpleasant effects of the bomb's radioactivity had been overestimated. Hersey's story, with its first-person accounts of devastation and suffering, awoke the American public to the horrifying power that had been unleashed. *Hiroshima* was so popular because Hersey "did what no one had accomplished before: he recreated the entire experience of atomic bombing from the victims' point of view," Michael J. Yavenditti explained in the *Pacific Historical Review.* "The contrast between the apparently objective simplicity of his prose and the enormity of the phenomenon he described made *Hiroshima* all the more graphic and frightening for most readers."

Contemporary reviews of *Hiroshima* reflected the public's wholehearted acceptance of it. Calling it "one of the great classics of the war," *New Republic* contributor Bruce Bliven praised the author's "simplicity of genius": "Hersey does no editorializing, passes no judgments; he does not try to say whether the atomic bombing of Japan was justified, or to compare its results with, for instance, the sack of Nanking [China, by the Japanese]. He just tells the story." Ruth Benedict noted in the *Nation* that *Hiroshima* was not only important because it brought readers to a fuller understanding of the horrors of nuclear war, but also because it was "a capsule of Japanese life, and it tells more about our ex-enemy Japan than many learned books." Other critics hailed not just the content, but the presentation of the book: "The style is clear and pure," George Herbert Clarke stated in *Queens Quarterly,* "and the organization uses balance and cross-reference with delicate skill." *New York Times Book Review* contributor Charles Poore wrote that "*Hiroshima* seems destined to become about the most widely read—and heard—article and book of our generation." Despite all the commentary, the critic concluded, "Nothing that can be said about the book can

equal what the book has to say. It speaks for itself, and, in an unforgettable way, for humanity."

In the more than fifty years since its publication, *Hiroshima* has become one of the most widely read works from the war, and has inspired much analysis. Some critics, such as Kingsley Widmer, faulted the book for failing to address moral issues directly; Widmer noted in *The Forties* that while *Hiroshima* is "competently written," the "unreflective and finally rather decorous treatment . . . manages to suggest some of the commonplaces of horror but loses fuller individual response as well as any larger issue." Other observers, however, have affirmed the enduring quality of the work. Reviewing the 1985 edition of *Hiroshima,* which included updates on the six individuals originally profiled, *New York Times Book Review* contributor John Toland commented that "the years have not dimmed the luster or import of what Mr. Hersey wrote 40 years ago. . . . As he did in 1946, Mr. Hersey again pricks the American conscience, compelling us to re-examine the issue of nuclear weapons and our responsibility for having dropped the first two atom bombs." Calling it Hersey's "masterpiece," David Gates similarly asserted in *Newsweek* that *Hiroshima* "is the [book] that will live as long as there *are* books. It offers no screed against the bomb: just unforgettable details (potatoes baked in the ground, soldiers with melted eyes) and six ordinary people." "There were to be other compelling books about the bomb, its history, use and effect, but none has had such a lasting impact," Chalmers M. Roberts asserted in the *Washington Post Book World.* In this "now completed version of *Hiroshima,*" the critic concluded, Hersey has demonstrated "that he remains one of the most magnificent and powerful writers of modern times. This little book brings the central problem of human existence today down from the often stupefying technical and theoretical to a reality no one can miss. You must not fail to read it."

Novels over News

After the success of *Hiroshima,* Hersey nevertheless focused primarily on writing fiction to express his concerns. As he wrote in the *Atlantic Monthly* in 1949: "Fiction is a clarifying agent. It makes truth plausible," he explained. "Among all the means of communication now available, imaginative literature comes closer than any other to being able to give an impression of the truth." When it came time to write about the evil of the Holocaust, in which millions of Jews were murdered by the Nazis, Hersey chose to write a novel. 1950's *The Wall* tells the story of the Jewish ghetto of Warsaw, Poland, as its inhabitants tried to survive the Nazi occupation of World War II. In writing the novel, Hersey drew on his experiences reporting on the ruins of Warsaw in 1944, and he also spent two years reviewing translated documents and interviewing survivors. The author used all this information to create the diary of a single person, Noach Levinson, as he witnesses the German occupation of Warsaw from the fall of 1939 to the escape of the last survivors of the Jewish resistance in 1943. Although the journal details a relatively short period, "Levinson's clear memory allows him to see the connection of the present crisis to the past," Girgus explained, thus giving a deeper look into the nature of "individual and group identity." The book scored a second critical and popular success for Hersey, winning several awards and finding its way into the hands of a public that was only just coming to understand the depth of suffering European Jews endured during the war.

Despite the positive public response to *The Wall*, its form led to some of the criticism that would follow much of Hersey's work. This new type of "documentary novel," some critics charged, emphasized facts over character and issues over story. Leslie Fiedler, for instance, faulted the novel for its awkwardness of form; he noted in "Straddling the Wall" that Hersey "merely flirts with fiction: sketching characters, tentatively striving for inwardness, but always retreating to the 'facts' of the researcher." In contrast, David Sanders asserted in *New Voices in American Studies* that the main character Levinson becomes "a complex and compelling person" and that "complexities beyond a reporter's grasp were breached in the writing of this novel." The end result, the critic suggested, is "a novel which goes beyond recording its day to affirm that survival from the ghetto was an instance of a universal theme."

Although there are obvious comparisons between this novel and *Hiroshima*, Sanders observed in his study *John Hersey* that "*The Wall* is beyond the brilliant journalism of *Hiroshima* because of Hersey's determination to make fiction of the history of his time." Maxwell Geismar similarly noted in *American Moderns* that in this work

Hersey's "virtuosity as a craftsman met a large moral and social drama," in the same manner that the works of John Steinbeck did. "A classic description of the Holocaust," as Girgus termed it, "it still stands as one of the few books that has been able to relate in human terms the destruction of European Jewry by the Nazis."

With his third novel, 1953's *The Marmot Drive*, Hersey moved away from the contemporary historical issues that had defined his previous work and began using more literary methods to explore the pitfalls of modern life. This novel takes place in the Connecticut town of Tunxis, where the town's Selectman is attempting to convince his fellow citizens that it is necessary to destroy a colony of marmots (woodchucks) that periodically invade the village. His efforts fail and he is punished by the townspeople for a crime he didn't commit, in an abstract allegory about the nature of government and the governed. Several critics faulted the novel as unsatisfactory; Irving Howe noted in the *New Republic* that "this novel is likely to be tagged a parable; I think it more accurate to call it a catastrophe." While the novel was not particularly successful, it still marks an interesting turning point in the author's career as a novelist.

Hersey's next novel, *A Single Pebble*, was similarly constructed as a parable, but this time used his considerable knowledge of the country of his birth, China. On the surface the novel follows the journey of a young American engineer up the Yangtze River during the 1920s, but it also reveals some thoughts on issues of East vs. West. Critics were also severe in their judgment of this work, faulting the characterization as weak and finding its moralizing obvious. They did recognize, however, Hersey's success in portraying the spectacle of the Yangtze: "The account of the junk's progress up the river is utterly convincing, and a triumph merely as the communication of experience," R. T. Horchler remarked in *Commonweal*.

Allegories and Alternate Worlds

In 1959's *The War Lover*, Hersey "was far more successful . . . in finding an adequate means to dramatize a complex set of ideas," Girgus declared in *Dictionary of Literary Biography*. The author once again used World War II as his setting, following two airmen who pilot a Flying Fortress they name

The Body. Captain Buzz Marrow is a loud, aggressive fighter whose devil-may-care declarations of bravery mask his fear of death; his copilot, Lieutenant Charley Boman, is short, self-deprecating, and feels himself inferior to Marrow. It is Boman, however, aided by his romance with an Englishwoman, who finds the psychological strength to survive the war, while Marrow finally gives in to his fear. Their story is told in alternating accounts of their twenty-five flying missions and a single mission to bomb some ball-bearing factories in Germany. Throughout Hersey vividly re-creates the experience of the airmen, making for "a fascinating novel of wartime flying," as Arthur Mizener described it in the *New York Times Book Review.* The critic explained that "Hersey has always had a knack for getting inside a special way of life . . . and it has never served him better than here. The very quietness of his sympathy with such men is his greatest strength."

Critics were less certain about the effectiveness of the novel's message, however, which *Saturday Review*'s Granville Hicks summed up as "'the reason for war' is the fact that some men enjoy it." The result, Hicks stated, is that *The War Lover* "is neither satisfying as a piece of fiction nor convincing as a message. That is a pity, for one has to respect Hersey's seriousness, his conscientiousness as a reporter, and the literary competence he always displays." On the other hand, Taliaferro Boatwright found the philosophical questions about death and war that Hersey raises interesting, if perhaps not as attention-getting as the story itself. "There can be only admiration for the story itself, for its thesis that the war lover is the death lover, for the characterizations . . ., and above all for the blinding impact of the air and its climax." As the critic concluded in the *New York Herald Tribune Book Review:* "This is an exceptionally fine war novel on first reading and an even better one on the second."

In one of his most thought-provoking works, 1960's *The Child Buyer,* Hersey turned his talent for allegory into a satire on American education and morals. The "child buyer" of the title is Wissey Jones, who is attempting to buy the ten-year-old genius Barry Rudd so that the giant United Lymphomilloid corporation can harness the power of his brain. The novel is related entirely in the form of transcripts of a state hearing on education, welfare, and public morality. "The potential deadliness of this becomes instead a drama with the electrical immediacy of good dialogue," Edmund Fuller stated in the *New York Herald Tribune Book Review.* Jones testifies of big business' need for powerful minds unspoiled by "what passes for education"; educational administrators and testers explain why their system never identified Barry Rudd as anyone with potential; the politicians reveal themselves as interested more in their political careers than the subject at hand; and the testimony of a principal, a librarian, and Barry Rudd himself highlight how all sides fail to see the boy as an individual. Hersey spent almost a decade on various public commissions on education, and his familiarity with the subject helps deepen the satire. "Hersey spins his satires of big business as an end of life and education as a gang press for citizenship," Robert Hatch remarked in the *Nation,* hailing this "brisk, stylish performance of a book." Fuller similarly praised the work as "essential reading for all concerned with education" and stated that *The Child Buyer* "is John Hersey at his best and most original, disclosing again one of our ablest, most serious and bold writers." The provocative ideas addressed in the novel led the *New Republic* to devote much of its October 30, 1960 issue to the educational concerns raised by the novel.

Similar to *The Child Buyer,* the 1965 novel *White Lotus* uses an alternate world to illuminate a problem of modern American society. In this world, white Americans have been rounded up from their homes and sold into slavery into China. The journey of one such slave, a young girl now known as White Lotus, parallels the progress of blacks in America, from slavery to the civil rights movement. Girgus claimed that "Hersey demonstrates an acute historical, sociological, and psychological insight into black history in America as well as a deep knowledge of the Orient of his youth." While *New York Times Book Review* contributor Webster Schott found the idea of the novel "startling" and the parallels "fascinating," he stated that "*White Lotus* misses because the author's characters generally are rice-paper thin, as impulsively motivated as Pinocchio, and as chained to their analogous environment." In contrast, Edwin Morgan wrote in the *New Statesman* that Hersey has addressed the problems of dealing with such heavy themes "head-on and produced one of the most remarkable books to come out of the present vigorous phases of the American novel." The critic hailed how the author uses his knowledge of stratified Chinese society to illuminate his theme

Hersey introduced readers to the horrors of the Holocaust in this 1950 novel about a group of men and women trying to escape Nazi-occupied Warsaw.

of freedom: "The overall impression is of a wealth of experience and invention; and of a deeply felt theme. This, I think," Morgan concluded, "is John Hersey's most creative and rewarding novel."

Hersey's next two novels dealt with issues of individual freedom, examining the pitfalls which people can face when trying to discover their identity in an alienated society. The 1966 novel *Too Far to Walk* is Hersey's version of the Faust legend, in which a man sells his soul to the devil in exchange for knowledge and power. Hersey's Faust is John Fist, a sophomore at an Eastern college who is having difficulty finding meaning in his life; the devil in this case is Chum Breed, who tells Fist that drugs are the way to self-discovery. Eventually, however, Fist comes to under-

stand that "there can't be any shortcut to those breakthroughs I yearn for. You can't imbibe them, or smoke them, or take them intravenously, or get them by crossing your legs and breathing deeply for twenty minutes." While *New York Times* reviewer Eliot Fremont-Smith believed the novel "challenged one's disbelief and lost," other critics found it more true-to-life, a result of the author's several years experience teaching at the university level. Peter Buitenhuis, for instance, noted in the *New York Times Book Review* that this "unusual and witty" story "captures brilliantly and amusingly a mood of restlessness and boredom so common to the sophomoric experience." The novel contains "the best and clearest portrait yet of the campus protestor," *National Review* contributor Guy Davenport similarly reported, and concluded that *Too Far to Walk* "is a book to be grateful for. . . . It opens our eyes, which is the last thing we can expect of a popular novel with a fashionable subject."

A similar voyage of discovery takes place in the 1967 novel *Under the Eye of the Storm*. Dr. Tom Medlar is a liver specialist, and at age thirty-five he is already sick of his job, his wife, and everything else about his life except his boat, the *Harmony*. The catalyst for his self-examination is the hurricane that strikes after Tom, his wife Audrey, and another couple embark on a leisurely cruise. This novel was not as well received as Hersey's others, as critics remarked that the characters were flat and the allegory was obvious. "That he gets away with any of it—and he does, without a single laugh: the book is what is called readable, at times even vivid—is a tribute to Mr. Hersey's craftsmanship," the *New York Times'* Eliot Fremont-Smith observed. The author's description of the storm is particularly powerful, and serves his theme well, according to F. W. J. Hemmings in the *Listener*: "In the last analysis, Mr. Hersey will be found to have written one more allegory of the aloneness of every human being. . . . There is nothing new in the message, but it comes to us on a new wavelength, powerfully transmitted."

Stories of Survival

The "overriding concern" of Hersey's work is the theme of "human survival with freedom and dignity," Girgus wrote in *Dictionary of Literary Biography*, and Hersey continued exploring this theme in nonfiction as well as novels during the 1960s.

In the 1988 preface to his 1962 nonfiction work *Here to Stay: Studies on Human Tenacity,* Hersey explained his fascination with this "most mysterious" of all questions: "What is it that, by a narrow margin, keeps humankind going, in the face of its crimes, its follies, its greed, its passions, its sorrows, its panics, its hatreds, its hideous drives to pollute and waste and dominate and kill?" *Here to Stay* collects nine true-life tales of survival, examining how people have survived war, concentration camps, and natural disasters; the collection concludes with the full text of *Hiroshima*. "While claiming to remain faithful to the factual demands of journalism, Hersey imbues his tales with a parable-like quality consistent with the thematic character of fiction," Jones observed in *Dictionary of Literary Biography.*

Hersey was not as successful in his approach to the 1968 work *The Algiers Motel Incident,* an account of the shooting of three young black men during the Detroit riots of 1967. The book contained Hersey's usual meticulous research, but the author also inserted his own comments on the matter. *The Algiers Motel Incident* "is presented as a parable of race relations and the malignant effects of prejudice," Jones related, "but the victims are not sufficiently ennobling, nor are the perpetrators sufficiently malicious, to reduce the tale to these terms." Because of this kind of difficulty, the author most often preferred fiction as a method of communicating with his readers. "The journalist is always a mediator between the material and the reader," Hersey told interviewer Tom Spain. "And the reader is always conscious of the journalist interpreting and reporting events. If the novelist is successful, he vanishes from the reader's perception except through his voice in the work, and the reader has direct access to experiences. So, to me, fiction is much the more challenging and desirable medium for dealing with the real world."

The 1972 novel *The Conspiracy* was the first work in which Hersey used a historical setting other than the twentieth century. The author uses letters, reports, files, and transcripts of interrogations to relate the strange plot to assassinate the Roman Emperor Nero in 65 A.D. Although the events upon which the novel was based occurred some two thousand years ago, the political intricacies of Nero's time were very relevant for the early 1970s, a time when President Richard Nixon was beginning to come under scrutiny for his

---

If you enjoy the works of John Hersey, you may also want to check out the following books and films:

Brian Garfield, *The Paladin: A Novel Based on Fact,* 1979.
Christa Laird, *But Can the Phoenix Sing?,* 199495.
Laurence Yep, *Hiroshima,* 1995.
Saving Private Ryan, a film by Steven Spielberg, 1998.

---

abuse of political power. "His inspiration for the novel comes more from recent American history rather than from Roman history," Girgus stated in *Dictionary of Literary Biography,* as the author examines "the problems of freedom and political corruption."

Noting that Hersey "is the sort of writer who always seems better at first glance than he turns out to be," *Washington Post Book World* contributor L. J. Davis found *The Conspiracy* "good light reading" which "under no circumstances should . . . be confused with anything else." Josephine Hendin similarly observed in the *New York Times Book Review* that "Hersey's moral may be uninspiring," but added that "his novel is so alive, so full of the whispers, the greed, the hope and the quirky nobility of even Rome's worst that it's a delight to read." Bernard F. Dick, however, stated that *The Conspiracy* is the author's "finest novel to date," and added in his *Saturday Review* assessment that "Hersey has discovered the ideal medium for his twin talents. . . . In the epistolary form he has found a means to transform the facts of history into compelling fiction." A *New Republic* critic likewise hailed the work as perhaps Hersey's "most distinguished in more than twenty [years]," and explained that "the reader comes to know not only the characters but a questing intelligence not ashamed to think about philosophy, and to pose large unfashionable questions."

Hersey's next novel, 1974's *My Petition for More Space,* was a quite a departure from his previous works because of its futuristic setting. In a country reminiscent of George Orwell's *1984* or Aldous Huxley's *Brave New World,* individuals must petition the government to approve any change in their lives—marriage, a new job, having a child, even getting more food rations or living space. Each day huge lines form in front of the government petition offices, and people wait for days in hopes of reaching a petition window, even though petitions are almost always denied. Sam Poynter is one such petitioner, hoping for an increase in his already close-to-maximum living space of seven by eleven feet. While Sam and his neighboring petitioners know their efforts are most likely pointless, the shared experience of standing in line somehow brings them together in an otherwise alienated world. Many reviewers drew comparisons—both positive and negative—between *My Petition for More Space* and the works of not just Orwell and Huxley but also Franz Kafka and Samuel Beckett. Rene Kuhn Bryant, for instance, observed in *National Review* that because Hersey's characters were not as credible as those of Orwell or Huxley, the novel "produces an effect more like the feeble fizzle of a damp squib than the awesome resonances of Doomsday he seems to have intended." In contrast, *Saturday Review/World* contributor Susan Heath praised the novel for a "mounting tension [which] sustains the action of the novel and compels you to keep turning the pages." The critic concluded that like the author's other works, *My Petition for More Space* had its own relevance to today's society: "Hersey's is a vision that belongs, dreadfully, to our time; its greatest power is, simply, that it is unbearably close to being true."

Hersey's 1977 novel *The Walnut Door*, which deals with a strangely obsessive love affair, also "seems to mark a kind of departure" for the author, according to *New York Times Book Review* writer Gene Lyons. Instead of dealing with larger public events, *The Walnut Door* tells the story of two young adults, Elaine and Eddie, who meet after Elaine's apartment is ransacked. Eddie arrives to install a secure walnut door for Elaine, and makes her his prisoner in turn. Lyons noted that while "Hersey's mastery of plot is as sure as ever," the characters left something to be desired: "what makes these characters compelling to each other will remain a mystery to most readers." *Washington Post Book World* critic Jonathan Yardley similarly found fault with the "too ordinary" characters, and added that while the novel "is intended, clearly, as a parable about the real and imagined fears of contemporary urban existence, . . . the parable overwhelms the story." Peter Gardner, however, praised the "upbeat message" of *The*

Walnut Door and stated in *Saturday Review* that "Hersey shows himself at the peak of his form in this love story that positively shimmers with vitality and controlled suggestiveness." *The Walnut Door* "integrates many of Hersey's pervasive themes into an artistic whole," concluded Girgus, "illustrating his belief that a changing and dangerous world provides a continuing challenge to individual freedom."

Hersey also produced several nonfiction works during the 1970s, including the 1975 work *The President*, which followed the activities of the author's former football coach, Gerald Ford, during a typical week of his presidency. Hersey was specially selected by the administration for this assignment, and he was given unlimited access as he followed President Ford through various meetings with staff, advisors, and congressmen. "Hersey avoids the temptation to position himself as a political sage who has been granted a rare privilege," Jones wrote in *Dictionary of Literary Biography*. "Rather, he becomes the reader's stand-in, a journalistic Everyman whose questions and perceptions are likely to be those of his readers." While not one of Hersey's most acclaimed works, *The President* "demonstrates that Hersey's strength as a journalist lay not in his investigatory skills but in his powers of observation." The author also used his experience with the President for his 1980 study *Aspects of the Presidency: Truman and Ford in Office.*

Returning to China

Hersey returned to the novel format in 1985 with one of his longest and most complex works, *The Call: An American Missionary in China*. The work is reminiscent of *A Bell for Adano* in that the protagonist is trying to change the lives of people in a foreign country for the better. Unlike Major Joppolo, however, David Treadup is a religious missionary, come to China in 1905 to spread the gospel. As Treadup comes to know the Chinese and understand the problems they face, he finds it increasingly difficult to keep faith in his mission. The novel is informed by the author's usual painstaking research, and he acknowledged that Treadup's character was based on several missionaries he knew in China during his childhood, including his own father. The result, Jonathan D. Spence commented in the *New Republic*, is "an extraordinary amount of powerful writing about

China, especially its poverty and its wars, its catastrophic floods and bungled relief missions."

While noting the impressive amount of detail in the novel, critics disagreed as to its effectiveness. Describing *The Call* as a "vastly ambitious, impressively erudite, and unfortunately flawed, undertaking," *New York Times* contributor Eva Hoffman thought the "amount of sheer information packed into this 'novel' is so overwhelming that it becomes difficult to focus on the significance of any one event or issue." *New York Times Book Review* contributor Robert McAfee Brown, however, believed the detail makes the reader "almost persuaded that one has not read fiction but biography," particularly since the protagonist David Treadup "has been endowed by Mr. Hersey with his own vibrant life." "*The Call* is big enough, subtle enough, and both historically and emotionally convincing enough to be one of those books we can lose ourselves in with profit and delight," Spence concluded in his *New Republic* review. "I think it will be deservedly popular, and perceived as the capstone to a writing career of enviable range and originality." *Dictionary of Literary Biography* contributor Dan R. Jones similarly noted that "as a novel *The Call* represents Hersey's most accomplished interweaving of factual content and fictional form."

Hersey once again returned to nonfiction with 1987's *Blues,* a meditation on the joys of bluefishing. Jones termed it "an engaging concatenation of scientific data, folklore, and wisdom set in a literary frame." The author followed that up two years later with *Life Sketches,* a collection of previously published portraits of people ranging from an illiterate World War II soldier who learns to read to the noted writers Sinclair Lewis and James Agee. "The skill that won Mr. Hersey a Pulitzer Prize in 1945 is more than evident," Helen Benedict observed in the *New York Times Book Review,* explaining that the author's decades-long career "adds up to an important collection of lives and their lessons." "The collection is a reminder that Hersey's journalistic talent lay in his ability to find extraordinary expressions of humanity in everyday experience," Jones commented, "whether that experience belonged to a president or to an uneducated army private."

Hersey created a similar assortment of memorable characters in his first short story collection, 1990's *Fling and Other Stories.* "Variety is the collection's

most striking overall attribute," Vance Bourjaily stated in the *New York Times Book Review,* adding that "the voices here are accurate, the insights convincing. *Fling* is a fine performance indeed." The following year Hersey published his last novel, *Antonietta,* which follows the history of a fictional Stradivarius violin from its creation in 1699 to its purchase by a Wall Street inside trader in the 1980s. Along the way it comes into contact with the composers Mozart, Berlioz, and Stravinsky, revealing something of their lives, times, and music. Critics found the novel not quite up to the standard of the author's previous work. "*Antonietta* is of a piece with everything else Hersey has written," Douglas Glover wrote in the *Los Angeles Times Book Review.* "It is painstakingly researched. It is slick and intensely readable. It employs a weirdly awkward linking image as a unifying device. . . . And, at the end, it turns preachy."

Hersey completed his final work, the story collection *Key West Tales,* shortly before his death from cancer on March 24, 1993. These stories recreate life in Key West, Florida, where the author spent much of his final years. "Like some of Hersey's best literary journalism," Jones noted, "the stories in *Key West Tales* have a fablelike quality, focusing on the compelling significance of everyday experience. In their seamless interweaving of fact and fiction one finds examples of some of Hersey's most mature writing. As a collection they display Hersey's finely honed eye for detail, his keen sense of narrative, and his shrewd understanding of the ingredients of human character."

Upon Hersey's death in 1993, critics remembered a writer who devoted his considerable literary skills to issues of importance, even if it was unfashionable to do so. "In the course of his five decades as a writer, Mr. Hersey emerged not only as a first-rate reporter but also as a storyteller who nurtured the idea that writers had to pursue a moral goal," Richard Severo noted in the *New York Times.* As David Sanders similarly remarked in his study on the author, "Hersey is a skillful writer who is devoted to the profound treatment of several of the most serious topics his era affords. He cannot be ignored because he treats these topics directly." Hersey himself was philosophical about the reception his works had received, having never quite repeated the level of success he achieved with his early works. In his interview with Spain, the author noted that both *Hiroshima* and *The Wall* "came at the right moment. From then on I was writing books that didn't have their exact moment. Some have had a life of their own, and some haven't, and that's the way things go." But no matter what the topic or however successful the work, Robert McAfee Brown concluded, Hersey gave his readers "the quests, bafflements, frustrations and modest triumphs of the human spirit in ways that leave our minds sometimes ennobled and always stretched in new directions."

■ Works Cited

Benedict, Helen, review of *Life Sketches, New York Times Book Review,* May 7, 1989, p. 25.

Benedict, Ruth, "The Past and the Future," *Nation,* December 7, 1946, pp. 656, 658.

Bliven, Bruce, review of *Hiroshima, New Republic,* September 9, 1946, pp. 300-1.

Boatwright, Taliaferro, "An Airman Who Gave His Soul to the God of Battle," *New York Herald Tribune Book Review,* October 4, 1959, p. 1.

Bourjaily, Vance, "Venus Was a Gibson Girl," *New York Times Book Review,* April 8, 1990, p. 24.

Brown, Robert McAfee, "All His Losses Were Gains," *New York Times Book Review,* May 12, 1985, p. 3.

Bryant, Rene Kuhn, "More Worrier Than Philosopher," *National Review,* December 6, 1974, pp. 1421-22.

Buitenhuis, Peter, "Sophomore Slump," *New York Times Book Review,* March 13, 1966, pp. 4, 38.

Clarke, George Herbert, review of *Hiroshima, Queens Quarterly,* summer, 1947, p. 251.

Review of *The Conspiracy, New Republic,* April 1, 1972, p. 31.

Cowley, Malcolm, "Novels after the War," *New Republic,* February 14, 1944, pp. 216-17.

Davenport, Guy, "Deep Waters and Dark," *National Review,* May 3, 1966, pp. 424-27.

Davis, L. J. "The Plot to Kill Nero," *Washington Post Book World,* March 26, 1972, p. 4.

Dick, Bernard F., review of *The Conspiracy, Saturday Review,* March 18, 1972, p. 74.

Fadiman, Clifton, review of *Men on Bataan, New Yorker,* June 6, 1942, p. 78.

Fiedler, Leslie A., "Straddling the Wall," in *The Collected Essays of Leslie Fiedler,* Volume 2, Stein & Day, 1971, pp. 36-40.

Fremont-Smith, Eliot, "Some Faust," *New York Times,* February 28, 1966, p. 25.

Fremont-Smith, Eliot, "Smug in a Tub," *New York Times,* March 17, 1967, p. 39.

Fuller, Edmund, "Hersey's Dramatic Satire on Education," *New York Herald Tribune Book Review,* September 25, 1960, p. 3.

Gardner, Peter, review of *The Walnut Door, Saturday Review,* September 17, 1977, p. 39.

Gates, David, "An All-American Foreigner," *Newsweek,* April 5, 1993, p. 70.

Geismar, Maxwell, "John Hersey: The Revival of Consciousness," in his *American Moderns: From Rebellion to Conformity,* Hill & Wang, 1958, pp. 180-86.

Girgus, Sam B., "John Hersey," *Dictionary of Literary Biography,* Volume 6: *American Novelists since World War II,* Gale, 1980, pp. 137-44.

Glover, Douglas, "Hersey Strings Us Along," *Los Angeles Times Book Review,* August 11, 1991, p. 9.

Hatch, Robert, "The Brain Market," *Nation,* October 8, 1960, pp. 231-33.

Heath, Susan, review of *My Petition for More Space, Saturday Review/World,* September 21, 1974, p. 26.

Hemmings, F. W. J., "Robbing Grillet," *Listener,* September 7, 1967, p. 312.

Hendin, Josephine, review of *The Conspiracy, New York Times Book Review,* April 2, 1972, p. 6.

Hersey, John, "The Novel of Contemporary History," *Atlantic Monthly,* November, 1949, pp. 80-84.

Hersey, John, "The Mechanics of a Novel," *Yale University Library Gazette,* July, 1952, pp. 1-11.

Hersey, John, preface to *Here to Stay: Studies on Human Tenacity,* new edition, Knopf, 1988.

Hersey, John, introduction to *Life Sketches,* Knopf, 1989.

Hicks, Granville, "John Hersey's Message," *Saturday Review,* October 3, 1959, p. 18.

Hoffman, Eva, review of *The Call, New York Times,* April 22, 1985, p. C16.

Horchler, R. T., "Serious Fable," *Commonweal,* June 29, 1956, pp. 329-30.

Howe, Irving, "Symbolic Suburbia," *New Republic,* November 16, 1953, p. 17.

Jones, Dan R., "John Hersey," *Dictionary of Literary Biography,* Volume 185: *American Literary Journalists, 1945-95, First Series,* Gale, 1997, pp. 115-26.

Lyons, Gene, "What Remains Is Sexual Melodrama," *New York Times Book Review,* September 18, 1977, pp. 9, 48.

Mizener, Arthur, "Death Always Flew the Mission," *New York Times Book Review,* October 4, 1959, pp. 1, 16.

Morgan, Edwin, "Sleeping Birds," *New Statesman*, June 25, 1965, p. 1018.

Poore, Charles, "The Most Spectacular Explosion in the Time of Man," *New York Times Book Review*, November 10, 1946, pp. 7, 56.

Redman, Ben Ray, "A Man of Good Will," *Saturday Review of Literature*, February 12, 1944, p. 8.

Roberts, Chalmers M., "John Hersey Returns to Hiroshima," *Washington Post Book World*, August 11, 1985, p. 3.

Sanders, David, "John Hersey: War Correspondent into Novelist," in *New Voices in American Studies*, edited by Ray B. Browne, Donald M. Winkelman, and Allen Hayman, Purdue University Studies, 1966, pp. 49-58.

Sanders, David, *John Hersey*, Twayne, 1967.

Sapieha, Virgilia, "With the Americans in a Sicilian Village," *New York Herald Tribune Weekly Book Review*, February 6, 1944, p. 1.

Schott, Webster, "White Is to Yellow as Black Is to White," *New York Times Book Review*, January 24, 1965, pp. 5, 26.

Severo, Richard, "John Hersey, Author of 'Hiroshima,' Is Dead at 78," *New York Times*, March 25, 1993, p. B11.

Spain, Tom, "PW Interviews: John Hersey," *Publishers Weekly*, May 10, 1985, pp. 232-33.

Spence, Jonathan D., "Emissary in the East," *New Republic*, May 13, 1985, pp. 28-30.

Toland, John, "Beyond the Brink of Destruction," *New York Times Book Review*, August 4, 1985, pp. 3, 24.

Widmer, Kingsley, "*American Apocalypse:* Notes on the Bomb and the Failure of Imagination," *The Forties: Fiction, Poetry, Drama*, Everett/Edwards, 1969, pp. 141-54.

Williamson, B. T., "A Report on a Jungle Skirmish," *New York Times Book Review*, February 7, 1943, p. 4.

Yardley, Jonathan, "Lost in the Country of the Young," *Washington Post Book World*, October 16, 1977, p. E5.

Yavenditti, Michael J., "John Hersey and the American Conscience: The Reception of *Hiroshima*," *Pacific Historical Review*, February, 1974, pp. 24-49.

■ For More Information See

BOOKS

Contemporary Literary Criticism, Gale, Volume 1, 1973, Volume 2, 1974, Volume 7, 1977, Volume 9, 1978, Volume 40, 1986, Volume 81, 1994, Volume 97, 1997.

Huse, Nancy Lyman, *John Hersey and James Agee: A Reference Guide*, G. K. Hall, 1978.

Huse, Nancy Lyman, *The Survival Tales of John Hersey*, Whitston, 1983.

Sanders, David, *John Hersey Revisited*, Twayne, 1991.

PERIODICALS

Catholic World, July, 1962, pp. 240-45.
Commonweal, March 5, 1965, pp. 743-44.
Detroit Free Press, March 25, 1993, p. 6B.
Harper's, May, 1967, pp. 116-17.
Life, March 18, 1966.
Los Angeles Times, March 25, 1993, p. A32.
National Observer, February 8, 1965.
New Republic, October 10, 1960.
Newsweek, January 25, 1965; June 7, 1965.
New York Herald Tribune Book Review, August 29, 1946; March 5, 1950; August 20, 1950; June 3, 1956.
New York Times Book Review, February 6, 1944; February 26, 1950; November 8, 1953, pp. 4, 44; June 10, 1956; September 25, 1960; January 19, 1965; May 10, 1987; May 19, 1991, p. 13; February 13, 1994, p. 22.
Saturday Review, November 2, 1946, p. 16; March 4, 1950; November 7, 1953, p. 22; June 2, 1956; January 23, 1965.
Tamkang Review, Autumn 1983-Summer 1984, pp. 85-100.
Time, June 4, 1956; January 29, 1965; March 25, 1966.
Tribune Books (Chicago), March 13, 1994, p. 3.
Washington Post, March 25, 1993, p. B5, D5.
Washington Post Book World, August 7, 1994, p. 6.
World Literature Today, autumn, 1994, p. 812.
Yale Review, winter, 1987.*

—Sketch by Diane Telgen

Minfong Ho

■ Personal

Born January 7, 1951, in Rangoon, Burma; daughter of Rih-Hwa (an economist) and Lienfung (a chemist and writer; maiden name, Li) Ho; married John Value Dennis, Jr. (a soil scientist), December 20, 1976; children: Danfung, MeiMei, Christopher. *Education:* Attended Tunghai University, Taichung, Taiwan, 1968-69; Cornell University, B.A. (honors) in history and economics, 1973; M.F.A. in creative writing, 1980. *Religion:* Agnostic. *Hobbies and other interests:* Swimming, hiking, growing things.

■ Addresses

Home—893 Cayuga Heights Rd., Ithaca, NY, 14850. *Agent*—Renee Cho, McIntosh and Otis, Inc., 310 Madison Ave., New York, NY 10017.

■ Career

Writer. *Straits Times* newspaper, Singapore, journalist, 1974-75; Chiengmai University, Chiengmai,

Thailand, lecturer in English, 1975-76; Cornell University, Ithaca, NY, English literature teaching assistant, 1978-80; Catholic Relief Services, Thai-Cambodian border, nutritionist and relief worker, 1980; Singapore University, writer-in-residence, 1983. Also presenter of various writing workshops in middle schools and high schools in Ithaca, NY, and international schools in Switzerland, Indonesia, Thailand, and Malaysia, 1990-96. *Member:* Authors Guild, PEN America.

■ Awards, Honors

First prize from Council of Interracial Books for Children, 1975, for *Sing to the Dawn;* first prize, Annual Short Story Contest of Singapore, Ministry of Culture, Singapore, 1982, and first prize, Annual Short Story Contest, *AsiaWeek Magazine,* Hong Kong, 1983, both for *Tanjong Rhu;* second place, prose section, Commonwealth Book Awards, Commonwealth Book Council, 1987, first prize, National Book Development Council of Singapore, 1988, Parents Choice Award, 1990, and Best Books for Young Adults, American Library Association (ALA), Editor's Choice, *Booklist,* and Books for the Teen Age selection, New York Public Library, all 1991, and all for *Rice without Rain;* National Council on Social Studies/Children's Book Council (NCSS-CBC) Notable Children's Book in the Field of Social Studies and Best Books selection, *Parents Magazine,* both 1991, "Pick of the Lists," American Booksellers Association (ABA), Notable

Children's Trade Books in the Language Arts, and Children's Book of Distinction, Hungry Mind Review, all 1992, all for *The Clay Marble*; Southeast-Asian Write Award, conferred by the Crown Prince of Thailand, 1996; *Horn Book* Fanfare, Notable Book designation, ALA, Children's Book of Distinction, *Hungry Mind Review,* and Caldecott Honor, all 1997, all for *Hush!: A Thai Lullaby*; Notable Book designation, ALA, Best Books selection, New York Public Library, and Children's Book of Distinction, *Hungry Mind Review,* all 1997, all for *Maples in the Mist: Children's Poems from the Tang Dynasty*; "Pick of the Lists," ABA, 1997, for *Brother Rabbit: A Folktale from Cambodia.*

■ Writings

Sing to the Dawn, illustrated by Kwoncjan Ho, Lothrop, Lee and Shepard (New York), 1975.

Tanjong Rhu and Other Stories, Federal Press (Singapore), 1986.

Rice without Rain, Andre Deutsch (London), 1986, Lothrop, Lee and Shepard, 1990.

The Clay Marble, Farrar, Straus and Giroux, 1991.

(With Saphan Ros) *The Two Brothers,* illustrated by Jean Tseng and Mou-sien Tseng, Lothrop, Lee and Shepard, 1995.

Hush!: A Thai Lullaby, illustrated by Holly Meade, Orchard Books, 1996.

(Translator and compiler) *Maples in the Mist: Children's Poems from the Tang Dynasty,* illustrated by Jean and Mou-Sien Tseng, Lothrop, Lee and Shepard, 1996.

(With Saphan Ros) *Brother Rabbit: A Cambodian Tale,* illustrated by Jennifer Hewitson, Lothrop, Lee and Shepard, 1997.

Ho's work has been anthologized in *Starwalk,* Silver, Burdett and Ginn, 1989; *Prizewinning Stories: Asian Fiction,* Times Edition, 1991; *Ripples: Short Stories,* EPB Publishers, 1992; *Tapestry: Selected Short Stories from Singapore,* Heinemann, 1992; *Join In: An Anthology of Multicultural Short Stories,* Dell, 1994; and *Battling Dragons,* Heinemann, 1995. Ho's work has also been translated into Thai, Chinese, Japanese, Tagalog, and French.

■ Adaptations

Sing to the Dawn was adapted as a musical in 1996 for the Singapore Arts Festival. Ho co-wrote the libretto with Stephen Clark, music by Dick Lee, performed by the Singapore Repertory Theatre, and published by Times Edition, 1996.

■ Work in Progress

Motherless Malik, for Lothrop, Lee and Shepard; "Turning Thirty," for the anthology *More Than Half the Sky,* Times Publishing Group, Singapore; *Jataka Tales: A Selection of Buddha's Birth Stories; Surviving the Peace,* a nonfiction book about the children born after 1975 now living in Vietnam, Laos, and Cambodia, for Lothrop, Lee and Shepard; *Mosaic: An Anthology of Short Stories from Southeast Asia; Duty Free,* a novel of Singapore in the 1840s; *The Great Pond,* a translation from the Thai novel by Thepsiri.

■ Sidelights

Minfong Ho, in award-winning novels such as *Sing to the Dawn, Rice without Rain,* and *The Clay Marble,* presents realistic depictions of her native Southeast Asia, avoiding the romanticism of many writers on the subject. Characteristically focusing on strong female protagonists who interact with their families and friends against the backdrop of real events, she is often recognized for the sensitivity and understanding with which she treats the feelings of her characters as well as for her depiction of Asian life and locale. Her books include stories for young adult readers and middle graders as well as picture books for younger children. In all of these works, Ho does not back off from harsher elements such as poverty and violent death, but she also weaves the theme of the stabilizing influence of family throughout her work.

Ho's own life reflects an ability to interpret the East to the West, to adapt to new and sometimes confusing and troubling circumstances. Born in Burma in what might be called privileged circumstances, Ho grew up in both Singapore and Thailand. She also did most of her studying in English, so that she is fluent in three languages. More than that, each language rules a separate part of her, as she noted in a biographical sketch for *Seventh Book of Junior Authors and Illustrators.* Chinese, Ho's first language, is the language of her "heart," while Thai, her workaday language, is that of her "hands." English, the language of study, is the language of her "head." The resulting fragmentation, or "linguistic schizophrenia" as she terms it, has never been resolved for Ho. Though she writes in English, she feels that she has never been able to bridge the languages of her life; having lived in the United States for two decades, she notes that "even now, when I cry, I cry in Chinese."

In part it is this very fragmentation—linguistic as well as cultural—that led Ho into writing stories. Educated at Bangkok's Patana School and the International School as well as at Taiwan's Tunghai University, Ho came to Cornell University in Ithaca, New York, to complete her undergraduate degree. At Cornell, she began a short story that later became her first novel, *Sing to the Dawn*. "When I wrote *Sing to the Dawn*, it was in moments of homesickness during the thick of winter in upstate New York, when Thailand seemed incredibly far away," Ho once commented. "Writing about the dappled sunlight and school children of home brought them closer to me; it aired on paper that part of me which couldn't find any place in America. That story was not meant to be read—it was only one hand clapping." But Ho found another hand, a reader, in the Council for Interracial Books for Children to whom she submitted the work for their annual short story contest. The original story describes how Dawan, a schoolgirl from a rural Thai village, encounters resistance from her father and brother when she wins a scholarship to the city high school. Ho won the award for the Asian American Division of unpublished Third World Authors, and she was then encouraged to enlarge the story into a novel. "The manuscript was later published (through no effort of mine)," Ho recalled. "Suddenly a whole new dimension of writing opened to me: it became a communicative rather than a cathartic activity. I had always written, but now I would have readers!"

Realistic Portraits of Asian Life

Ho also began to see the writing process as one that was inherently "a political expression," as she once wrote in *Interracial Books for Children Bulletin*. "I had never enjoyed reading stories of Asia in my own childhood. . . . Children's books about Thailand, China, Burma, etc. were invariably about princes and emperors and/or their elephants, peacocks and tigers. The few about village life portrayed it as idyllic and easy-going, full of kites and candles and festivals at the temples. This was

Life changes for seventeen-year-old Jinda and her family of rice growers when some college students visit her small village outside Bangkok.

not the Asia I knew, and I had resented the writers—usually white—who out of condescension and ignorance misrepresented these countries." With *Sing to the Dawn*, Ho attempted to avoid these pitfalls and created a realistic story of one girl's struggles to get an education. Dawan has won a government exam for a high school scholarship, an exam in which her younger brother has come in second. But her real fight comes after the test: now she must convince her father and her brother that she—the girl of the family—should be allowed to go to the city and study. She enlists the aid of her timid mother, of a Buddhist monk, and of a cousin who has lived in the city. Support also comes from her grandmother and from a flower girl named Bao. Dawan learns an important lesson along the way—that she must struggle to become free. Finally she convinces her brother to give his blessing and she leaves for school, her father still resistant.

"The author's love of her native countryside is evident in her vivid descriptions," commented Cynthia T. Seybolt in a *School Library Journal* review of the book. Seybolt also noted that Dawan's story "provides a perspective on women's liberation far removed and much more important than breaking into the local Little League." Though many reviewers noted that this first novel was slow in parts because of frequent descriptive passages, a *Kirkus Reviews* critic maintained that, "underneath the delicate lotus imagery, this small, understated story is infused with passion and determination," such that Dawan confronts her battle for freedom and equality with a "rage so powerful" that it makes "this otherwise modest narrative vibrate." The book was illustrated by Ho's younger brother, Kwoncjan, and proceeds from its sales were used to help set up a nursing scholarship for village girls in Thailand.

Meanwhile, Ho had graduated from Cornell and returned to Asia, working as a journalist on the Singapore *Straits Times* and then as a lecturer at Chiengmai University in Thailand. While in Thailand, she observed firsthand the military coup of October 6, 1976. During these post-college years, Ho worked in "prisons and plywood factories," as she once stated. "I have transplanted rice seedlings and helped a peasant woman give birth; I have attended trade union meetings in stuffy attics and international conferences in plush hotels. There is so much, so much beauty and so much pain in the world around me which I want to write about—because I want to share it." But it would be another decade before she wrote her second book, using much of this material. Married in 1976 to a soil scientist she had met during her Cornell years, Ho returned to the United States and settled in Ithaca, New York. She finished an M.F.A. in creative writing at Cornell while working as a teaching assistant. She also spent some time in relief work along the Thai-Cambodian border in 1980, gaining experience that would inform yet another novel.

Return to Writing

In 1986, after starting a family, Ho returned to writing fiction, publishing *Rice without Rain,* a book which retells the experiences of another village girl in Thailand. This time, however, the stakes are higher than in *Sing to the Dawn.* Jinda is seventeen the summer when young intellectuals arrive in her remote village from Bangkok. Two years of drought have brought deprivations to the village: Jinda's sister has no milk and her baby starves to death. Still, the villagers greet these outsiders with suspicion, especially when they encourage the men to form a rent resistance movement. Slowly the villagers, including Jinda's father, the headman, take up the rallying cry, and slowly too does Jinda fall in love with Ned, the leader of the student radicals. When Jinda's father is arrested, she follows Ned to Bangkok

Will Dara survive in war-torn Cambodia?

Twelve-year-old Dara and her new friend Jantu struggle to survive after they become separated from their families during a rebel skirmish shortly after the fall of Cambodia's Khmer Rouge.

where he organizes a demonstration that might help free Jinda's father. However, the military put down the demonstrators in a bloody massacre. Returning to her village, Jinda discovers that her father has died in prison. Ned and she part ways, he to join communist guerrillas fighting the government, and she to "grow things and be happy" in her village. The title, taken from a Thai folk ballad, points to the fundamental importance of rice—of agriculture—in the life of the common people. Caught up in the larger ideologies of the college students, the villagers have become pawns. Jinda chooses the simpler path in life, the eternal way. Hazel Rochman, writing in *Booklist*, maintained that though the book has violent and sometimes gritty passages, "The violence is quietly told, never exploited." *School Library Journal* contributor John Philbrook, despite finding some of the characters too "predictable," felt on the whole that Ho's novel "gives an interesting and at times absorbing glimpse of class struggle in the Thailand of the 1970s. . . . Not a masterpiece, but a novel from an author to watch." A *Kirkus Reviews* commentator called *Rice without Rain* "a valuable, memorable portrait of a little-known country."

Ho stayed with the land of her childhood for her third novel, incorporating experiences she had gleaned while serving as a relief worker along the Thai-Cambodia border. But with *The Clay Marble*, Ho created a book for middle grade readers rather than strictly young adults. Twelve-year-old Dara, with her mother and older brother Sarun, journeys to the Thai border in search of food after the fall of Cambodia's Khmer Rouge. At a refugee camp, Dara meets another Cambodian family and becomes fast friends with Jantu, while Jantu's sister falls in love with Sarun. Jantu gives Dara a clay marble which Dara believes has magical properties. When fighting breaks out between rival guerrilla factions, Dara and Jantu are cut off from their families. Surviving several adventures, the two are finally reunited with their families, but Jantu is mistakenly shot and killed by Sarun— overly zealous on watch duty. Dara, in the end, convinces Sarun not to go off with the army, but to return home with his family. Once again, Ho presents a strong female protagonist and employs the theme of family unity in the face of adversity. Though some reviewers felt that Ho's characters lacked depth and that her language was at times too sophisticated for a twelve-year-old protagonist, many found, as does Maeve Visser Knoth in *Horn Book*, that Ho's story was "moving."

If you enjoy the works of Minfong Ho, you may also want to check out the following books and films:

Allan Baillie, *Little Brother*, 1992.
Linda Crew, *Children of the River*, 1989.
Louise Moeri, *The Forty-Third War*, 1989.
William Sleator, *Dangerous Wishes*, 1995.
Suzanne Fisher Staples, *Shabanu: Daughter of the Wind*, 1989.
The Killing Fields, an Academy Award-winning film, 1984.

Knoth noted that the book depicted a "people who have rarely had a voice in children's literature." A *Kirkus Reviews* critic commented that Ho "shapes her story to dramatize political and humanitarian issues," and concluded that the book was "touching, authentic," and "carefully wrought."

A change of pace for Ho came with her third child and next few books. *The Two Brothers*, a picture book for young readers, was co-written with Saphan Ros. Ho again teamed up with Ros on 1997's *Brother Rabbit*, a story about a crocodile, two elephants and an old woman who prove to be no match for a mischievous rabbit. Other picture books by Ho include *Maples in the Mist*, her translations of sixteen short Tang Dynasty unrhymed poems, and *Hush!: A Thai Lullaby*, a bedtime tale that requests various animals including a lizard and monkey to be quiet and not disturb a sleeping baby.

Ho continues to write novels for young people, and is presently at work on a story set in eighteenth century Nantucket Island, focusing on its links with the Far East through its China Trade. Infusing all of her work is her emphasis on sharing her cross-cultural experiences with others, sometimes in the guise of fiction, sometimes in retellings of folktales or poems. "I have grown up in Thailand and Singapore, and lived in Taiwan, Laos and the United States—and yes, sometimes it's been a bit of a stretch, to try to absorb and adapt to the different cultures, but it's been very enriching as well," Ho once commented. "If my writing has helped other children become more 'elastic' in their appreciation of Southeast Asian cultures, then my stretching would have been truly worthwhile!"

■ Works Cited

Review of *The Clay Marble*, *Kirkus Reviews*, October 1, 1991, p. 1287.

Ho, Minfong, "Writing the Sound of One Hand Clapping," *Interracial Books for Children Bulletin*, Volume 8, No. 7, 1977, pp. 5, 21.

Ho, Minfong, *Rice without Rain*, Lothrop, Lee and Shepard, 1990.

Ho, Minfong, autobiographical essay in *Seventh Book of Junior Authors and Illustrators*, edited by Sally Holmes Holtze, H. W. Wilson, 1996, pp. 131-33.

Knoth, Maeve Visser, review of *The Clay Marble*, *Horn Book*, January-February, 1992, p. 71.

Philbrook, John, review of *Rice without Rain*, *School Library Journal*, September, 1990, p. 250.

Review of *Rice without Rain*, *Kirkus Reviews*, May 1, 1991, p. 649.

Rochman, Hazel, review of *Rice without Rain*, *Booklist*, July, 1990, p. 2083.

Seybolt, Cynthia T., review of *Sing to the Dawn*, *School Library Journal*, March, 1976, p. 104.

Review of *Sing to the Dawn*, *Kirkus Reviews*, June 1, 1975, p. 604.

■ For More Information See

BOOKS

Children's Literature Review, Volume 28, Gale, 1992, pp. 131-34.

PERIODICALS

Bulletin of the Center for Children's Books, November, 1975, p. 46; June, 1990, p. 241; December, 1991, p. 92; April, 1996, p. 266; May, 1997, p. 324.

Horn Book, November, 1990, p. 749; July, 1995, p. 471; May-June, 1997, pp. 333-34.

New York Times Book Review, October 7, 1990, p. 30; April 26, 1992, p. 25; August 13, 1995, p. 23.

Publishers Weekly, March 25, 1996, p. 82; April 14, 1997, p. 75.

School Library Journal, June, 1995, p. 102; March, 1996, p. 175; September, 1996.

Times Educational Supplement, February 13, 1987, p. 44; September 22, 1989, p. 30.

Voice of Youth Advocates, December, 1995, p. 302.

—Sketch by J. Sydney Jones

Lesley Howarth

Personal

Born in Bournemouth, England, 1952; married Phil Howarth (a civil engineer); children: Sadie, Georgia, Bonnie. *Education:* Studied at Bournemouth College of Art; Croydon College of Art.

Addresses

Home—Callington, Cornwall, England.

Career

Writer, 1993—.

Awards, Honors

Shortlisted, Whitbread Award for a Children's Novel, 1993, and shortlisted, *Guardian* Children's Fiction Award, 1994, both for *The Flower King;* highly commended list, Carnegie Medal, 1995, for *MapHead.*

Writings

The Flower King, Walker, 1993.
MapHead, Walker, 1994, Candlewick, 1994.
Weather Eye, Walker, 1995, Candlewick, 1995.
The Pits, Walker, 1996, Candlewick, 1996.
Fort Biscuit, illustrated by Ann Kronheimer, Walker, 1997.
MapHead: The Return, Candlewick, 1997.

Sidelights

With her first young adult novel, *The Flower King,* British author Lesley Howarth made it to several shortlists for fiction awards. With her second book, *MapHead,* she served up a fictional brew that "one only occasionally happens upon," according to Robyn Sheahan in a cover story in *Magpies.* Sheahan went on to note that Howarth writes the sort of book that "is respectful of its readers' imaginative and intellectual capabilities, and which offers real insights into the difficult business of growing up." Howarth herself was coming of age as a writer with these first published books and has since broadened her fictional universe to encompass not only a turn-of-the-century world filled with flowers and a modern country town with alien visitors in its midst, but also a wind farm in the near future in *Weather Eye,* and the chilly world of prehistory in *The Pits,* a story of an ice-age man told by a chatty ghost. These are all parts of Howarth and are indicative of the varied life she herself has led.

Born in Bournemouth, England, she attended grammar school there and at the Bournemouth School for Girls. A self-confessed lazy student, she commented in an interview with Stephanie Nettell for *Magpies* that she puts her lack of success in school down to stubbornness and a "fierce strain of individualism: the more people told me to buckle down the less likely I was to do it." But she did develop a love for story at an early age; as an only child she created a rich interior life. "I'd live in a story, in its atmosphere, for days," she told Nettell, "and spent long hours plonking out stories on my Dad's typewriter." Growing up in the Westbourne district of Bournemouth, she was also in close proximity to the house where Robert Louis Stevenson lived while writing *Dr. Jekyll and Mr Hyde* and *Kidnapped*. Howarth would sit in the garden of the house where Stevenson created those classics and marvel at how close the past was to her. Stevenson continues to be a major influence in her own writing—especially his sense of adventure and his ability to use "just the right word every time," as she explained to Nettell.

Upon graduation, Howarth attended the Bournemouth College of Art for a time, but soon met her future husband, Phil. Married at age eighteen and off to London where Phil had a job, Howarth attended the Croydon College of Art for three years. Quite by accident, she became involved in fashion designing, a course of study that did her little good when returning to the country with her husband for a new job. Instead, in the country Howarth worked various casual labor jobs, including gardening and assisting in a retirement home. Her days spent in the flower beds and the tomato hothouses stood her in good stead with material when later she took up writing. Together with her husband, Howarth built the family house in Cornwall. One night while soaking in the bath after a particularly strenuous day of building, she suddenly felt she was "burning to write all these rather quirky stories," as she said in her interview with Nettell.

Howarth proceeded to write short stories and short screenplays which were submitted for a BBC video project. Though the films were not accepted, the process of writing them spurred Howarth into

After thirteen-year-old Telly recovers from a near-death accident, she believes she possesses magical powers in this 1995 novel.

taking evening classes in creative writing. Soon her stories were expanding, turning into novels, and the voice she consistently wrote in was one directed at children. Finally, with three novels under her belt—none of them accepted by a publisher—she was able to place her fourth with the British publisher, Walker Books. This was "only the second unsolicited novel published by Walker," according to Kevin Steinberger in *Reading Time*. As Steinberger goes on to point out, Howarth's varied background in work and family all play a large part in her fiction. This first young adult novel, *The Flower King*, is a "gentle turn-of-the century story," according to *Magpies*, and some of the characters that she worked with in the retirement home find their way into the novel, as well as Howarth's experiences working in flower gardens. Shortlisted for both the Whitbread and *Guardian* children's fiction prizes, *The Flower King* won Howarth recognition and an agent. The novel has not been published in the United States.

A Boy's Search

For her second published novel, *MapHead,* Howarth adopted a science fiction format. Alien beings from the Subtle World, twelve-year-old MapHead and his father, Ran, come to Earth to search for the boy's mother, Kay. Before MapHead's birth, Ran saved the Earthling woman from death by a lightning bolt, and she returned with him to the Subtle World where they had a baby. But pining for her home, Kay returned to

When an archeologist discovers a frozen 9,000 year-old-man, his daughter's curiosity leads her to her own discoveries about iceman.

Earth with no memory of her encounter with Ran nor of her son. Now MapHead—so-called because of his ability to project a map of the terrain on his face and bald head—needs to find his mother before he can enjoy the Dawn of Power. Under the names of Boothe and Powers, the son and father take up residence in a tomato glasshouse on Earth, and Boothe enrolls in the local school where he meets the boy who is his half-brother and will take him to find his mother. In the process, he and his half-brother, Kenny, become friends, and MapHead begins to fit in and know what it means to be loved. Meeting his mother, he experiences an internal integration that gives him power equal to his father's, but the actual process of his search has led him to this self-integration.

Told with humor and attention to detail, *MapHead* "is a sweet, tender, coming-of-age story . . . a marvelous read," according to Dorothy M. Broderick in *Voice of Youth Advocates*, and a "deliciously grotesque tale," according to John Peters in *School Library Journal*. Merri Monks in *Booklist* noted that "Howarth skillfully evokes the internal landscapes of a young man's emotions and imagination," while *Magpies*' Sheahan praised the novel's "felicitous turns of phrase," noting that it was "brimful with lyrical, luscious language; written with an intensity, a distillation of the senses. . . ." Though MapHead eventually leaves Earth without his mother, he has most definitely found himself: "Don't you know?" he asks toward the end of the book. "Can't you see? I'm not a little kid anymore. No one's got me, because I've got myself." In *Junior Bookshelf* a reviewer concluded that "Lesley Howarth has mixed the imaginary and the real ingredients with great skill."

Howarth reintroduced MapHead and his adventures in a 1997 sequel, *MapHead: The Return,* in which the title character finds himself alone without his father for the first time and must return to Earth to find his destiny. In his loneliness MapHead misuses his powers, transferring his memories into the mind of his newfound friend Jack Stamp, an action that has unintended consequences. *Voice of Youth Advocates* critic Roxy Ekstrom applauded the work, calling it a "great coming-of-age story that dwells on a respect for freedom, the desire for autonomy, and the fear of that independence." A reviewer in *Horn Book* also praised *MapHead: The Return,* stating, "Insightful characterization, concise prose, and sophisticated

Twelve-year-old Maphead and his father, aliens from Subtle World, return to Earth in search of Maphead's human mother in this fantasy novel.

humor distinguish the fantasy." Steven Engelfried, writing in *School Library Journal*, remarked that MapHead's "deep concern for the humans he comes to love and his burning need to find his own place in the world are truly touching."

With increased recognition came the working hours of a full-time novelist. Howarth begins work at nine—once her children are off to school—and works until two, after which she takes a walk to clear her head and work out plot twists for the next day's writing. "I'm not interested in oral storytelling," Howarth told Steinberger for his *Reading Time* article. "For me the whole buzz is

the word—the word making an effect on the page; that's what interests me." Normally Howarth does not begin her novels with a grand plan, but once in the story, she relishes in doing research and gathering more information than she'll ever need. "Then I let the stuff percolate for a long time," she told Steinberger. "You have to edge up to a story. . . . The whole essence of storywriting is to be excited. Once I get bored or find it a slog I decide to let it go."

Fictional Brush with Death

Howarth's third novel is sometimes typified as an environmental story, though the author herself rejects the notion that she begins with a theme. For her, story is paramount and meaning follows

In this 1997 sequel to *MapHead*, the title character comes back to Earth alone to find his destiny.

story. With *Weather Eye*, Howarth was influenced both by an article about a near-death experience and by an apocalyptic feeling engendered in the novel by changing weather patterns. Thirteen-year-old Telly lives with her parents on a weather farm in Cornwall in 1999, just before the millennium. She helps her parents on this farm which generates electricity with huge windmills. All around the world unseasonal weather patterns are causing immense damage to property and life; in Cornwall strong winds have been blowing for days, and Telly is almost killed when struck on the head by a damaged turbine blade from one of the giant windmills. Telly feels she is imbued with special powers after this close scrape with death and resolves to do something to alter the human destructiveness responsible for the severe weather. Networking with youths around the world via computers, Telly, the Weather Eye, hopes to save the planet by redirecting energies. After many adventures and much hard work, a new turbine is brought on line at the climax of the novel, just in time for the new millennium. Telly describes it, "wheeling into the twenty-first century. Dad has the right idea: 'Next century belongs to you lot. . . . I've a feeling you'll all make the best of it.'"

In a *Magpies* review of the novel, Steinberger noted that *Weather Eye* "may be read as a very reassuring 'environmental' novel but it is immediately a humorous, suspenseful, thoughtful narration. . . . It is a story for, and of, our times, but in Howarth's inimitable style." Other critics, including Maeve Visser Knoth in *Horn Book*, also commented on Howarth's humor: "The author . . . has written an unusual novel that will appeal to readers with its empowering theme and its strong element of humor." In *Junior Bookshelf*, a critic also remarked on Howarth's use of humor, saying "[Howarth's] vision of the world is essentially comic as well as profoundly moral." The reviewer went on to conclude that young readers "will read her book with joy and satisfaction because her children are drawn clearly and with humour as well as understanding."

Steinberger, in his *Reading Time* article on Howarth, noted that her use of idiom for both comic effects and depth of story set her apart from other writers. In *The Pits* she uses idiom to heightened effects. The book was inspired by news reports of the discovery of an iceman in the west of Austria and also by an article relating the discov-

If you enjoy the works of Lesley Howarth, you may also want to check out the following books and films:

Bill Brittain, *Wings*, 1992.
Ivy Ruckman, *Night of the Twister*, 1984.
G. Clifton Wisler, *The Seer*, 1988.
Edward Scissorhands, a film by Tim Burton, 194890.

ery of an Ice-Age pine chewing gum. This started Howarth looking for parallels between that time and ours and ended up with "a *West Side Story*-like gang rivalry set in Ice Age coastal Britain," according to Steinberger. The archaeologist Needcliff discovers Arf, the Iceman, a relic of a distant age, but his daughter, with him for the summer, wonders all the time what really made the Iceman tick. Such particulars are supplied by an adolescent ghost, Broddy Bronson, who was a pal of Arf's. Broddy has been drifting around for some 9,000 years, picking up the speech and experiences of each succeeding age, and it is his voice—entered into the archaeologist's computer—that relates the story of Arf, and of Broddy. It is Broddy's distinctive idiom that gives life to the tale. There are parallels between Broddy's time and ours, especially the gang fighting and turf wars. There is also "much humor," according to a reviewer in *Magpies*, who went on to conclude that *The Pits* is a great read. It rollicks along . . . and rejoices in telling an original story in an original way." Janice M. Del Negro, writing in the *Bulletin of the Center for Children's Books*, echoed this opinion of originality and commented that "what is most unusual about this book is that it works, and works remarkably well. Howarth creates a prehistoric world that is eminently credible, peopled by individuals with complex personalities."

Howarth, who complains that she is easily bored, has created in a short span of time, a most original group of works, full of adventure, humor, and meaning. As she concluded in her interview with Nettell, she feels that writing children's books is essentially fun. She sets out both to provide it and receive it. "Adult novelists could learn a thing or two about plotting and pace from children's fiction," Howarth said. "It's a world of the imagination I particularly enjoy roaming around in. . . . It's the best job ever."

■ Works Cited

Broderick, Dorothy M., review of *MapHead, Voice of Youth Advocates*, February, 1995, p. 348.

Del Negro, Janice M., review of *The Pits, Bulletin of the Center for Children's Books*, December, 1996, pp. 138-39.

Ekstrom, Roxy, review of *MapHead: The Return, Voice of Youth Advocates*, April, 1998, pp. 55-56.

Engelfried, Steven, review of *MapHead: The Return, School Library Journal*, January, 1998, p. 112.

Howarth, Lesley, *MapHead*, Walker Books, 1994.

Howarth, Lesley, *Weather Eye*, Walker Books, 1995.

Knoth, Maeve Visser, review of *Weather Eye, Horn Book*, March-April, 1996, pp. 208-09.

Review of *MapHead, Junior Bookshelf*, August, 1994, p. 145.

Review of *MapHead: The Return, Horn Book*, January-February, 1998, pp. 74-75.

Monks, Merri, review of *MapHead, Booklist*, October 1, 1994, p. 319.

Nettell, Stephanie, "Know the Author: Lesley Howarth," *Magpies*, May, 1996, pp. 18-21.

Peters, John, review of *MapHead, School Library Journal*, October, 1994, p. 124.

Review of *The Pits, Magpies*, May, 1996. p. 21.

Sheahan, Robyn, review of *MapHead, Magpies*, July, 1994, p. 4.

Steinberger, Kevin, review of *Weather Eye, Magpies*, July, 1995, p. 25.

Steinberger, Kevin, "Lesley Howarth," *Reading Time*, May, 1996, p. 12.

Review of *Weather Eye, Junior Bookshelf*, June, 1995, p. 108.

■ For More Information See

PERIODICALS

Books for Keeps, November, 1993, p. 14; July, 1994, pp. 6, 28; July, 1995, p. 12; January, 1996, p. 11.

Bulletin of the Center for Children's Books, November, 1995, p. 93; March, 1998, p. 246.

Kirkus Reviews, October 15, 1997, p. 1583.

Horn Book Guide, spring, 1995, p. 78; spring, 1996, p. 73.

Magpies, May, 1994, p. 24.

Publishers Weekly, November 14, 1994, p. 69.

Times Educational Supplement, November 12, 1993, p. R12; December 24, 1993, p. 8.

U.S. News & World Report, December 5, 1994, p. 97.*

—Sketch by J. Sydney Jones

Laurie R. King

and as a counselor for La Leche League International. *Member:* International Association of Crime Writers, La Leche League International, Crime Writers of America, Mystery Writers of America, Sisters in Crime.

■ Personal

Born September 19, 1952, in Oakland, CA; daughter of Roger R. (a furniture restorer) and Mary (a retired librarian and curator; maiden name, Dickson) Richardson; married Noel Q. King (a retired professor), 1977; children: Zoe, Nathanael. *Education:* University of California at Santa Cruz, B.A., 1977; Graduate Theological Union, M.A., 1984. *Politics:* "Nonc." *Religion:* Episcopal. *Hobbies and other interests:* Swimming, gardening, travel.

■ Addresses

Home—P.O. Box 1152, Freedom, CA 95019. *Agent*—Linda Allen, 1949 Green St., #5, San Francisco, CA, 94123.

■ Career

Writer, 1987—. Worked as a manager of Kaldi's (now Los Gatos Coffee Roasters), at various volunteer posts in the Pajaro Unified School District,

■ Awards, Honors

Edgar Allan Poe Award, Best First Novel, 1993, and the British John Creasey Dagger, both for *A Grave Talent;* nominee, Agatha award, 1994, for *The Beekeeper's Apprentice;* Nero Wolfe award, 1995, for *A Monstrous Regiment of Women;* nominee, Edgar Award, and American Library Association Best Book, 1996, for *With Child.*

■ Writings

NOVELS

A Grave Talent, St. Martin's, 1993.
The Beekeeper's Apprentice: On the Segregation of the Queen, St. Martin's, 1994.
To Play the Fool, St. Martin's, 1995.
A Monstrous Regiment of Women, St. Martin's, 1995.
With Child, St. Martin's, 1996.
A Letter of Mary, St. Martin's, 1997.
The Moor: A Mary Russell Novel, St. Martin's, 1998.
A Darker Place, Bantam, 1999.
O Jerusalem, St. Martin's, 1999.
Night Work, St. Martin's, in press.

■ Adaptations

A Monstrous Regiment of Women, 1995, and *The Beekeeper's Apprentice: On the Segregation of the Queen,* 1996, were recorded on cassette.

■ Work in Progress

Further titles in the "Mary Russell" and "Kate Martinelli" series, and a sequel to her thriller *A Darker Place.*

■ Sidelights

The words "smart" and "thoughtful" crop up a lot when reading reviews of Laurie R. King's mystery novels. King, the author of ten books in two separate series plus a stand-alone thriller, has captured a legion of faithful readers of all ages and genders—especially YAs—with her sassy and intellectual Mary Russell who won the head and heart of that crustiest of detectives, Sherlock Holmes. Russell, a historical invention, first encounters the great detective as a fifteen-year-old with her nose stuck in a book; Holmes himself is in retirement, raising bees and his consciousness in Sussex. Over the course of five books, their relationship has grown from mentor-student to equals in crime detection and in the home, for by the end of book two they marry.

King's other main female protagonist is Kate Martinelli, a strong and dedicated cop. No history here; Martinelli's tales take place in the here and now of northern California. The first Martinelli mystery, *A Grave Talent,* won an Edgar Allan Poe Award and set the tone for the series. Again King's female lead is independent and intelligent, and Martinelli's sexual orientation adds to her sense of apartness from the mainstream. Dick Adler, reviewing the third Martinelli mystery in the *Chicago Tribune Book World,* noted that this female police officer "is the kind of person you'd like to know and talk with over many lunches, a smart and tough woman confident in her lesbian sexuality. . . ."

Part of King's winning formula is, ironically, her lack of formula. Strong female protagonists who display humor and intelligence form the core of her books, yet the plotting is anything but standard crime format. "I don't work from an outline

Newly promoted Detective Kate Martinelli and her new partner delve into a famous artist's past to solve a string of murders in this Edgar Allan Poe Award-winning novel.

or plot out my books before I start writing," King told *Authors and Artists for Young Adults (AAYA)* in an interview. "I have a clear idea of how it will end, but otherwise I just have faith that it will get there." And it is matters of faith, or more properly theology and religion, that drive much of the intellectual content of King's books, another thing that sets them apart from the rest of the pack of crime fiction.

Literature was a part of the author's life since she was a young girl. "We moved a lot when I was young," King explained, deadpan, in her *AAYA* interview. "My father had itchy feet and liked to experiment with different places. In fact we moved so much that I can recall only three or four times that I was in the same school come September that I had been in the previous year. After about six or eight years of this I just gave up on having friends and turned to books instead. They're a lot more portable."

Books for Comfort

Born in the San Francisco Bay area, King and her family lived in several communities before moving north, to Tacoma, Washington. "I believe I was the only hippie in Tacoma at the time," King told *AAYA*. "I felt a little out of place." Books, as usual, provided solace. "I loved libraries when I was young. They were like a permanent home for me. They all have a familiar quality to them wherever they are, they even smell the same." Books were in the home as well: "I remember my father would sit after dinner reading a book and watching television at the same time. Books formed a major part of our lives growing up. I read lots of science fiction—Heinlein and such—and of course all the horse books. But books were also holy objects almost. I figured real people had nothing to do with writing them. I didn't know anybody who'd written a book, and this was prior to the time when authors would visit the schools. So I never thought I could be a writer. It was not until my thirties that I started to think about being a writer myself."

At school, King worked just hard enough to get by. "I guess you might say I was a mediocre student," King told *AAYA*. "If I'd worked harder, I would have been a straight A student, but there was little encouragement for that in my family. College was for the males, but as it turns out I'm the first one in my family to get a college education. And it was in one of my first college classes that I calculated how many different homes I'd had in my first eighteen years of life and came up with the number of twenty-one. That's a lot of moving."

Another move brought King, on her own as a high school graduate, back to the Bay Area. As King put it, she "backed into college," attending a junior college for three years while working full time to support herself. Then she transferred to the University of California at Santa Cruz where she was a Religious Studies major. "This was one of those decisions that chose me," King told *AAYA*. "Of all the classes I took in junior college, the ones I liked the most were religious studies. So that's the degree I pursued in college, and then followed it up later with a masters at the Graduate Theological Union at Berkeley." Earning the bachelor's degree took King seven years, working again full time while going to school. Graduating in 1977, King also married a faculty member of the Religious Studies program.

King's graduate studies shared pride of place with being a new mother and with traveling around

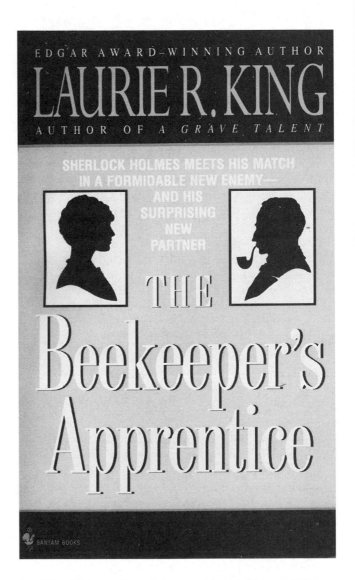

In this 1994 mystery King pairs intelligent fifteen-year-old Mary Russell with Sherlock Holmes to solve a murder.

the world. Following her master's degree in 1984, she first began experimenting with fiction: "My first project was a long futuristic novel that I put aside and never tried to sell." Then when her second child was four and beginning pre-school, King used the free daytime hours three times a week to get down to writing in a serious fashion. She wrote a first sentence: "I was fifteen years old when I first met Sherlock Holmes. . . ." Twenty-eight days later she had the first draft of a novel.

The "Mary Russell" Novels

"I'm not sure where that book came from," King told *AAYA*. "I'd been watching one of those excellent Holmes productions with Jeremy Brett on BBC, and perhaps that was playing in my subconscious. But Mary just came out on the paper." If the first draft was an easy birth, publication proved cantankerous and stubborn. King sent her manuscript out on her own for two years with no success; then in 1989 she started working with an agent. Meanwhile she continued with further Russell books, enjoying developing her teenage character into a full-blown woman. But finding a publisher proved no easy task. One interested house was scared off by potential copyright problems, though in the event no such problems met the publication of the books. After two finished manuscripts, King decided to adapt another possible Russell plot for a contemporary novel featuring a female cop, Kate Martinelli. This manuscript was taken by St. Martin's and paved the way for publication of the Russell series as well.

Thus King's first novel, *The Beekeeper's Apprentice: On the Segregation of the Queen*, was actually her second published book. In this first outing, Mary Russell, a recently orphaned heir to a sizeable fortune, living with her aunt, quite literally bumps into Sherlock Holmes on the Sussex Downs. She is fifteen, he fifty-four, yet the two form a friendship and bond. Holmes is taken by her intelligence and spunk, and she is not a little in awe of his powers of deductive reasoning, yet not so in awe that she will not deflate his ballooning ego from time to time. In short, they form an admirable partnership and soon begin taking on cases together in between Mary's studies at Oxford. They solve a local burglary, then save the kidnaped daughter of a U.S. Senator. This first title

is episodic in structure, with an end game in which the pair are forced to face a dangerous enemy from Holmes's past, dodging bombs and sniper bullets.

As Susan H. Woodcock noted in a *School Library Journal* review of *The Beekeeper's Apprentice*, "The story is well written in a style slightly reminiscent of Conan Doyle's, but is also very much King's own." Woodcock also went on to remark on the "excellent" characterization, the "skillfully evoked" sense of the time, and the "delightfully feminist" narrative. This combination attracted all

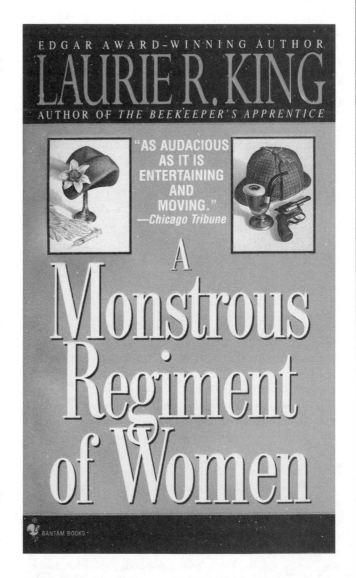

Mary Russell teams up with Sherlock Holmes once again to investigate the murders of several women belonging to a suffragette/religious organization.

sorts of readers, from those who love books about Holmes to adolescents looking for female role models. Addressing this last issue in particular, Pat Dowell wrote in the *Washington Post Book World* that "King has relieved Holmes of the worst effects of his misogyny and, by so doing, salved the old hurt that comes to every female reader of literature, usually at a very young age, when she realizes with great disappointment that she is excluded from the circle of presumed readers and fellow adventurers: that sinking feeling that 'They didn't mean *me*.'" In this case, King certainly did mean female readers to join in the fun as well: Mary Russell is Holmes's equal in detection and bravery, and she gets to dress up in all sorts of disguises, from a Gypsy girl to a young boy. Holmes even presents her with her own set of picklocks for her birthday. *Booklist*'s Emily Melton concluded that "Holmes fans, history buffs, lovers of humor and adventure, and mystery devotees will all find King's book absorbing from beginning to end."

In the second Russell title, *A Monstrous Regiment of Women*, a series of murders are claiming the lives of members of a suffrage organization that also serves as a feminist church. Its charismatic leader, Margery Childe, blends social activism with theological inquiries and feminist doctrine to make her New Temple of God a magnet for wealthy, educated women. Russell, a theology student at Oxford, is at first skeptical of Childe, then is slowly drawn into the inner circle of the Temple. When members begin dying, Russell becomes as much investigator as potential victim. In the course of the book, "the deeply rational, fiercely independent Mary . . . struggles to accept both Childe's possible mysticism and her deepening affection for Holmes," according to a *Publishers Weekly* reviewer, who concluded that "King's second Russell/Holmes tale lives up to all the accomplished promise of the first." Adler in the *Chicago Tribune Book World* called this second installment "as audacious as it is entertaining and moving," and noted that "King's research here and elsewhere is both prodigious and seamless: Fact and fiction blend smoothly." The Holmes-Russell relationship grows in this title, as well. Marilyn Stasio pointed out in the *New York Times Book Review* that Holmes "flings aside his idiosyncratic genius and his proud, disdainful ways to mince along in the shadow of his protege—even to the point of drawing her bath and preparing her meals. It is not a pretty sight."

If you enjoy the works of Laurie R. King, you may also want to check out the following books and films:

Carole Nelson Douglas, *Good Night, Mr. Holmes,* 1990, and *Good Morning, Irene,* 1991.

Arthur Conan Doyle, *The Complete Sherlock Holmes,* 1953.

The classic "Sherlock Holmes" films starring Basil Rathbone and Nigel Bruce, including *The Hound of the Baskervilles,* 1939.

The third book in the series, *A Letter of Mary,* finds Russell and Holmes settled down in 1923 to a "life of dull respectability in Sussex," according to Stasio in the *New York Times Book Review.* Such lassitude is interrupted by the visit of an archaeologist the couple met while hiding out in Palestine in *The Beekeeper's Apprentice,* Dorothy Ruskin. She produces an interesting artifact: an Aramaic papyrus supposedly written by one Mary of Magdala, and containing a secret which could rock christendom. Mary Magdalene refers to herself as an apostle. The murder of Ruskin makes Russell and Holmes take the papyrus seriously, and soon they are caught between Zionists and academics. "For all the disparity of their investigative techniques," Stasio wrote, ""the ultra-perceptive Holmes and the super-scholarly Russell make an engaging pair of sleuths." Woodcock, writing again in *School Library Journal,* remarked that the book would be a "sure hit with previous fans and a fine introduction to a dynamic duo." Maureen Corrigan concluded in the *Washington Post Book World* that this third title in the series "offers compelling characters, scrupulous period detail, and an absorbing, feminist-influenced mystery that would have made Sir Arthur Conan Doyle apoplectic."

King's fourth title in the Russell series, *The Moor,* brings loyal fans back to the scene of one of Holmes's most intriguing cases, *The Hound of the Baskervilles.* Getting word of mysterious doings on the moor, including the death of a tin seeker and the sighting of a ghostly-looking carriage and an enormous savage dog, Holmes and Russell set out to Dartmoor where they are in part aided by the Reverend Sabine Baring-Gould, an actual historical character, creator of the famous hymn "On-ward Christian Soldier" and an antiquarian and eccentric of more than local repute. Sorting through local legend and myth to get to the bottom of the mystery, Russell and Holmes once again tackle adventures and create "a superbly rich read that would please Doyle himself," Melton noted in *Booklist*. John Charles, writing in *Voice of Youth Advocates,* concluded that information about Dartmoor was "expertly woven into the plot" and that King "has a flair for bringing the bleak, harsh beauty of the moors to life."

Kate Martinelli

At the same time she has been writing the Mary Russell mysteries, King has also actively kept up the series that initially won her publication, those featuring the tough lesbian detective, Kate Martinelli. King seems to think in terms of both series and mystery or intrigue with her books. "As a writer I like the structure of a mystery," King told *AAYA* in her interview. "It enables me the skeletal structure upon which to hang story or plot, something to keep me going forward in narrative, to allow the people in the book to move around and develop while the plot unfolds. Mysteries also are often series, and you have the opportunity to get to know characters over a length of time. You can develop them and really get to know them in a series."

The author continued, "While the Russell books are pure fun for me, the Martinelli's are more serious. She's a more solid character. I mean I can't have Kate dressing up like a gypsy as Mary does. And the Martinelli books also require more research for me. While I am well grounded now in the world of the early twentieth century, and my religious studies continue to come in handy with the Russell books, when it comes to Kate Martinelli, I have to find out all about police procedure, what various officers are called, what weapons they carry—all that. But I am becoming very fond of Kate."

As are King's fans. The first title, *A Grave Talent*, which introduced the San Francisco cop, won an Edgar award, an auspicious enough beginning for a series. Martinelli needs to solve the murders of three small children in the Bay Area whose bodies have been found near an isolated artists' colony. The investigation focusses on a famous

This 1995 sequel to *A Grave Talent* finds Detective Kate Martinelli investigating the murder of a homeless person and a possible link with a suspicious preacher.

painter who has a murder conviction in her past. *Booklist*'s Marie Kuda called this debut title "Well crafted" and "prickling with excitement, full of intriguing characters," and a reviewer for *Library Journal* commented that an "omniscient narrator endows this amazing first novel with intelligence, intrigue, and intricacy."

King has followed up this first book with two others, *To Play the Fool* and *With Child*. In the former, the author expanded an idea from her bachelor's thesis, the role of the holy fool, and set out to discover what such a person might look like in the twentieth-century. Investigating the wrongful death of a homeless person in Golden Gate Park, Martinelli is led into the world of Brother Erasmus, another of the homeless but one whose quotation-peppered speech and dignity have attracted a following. Kate must balance this investigation with caring for her lover who was badly wounded in the conclusion of the first book, and in the course of her work she bounces between ivy-covered towers and squalid districts. Gail Pool noted in the *Wilson Library Bulletin* that King's second Martinelli mystery "is filled with fascinating lore . . . an unusual and quite wonderful novel."

In *With Child*, Kate must find a missing twelve-year-old girl who disappeared from her hotel room while under Kate's care. That the disappearance has occurred in the middle of a serial killer's territory adds urgency to the matter, and that the girl is the stepdaughter of her police partner, Al, complicates things even more. As if things were not hard enough for Kate, her lover, Lee, has moved out and Kate is on the outs with her other police colleagues. *Booklist*'s Melton observed that "As usual, King delivers a gripping, suspense-filled story that will appeal to most mystery fans."

A Sense of Mystery

King's one stand-alone book is *A Darker Place*, which introduces Anne Waverley, a sociologist who investigates cult groups for the FBI. Waverley has lost members of her family to a cult suicide, so she knows firsthand what she's talking about; now she infiltrates and investigates such groups to see if they pose a threat to society. This thriller may also lead to a sequel—if not more. "I like the character of Anne Waverley," King explained to *AAYA*, "and after you've invested so much time getting to know a character, it is hard to just let her evaporate. I might work on another Waverley title, but I don't see it as a series; perhaps two or three titles at most."

Meanwhile King is hard at work juggling her two other series at the same time. Her next Russell book, *O Jerusalem*, is planned as a flashback to Palestine during a six-week period in 1918-19, and a subsequent book will bring characters from *O Jerusalem* forward in time and place to England in 1924. A further Martinelli title, *Night Work*, is also in the pipeline. "This has been a busy year for me," King told *AAYA*. "I've finished three books, and this is from someone who does not even like to plot a novel. I seem to always be breaking the rules about writing. All those things

they tell you—write every day, write what you know, write to an outline—I don't do any of them. But being a writer allows me to structure my own life. I don't like to have to write every day, but when I am writing, I may work ten hours a day."

King is not a message author, though Mary Russell and Kate Martinelli are both independent, intelligent, accomplished women working in what was traditionally considered the male sphere of crime. "Any good novel tells truth in some way," King told *AAYA*. "It's the responsibility of an author to entertain, but it's also the job of any good novel to allow us all to learn something about what it means to be a thinking human being, to see how we work and function in the world. A good novel is one with many dimensions to it. I'm proud of the fan mail I get about my books because I find that I am reaching a diverse audience and on many levels. Bright, adolescent girls are drawn to Mary—they have even created a fan Web site—and in a way she provides something of a role model for them. I did not set out to do that when writing the books, but I can see how it might happen. But my books appeal to men and women alike, and I am never happier than when someone writes to say they have re-read my books. This indicates that there is a depth to them that you don't get with just one reading."

■ Works Cited

Adler, Dick, review of *A Monstrous Regiment of Women*, *Chicago Tribune Book World*, September 13, 1995, p. 4.

Adler, Dick, review of *With Child*, *Chicago Tribune Book World*, January 7, 1996, p. 6.

Charles, John, review of *The Moor*, *Voice of Youth Advocates*, October, 1998, p. 274.

Corrigan, Maureen, review of *A Letter of Mary*, *Washington Post Book World*, December 15, 1996, p. 10.

Dowell, Pat, "Sherlock Rusticates," *Washington Post Book World*, February 20, 1994, p. 8.

Review of *A Grave Talent*, *Library Journal*, January, 1993, p. 169.

King, Laurie R., interview with J. Sydney Jones for *Authors and Artists for Young Adults*, conducted December 14, 1998.

Kuda, Marie, review of *A Grave Talent*, *Booklist*, February 1, 1993, p. 972.

Melton, Emily, review of *The Beekeeper's Apprentice, Booklist,* February 1, 1994, p. 997.

Melton, Emily, review of *With Child, Booklist,* February 1, 1996, p. 919.

Melton, Emily, review of *The Moor, Booklist,* January 1, 1998, p. 784.

Review of *A Monstrous Regiment of Women, Publishers Weekly,* July 10, 1995, p. 46.

Pool, Gail, "Murder in Print," *Wilson Library Bulletin,* February, 1995, p. 72.

Stasio, Marilyn, review of *A Monstrous Regiment of Women, New York Times Book Review,* September 17, 1995, p. 41.

Stasio, Marilyn, review of *A Letter of Mary, New York Times Book Review,* January 5, 1997, p. 20.

Woodcock, Susan H., review of *The Beekeeper's Apprentice, School Library Journal,* July, 1994, pp. 128-29.

Woodcock, Susan H., review of *A Letter of Mary, School Library Journal,* June, 1997, p. 151.

■ For More Information See

PERIODICALS

Armchair Detective, Summer, 1996, p. 377; January 1, 1998, p. 784.

Booklist, February 15, 1995, p. 1062; February 1, 1996, p. 919.

Chicago Tribune Book World, January 7, 1996, p. 6; January 5, 1997, p. 4.

Kirkus Reviews, December 15, 1992, p. 1539; December 1, 1993, p. 1491.

New York Times Book Review, February 19, 1995, p. 25; February 18, 1997, p. 20; March 7, 1999, p. 20.

Publishers Weekly, January 3, 1994, p. 73; December 12, 1994, p. 52.

School Library Journal, December, 1994, p. 27; April, 1998, p. 158.

Washington Post Book World, February 19, 1995.

—Sketch by J. Sydney Jones

Stephen R. Lawhead

■ Personal

Born July 2, 1950, in Kearney, NE; son of Robert and Lois Lawhead; married Alice Slaikeu, 1972; children: Ross, Drake. *Education:* Kearney State College, B.A.; attended Northern Baptist Theological Seminary. *Hobbies and other interests:* Playing guitar, watching television.

■ Addresses

Agent—c/o Avon Books, The Hearst Corporation, 1350 Avenue of the Americas, New York, NY 10019.

■ Career

Writer. Associated with *Campus Life* magazine for five years; managed a Christian rock band; managed Ariel Records.

■ Writings

"DRAGON KING" SERIES

In the Hall of the Dragon King, Crossway (Westchester, IL), 1982.

The Warlords of Nin, Crossway, 1983.
The Sword and the Flame, Crossway, 1984.

"EMPHYRION SAGA" SERIES

The Search for Fierra, Crossway, 1985.
The Siege of Dome, Crossway, 1986.
Emphyrion (contains *The Search for Fierra* and *The Siege of Dome*), Lion (Oxford), 1990.

"PENDRAGON CYCLE" SERIES

Taliesin, Crossway, 1987.
Merlin, Crossway, 1988.
Arthur, Crossway, 1989.
Pendragon, Avon, 1994.
Grail, HarperCollins, 1997.

"SONG OF ALBION" SERIES

The Paradise War, Lion (Batavia, IL), 1991.
The Silver Hand, Lion, 1992.
The Endless Knot, Lion, 1993.

"CELTIC CRUSADES" SERIES

The Iron Lance, HarperPrism/Zondervan, 1998.

CHILDREN'S BOOKS

Howard Had a Spaceship, Lion, 1986.
Howard Had a Submarine, Lion, 1987.
Howard Had a Shrinking Machine, Lion, 1988.

Brown Ears, Multnomah Press (Missoula, MT), 1988.

Brown Ears at Sea, Multnomah Press, 1990.

Also author of *Howard Had a Hot Air Balloon, The Tale of Anabelle Hedgehog, The Tale of Jeremy Vole,* and *The Tale of Timothy Mallard.*

NONFICTION

Rock Reconsidered: A Christian Looks at Contemporary Music, InterVarsity Press, 1981.

(With Karl Slaikeu) *The Phoenix Factor: Surviving and Growing through Personal Crisis,* Houghton, 1985.

(With wife, Alice Slaikeu Lawhead) *Judge for Yourself,* Victor Books, 1985.

(With wife,) *The Ultimate College Student Handbook,* Harold Shaw Publishers (Wheaton, IL), 1989, revised and updated as *The Total Guide to College Life,* Harold Shaw Publishers, 1997.

Also author of *After You Graduate, Welcome to the Family, Nightmare in Paradise, Decisions, Decisions, Decisions.*

OTHER

Dream Thief, Crossway, 1983.

Byzantium, HarperCollins, 1996.

■ Sidelights

Stephen R. Lawhead's parlayed his long-time interest in history and mythology into a successful career writing historical fantasy novels. His most successful series, "The Pendragon Cycle" follows the life of King Arthur and the magician Merlin. Though this subject had been tackled by many previous writers, Lawhead's innovative retelling of this story appealed to many young adult as well as adult readers, earning him a loyal following and brisk book sales. Lawhead has also branched out into several other successful book series, including the "Song of Albion" volumes, that chronicle two characters traveling between mythological Britain and the modern world.

Lawhead grew up in Kearney, Nebraska, during the 1950s. Always interested in music and the arts, he financed his way through Kearney State College by working in the rock band Mother Rush.

Years after Prince Elphin adopts him, the orphaned Taliesin meets and marries Charis, a princess from Atlantis, who eventually bears a son named Merlin.

While in college, he pursued a fine arts curriculum. The multi-talented Lawhead was also a good writer—several of his poems were published in the college journal and he also wrote a humor column for the newspaper there.

After graduation, he decided to attend Northern Baptist Theological Seminary in Chicago, Illinois. But Lawhead was not totally convinced that he would enter a religious career. "As a Christian," he told Bob Summer of *Publishers Weekly*, "I thought a dose of theology might not be a bad idea. But I enrolled also in some classes in a nearby graduate school in the Chicago area. One of them was on editing and writing taught by the publisher of *Campus Life*. One night—it was an evening class—he asked me if I would like a job on the magazine, and I said 'Yes, please.' So I jumped ship, and spent the next five years there."

His job exposed him to many musicians, and he decided to manage the Christian rock group DeGarmo & Key. This apparently got his interest in music back on the front burner, and he left the magazine to form a record company of his own—Ariel Records. Unfortunately, as many new businesses do, the company failed only a year after he started it. That left Lawhead, who had

AUTHOR OF GRAIL

STEPHEN R. LAWHEAD

He was the glorious King of Summer...
And his legend the stuff of dreams

ARTHUR

Book Three of
THE PENDRAGON CYCLE

In this 1989 fantasy Lawhead describes King Arthur's life from his lowly beginnings to his rise to the throne.

moved to Memphis, Tennessee, to find a way to support his family—a wife and a child, with another child on the way. The week after Lawhead closed his business, he began to write his first novel, *In the Hall of the Dragon King* (1982). He wanted to know if it would be possible to support his family on a writer's income. Luckily for Lawhead's fans, the answer to that question would be a resounding yes.

This book was picked up by Crossway, a Christian publisher, but Lawhead explains that he didn't insist that a religious publisher take his works. "I don't write for a particular market," he told Summer. "It just happens that my novels are published by . . . a Christian publisher, because that was where I started out, and they have been good enough to stay with me."

In the Hall of the Dragon King features fifteen-year-old Quentin, an acolyte in the temple of Ariel. Quentin, although young and inexperienced when the tale begins, has been prophesied to become a mighty Priest King by those who worship the Most High God. In the work Quentin delivers a message to the Queen. Her husband, King Eskevar, has been kidnapped by the evil magician Nimrood who is in alliance with the King's younger brother, Jaspin. Jaspin wants the throne for himself alone. The Queen takes Quentin and a few brave knights to try to reclaim the king and end Jaspin's plan. Kathy Piehl, writing in *School Library Journal*, claimed that the book "should please most fantasy and adventure fans."

Lawhead continued Quentin's tale in *The Warlords of Nin* (1983). Quentin has been named Prince of Dekra, and he has gone on a quest to find an ore, lanthanil, from which to forge a special sword, Zhaligker. Meanwhile, Quentin's love, Bria, and the people of her kingdom are threatened by the hordes of Nin, a fearsome and evil invader. Although King Eskevar falls victim to the barbarians, Quentin arrives and uses his new sword to bring peace—and a new rule—to the land. Susan H. Harper of *Science Fiction and Fantasy Book Review* thought that the book was too heavy-handed when it came to religious and scriptural connotations. *School Library Journal* reviewer Lyle Blake Smythers had a different take on this work. While he faulted the bad grammar and clichés which mar some of the passages, he felt that these lapses "do not detract from the spell of this entertaining story."

The concluding volume to the "Dragon King" trilogy, *The Sword and the Flame* (1984), takes place ten years after the crucial battle with Nin. Quentin and Bria have married and now have a family with three young children. All seems to be well within the kingdom until the magician Nimrood, who was thought to be dead, returns—more deceptive than ever. Things quickly go from bad to worse when Quentin's son is kidnapped, his good friend is killed, and his sword loses its power. With the strength of the sword gone, his kingdom soon rebels against him. Quentin's faith is severely tested, yet he finds the courage to fight back against his enemies.

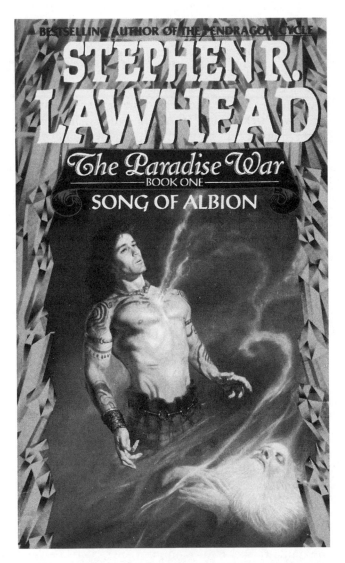

While investigating the sightings of a supposedly extinct beast in Scotland, two students, Lewis and Simon, stumble upon a mysterious Otherworld.

English Inspiration

After finishing these works, for which he had spent a year in England doing research, Lawhead moved back to Nebraska, but then decided to move permanently to Oxford, England, in 1990. This cemented his commitment to producing historical mythology. His most famous series, "The Pendragon Cycle" was inspired by a book he had in his house. "I have very eclectic interests and keep a lot of old things around," he told Summer. In his *Reader's Encyclopedia* he was reading about King Arthur when he discovered a tidbit about how Arthur had been tied to the mythological lost city of Atlantis. "That one sentence put a new slant on things," he told Summer. From this tiny bit of information, he began to create a new mythology of Arthur. Instead of setting his books in the medieval age, as most writers had done, he centered his work in the fifth century. In order to produce his works, Lawhead told Summer that "I had to master the archeology of the time, besides church history, Roman history and cultural anthropology."

His research gave him a different perspective on the old legends. In an interview in *Books*, Lawhead commented that "Mallory, Tennyson and Walt Disney have made us think of Arthurian legend as courtly medieval romances. That's far from the truth. As I read the old Welsh and Irish legends I found myself face to face with a fiercer, darker world, the world of Arthur the Celtic warlord, battling for Britain's survival in the power vacuum left by the withdrawal of the Roman legions." *Taliesin* (1987) is the first book in the series. The work follows Taliesin, who is found sewn into a sealskin sack as a child and adopted by Prince Elphin, and Charis, a princess living on Atlantis. Beautiful and graceful, she studies to become a bull-dancer on her island. When Atlantis is destroyed by a powerful earthquake, the refugees find their way to Britain. Charis and Taliesin fall in love and eventually marry. Taliesin is murdered by the prince's troops after Charis becomes pregnant with Merlin.

A *Kirkus Reviews* critic faulted Lawhead's sketchy portrayal of the main character, stating: "All in all, a mediocre warm-up." Sybil Steinberg, writing in *Publishers Weekly*, criticized Lawhead for flat characters who do not match the brilliance of his setting, calling the novel "more decorative than narrative." Jerome V. Reel, writing in *Kliatt*, had

Bestselling author of the PENDRAGON CYCLE

STEPHEN R. LAWHEAD
Byzantium

A GIFT
TENDERED,
A JOURNEY
UNDERTAKEN

Aidan's quiet life as a scribe ends when he is chosen to help deliver a hand-illuminated manuscript to the Emperor of Christendom in the city of Byzantium.

a different take on the narrative, believing that Lawhead has captured the period faithfully. He found that "the story is well paced, intriguing and informative."

Merlin (1988) follows the young magician in Britain during the end of Rome's rule of the country. Merlin must prove himself as a warrior before he assumes his role as protector of the future King Arthur. Along the way, however, he gains and loses a kingdom, as well as a young wife. Despite his personal pain, he remains faithful to the prophesy that he will be a prophet for the future king. Reviewer Anne Frost of *Voice of Youth Advo-*

cates admitted that the book is "beautifully written" and commented that "*Merlin* is as engrossing and spellbinding as the character himself."

Arthur (1989) chronicles Uther's illegitimate son's rise to rule Britain. Arthur begins as a savage brute; only with the help of Merlin does he become worthy of getting the Sword in the Stone that signifies that he is the Summer King. To accomplish this feat, Merlin takes Arthur away from his family. The story of his life is told by people in the court, giving the text a multi-layered quality. Reel praised the book, writing that "the story is so good and so well paced that I suspect most readers will love it." Carolyn Cushman, writing in *Locus*, felt that the story lacks a human element. "What doesn't make itself felt, unfortunately, is Arthur's personality. He is a mission and a symbol, not a man. . . . Lawhead's vision of Arthur is intellectually intriguing, and the action frequently enthralling, but it lacks much of the emotional involvement that makes other Arthurian tales so powerful."

The tales of King Arthur's early years at court are told in *Pendragon* (1994). He is crowned in Londonium and the Irish warrior princess Gwenhwyvar comes to the coronation to become his wife. Arthur soon has to go off to Ireland, where the Vandals have invaded. The Vandals are put off, but they then decide to rampage through Britain, a campaign that pits Arthur against his fiercest enemies ever. A reviewer in *Publishers Weekly* claimed that Lawhead "brilliantly creates an authentic and vivid Arthurian Britain."

In *Grail* (1997), Arthur makes peace with the Vandals but finds himself confronting another evil power—Morgian, the Queen of Air and Darkness. Irish knight Llenlleawg unites with Morgian in order to defeat Arthur and steal the Holy Grail. Arthur must fight off monsters and magic in order to remain King. A *Kirkus Reviews* critic praised the work, indicating that "Lawhead's interpretation is different and distinctive."

On to Albion

Lawhead's "Song of Albion" series has also enjoyed popularity among readers. The series chronicles the lives of two friends, Lewis Gillies and Simon Rawnson, who gain entrance to a mysterious Celtic Otherworld known as Albion. In

If you enjoy the works of Stephen R. Lawhead, you may also want to check out the following books and films:

Gillian Bradshaw, *Hawk of May*, 1980.
Mary Stewart's Merlin Trilogy (contains *The Crystal Cave*, *The Hollow Hills*, and *The Last Enchantment*), Morrow, 1980.
T. H. White, *The Once and Future King*, 1958.
Excalibur, a film by John Boorman, 1981.

the first book of the trilogy, *The Paradise War* (1991), Lewis and Simon travel to Scotland to check on a sighting of an aurochs, an ox thought to have been extinct. Other equally unusual events start taking place because of turbulence between the modern world and the Otherworld. Simon then disappears into Albion, and Lewis follows him. The two become fierce Celtic warriors and are drawn into battle when the powerful Lord Nudd, with whom Simon has aligned himself, threatens both worlds. Gladys Hardcastle of *Voice of Youth Advocates* found fault with the characters in the book. She observed, "Convincing as Oxford students, Lewis and Simon become stereotypical as Celtic warriors." Judith H. Silverman, writing in *Kliatt*, called the story "fast-moving . . . the series may be a successor to Tolkien."

In *The Silver Hand* (1992) Lewis, now named Llew, is chosen successor to the throne after the king of the Llwyddi is slain. Meldron, the King's son, is not happy with the choice, and he cuts off Llew's hand, preventing him from taking power, since a man with a disability is not allowed to rule. As Meldron assumes power, Llew and his friend, the bard Tegid Tathal, escape to found Dinas Dwr, a city they hope will act as a safe haven for those who are who are oppressed by the new king. A critic in *Publishers Weekly* stated that Lawhead "invests his often poetic vision of a Celtic land living by ancient laws with charm and dignity."

The Endless Knot (1993) finishes the story of Simon and Llew. Since Llew has restored hope to the kingdom of Albion, his friend in the modern world, professor Nettleton, urges him to come back to his previous life. Llew, however, believes

in the prophesy that would make him king in Albion, and he stays to marry Goewyn. Soon, Goewyn is kidnapped and Llew must do battle with magical creatures to reclaim her. Finally he meets up again with Simon, this time in charge of a band of marauders. Llew is able to defeat Simon, right Albion again, and return to his world. A critic in *Kirkus Reviews* called the series an "admirably restrained and above-average Celtic trilogy."

Despite Lawhead's commitment to solid research and well-developed works, he also knows that his works should be centered in solid storytelling. "I do try to give my readers a good story. The way I look at it, my license as a writer of popular fiction says 'license to entertain.'" he told Summer. Apparently, he has succeeded. His many fans and his well-traveled Internet Web site are a testament to his popularity. As for his future, readers should keep an eye on his homepage, which recently stated: "What is next? Perhaps a giant step backward. Books about ancient Egypt are beginning to fill his shelves."

■ Works Cited

Cushman, Carolyn, review of *Arthur*, *Locus*, August, 1989, p. 15.

Review of *The Endless Knot*, *Kirkus Reviews*, May 1, 1993, p. 561.

Frost, Anne, review of *Merlin*, *Voice of Youth Advocates*, April, 1989, pp. 43-44.

Review of *Grail*, *Kirkus Reviews*, May 1, 1997.

Hardcastle, Gladys, review of *The Paradise War*, *Voice of Youth Advocates*, December, 1993, p. 311.

Harper, Susan H., review of *The Warlords of Nin*, *Science Fiction and Fantasy Book Review*, Issue 18, October, 1983, pp. 26-27.

Interview with Stephen Lawhead, *Books*, November/December, 1994, p. 25.

Review of *Pendragon*, *Publishers Weekly*, October 3, 1994, p. 54.

Piehl, Kathy, review of *In the Hall of the Dragon King*, *School Library Journal*, November, 1982.

Reel, Jerome V., review of "The Pendragon Cycle," *Kliatt*, January, 1991, p. 24.

Review of *The Silver Hand*, *Publishers Weekly*, May 4, 1992, p. 45.

Silverman, Judith H., review of *The Paradise War*, *Kliatt*, September, 1992, p. 22.

Smythers, Lyle Blake, review of *The Warlords of Nin*, *School Library Journal*, October, 1983, p. 170.

Steinberg, Sybil, review of *Taliesin, Publishers Weekly,* August 14, 1987, p. 99.

Stephen R. Lawhead's Internet homepage is located at http://www.stephenlawhead.com, December, 1998.

Summer, Bob, "Crossway's Crossover Novelist," *Publishers Weekly,* October 6, 1989, pp. 28, 32.

Review of *Taliesin, Kirkus Reviews,* July 1, 1987.

■ For More Information See

PERIODICALS

Booklist, September 1, 1987, p. 31; October 1, 1988, p. 220; August, 1989, p. 1949; June 1, 1992, p. 1749; October 1, 1994, p. 245; September 1, 1996.

Kirkus Reviews, May 1, 1991, p. 571; July 15, 1996; October 1, 1998, p. 1422.

Publishers Weekly, April 19, 1991, p. 61; September 13, 1993, p. 124; June 16, 1997, p. 50; November 30, 1998, pp. 54-55.

Voice of Youth Advocates, February, 1990, p. 371; February, 1997, p. 336.*

—Sketch by Nancy Rampson

Spike Lee

■ Personal

Born March 20, 1957, in Atlanta, GA; son of William (a musician and composer) and Jacqueline (a teacher; maiden name, Shelton) Lee. *Education:* Morehouse College, B.A., 1979; New York University, M.A., 1983.

■ Addresses

Home—Brooklyn, NY. *Office*—Forty Acres and a Mule Filmworks, 124 DeKalb Ave., Brooklyn, NY 11217.

■ Career

Screenwriter, actor, and director and producer of motion pictures and music videos. Director of films, including *She's Gotta Have It*, 1986, *Do the Right Thing*, 1989, *Malcolm X*, 1992, *Get on the Bus*, 1996, *Girl 6*, 1996, and *4 Little Girls*, 1997. Founder and director, Forty Acres and a Mule Filmworks, Brooklyn, NY, 1986—.

■ Awards, Honors

Student Director's Award from Academy of Motion Picture Arts and Sciences, 1982, for "Joe's Bed-Stuy Barber Shop: We Cut Heads"; Prix de Jeunesse from Cannes Film Festival and New Generation Award from the Los Angeles Film Critics, both 1986, for *She's Gotta Have It. Member:* Screen Actors Guild.

■ Writings

Spike Lee's "Gotta Have It": Inside Guerrilla Filmmaking (includes interviews and a journal), illustrated with photographs by brother, David Lee, foreword by Nelson George, Simon & Schuster, 1987.

(With Lisa Jones) *Uplift the Race: The Construction of "School Daze,"* Simon & Schuster, 1988.

(With Lisa Jones) *"Do the Right Thing": The New Spike Lee Joint,* Fireside Press, 1989.

(With Lisa Jones) *Mo' Better Blues,* Simon & Schuster, 1990.

(With Ralph Wiley) *By Any Means Necessary: The Trials and Tribulations of the Making of "Malcolm X,"* Hyperion Adult, 1992.

Best Seat in the House: A Basketball Memoir, Crown, 1997.

SCREENPLAYS; AND DIRECTOR

She's Gotta Have It, Island, 1986.

School Daze, Columbia, 1988.

Do the Right Thing, Universal, 1989.

Mo' Better Blues, Forty Acres and a Mule Filmworks, 1991.

Jungle Fever, Forty Acres and a Mule Filmworks,
1991.

(With Arnold Perl, adapted from the James
Baldwin screenplay) *Malcolm X,* Forty Acres and
a Mule Filmworks, 1992.

(With Joie Lee and Cinque Lee) *Crooklyn,* Forty
Acres and a Mule Filmworks, 1994.

Clockers (based on the Richard Price novel of the
same name), Forty Acres and a Mule Filmworks,
1995.

Girl 6, Fox Searchlight, 1996.

Get on the Bus, Forty Acres and a Mule Filmworks,
1996.

He Got Game, Forty Acres and a Mule Filmworks,
1998.

Also writer and director of short films, including
"The Answer," 1980; "Sarah," 1981; and "Joe's
Bed-Stuy Barbershop: We Cut Heads," 1982. Contributor of short films to *Saturday Night Live* and
to MTV.

■ Sidelights

Few Americans in the arts are able to boast the
exhaustive list of achievements that Spike Lee has
accomplished before his fortieth birthday. Since the
mid-1980s, the Brooklyn-bred, New York Univer-
sity-trained filmmaker has written, directed, and
acted in several successful movies—creations all
the more remarkable for their unique look at African American life, in settings on the streets of
and in the mental landscapes of Brooklyn. Though
sometimes provocative and controversial in their
themes or characterizations, Lee's films transcend
color lines. Almost singlehandedly, he has changed
the relationship between the Hollywood film industry and African American audiences. Without
Spike Lee, it is hard to imagine that such films
as *Waiting to Exhale,* or even *Pulp Fiction,* would
have found commercial success.

Not surprisingly, Lee is an iconoclastic, outspoken,
and articulate public figure. But he is also a me-
dia-savvy one with a trenchant sense of humor.
Lee is particularly fluent on the subject of race in
America and the many shapes and forms by
which it disguises itself. After a solid childhood
and a positive college experience firmly grounded

in African American culture, Lee was well-
equipped to enter battle when he faced serious
obstacles as a neophyte filmmaker. As a writer
and top-notch observer of human experience, Lee
was no great exception to any rule; but the combination of his talents and his vision as a filmmaker and his intense, almost enthusiastic stubbornness have helped him to usher in a new and
significant era for American film.

Spike Lee was born Shelton Jackson Lee in Atlanta, the first of William and Jacqueline Lee's five
children. As the family grew, they moved around;
Bill Lee, a jazz musician, was drawn first to Chicago, then to the equally vibrant music scene in
New York City. The Lees settled in Brooklyn about
1959, when their first son was still a two-year-
old toddler—but already nicknamed "Spike" by
his mother as a result of his cantankerousness. The
family lived first on Union Street in the Crown
Heights neighborhood. They later moved to
nearby Cobble Hill, becoming the first African
American family on their street, before eventually
relocating to the Fort Greene area, which already
had a reputation as a dangerous place. However,
Lee recalled that the crime and violence of the
1960s were "tame" compared to more recent times,
and that his block was filled with kids around
his age, all of who played team-based street
games together. "You were told: 'Look, when it
gets dark, bring your butt home,'" Lee told Anna
Deavere Smith in *Premiere,* He would later depict
this world—first in narrative-framing glimpses in
Mo' Better Blues, and then more fully developed
in the saga of the Carmichael family of *Crooklyn.*
"I never had to worry about getting into fights,
or think, 'Am I going to get hit by that errant
bullet?'" Lee recalled in an interview with Patricia
Sellers in *Entertainment Weekly.*

Stubborn Streak

Like many other African American teens in northern cities, Lee spent summers with relatives down
South, usually his grandmother in Atlanta. After
graduating from John Dewey High School in
Brooklyn in 1975, Lee enrolled at Morehouse College in Atlanta, an historic African American college from which both his father and grandfather
had graduated; Lee's mother had gone to nearby
Spelman College. His grandmother paid his tuition, for his parents were still struggling financially. Lee's father had played bass for a number

of big-name folk singers and their album sessions during the 1960s, but being a "jazz purist," he lost work when he refused to make the switch to the electric bass. Lee would later say he most certainly inherited his stubborn streak from his father. Lee's mother Jacqueline, a teacher of art and black literature at St. Ann's School in Brooklyn, supported the family. But she died of liver cancer in 1977, when her eldest son was in college.

At Morehouse, Lee studied mass communications, and decided to become a filmmaker halfway through. "Being the first born, not becoming a musician was part of my rebelliousness," Lee wrote in *Spike Lee's "Gotta Have It": Inside Guerrilla Filmmaking*. One of his first short films was a romance he titled "Black College: The Talented Tenth," and the female lead was played by a student named Rolanda Watts, who would later become a television reporter and host of her own

daytime show. Lee also did another short he called "Last Hustle in Brooklyn," set in the disco summer of 1977, when New York City suffered the last of its famous blackouts. During his Morehouse years, Lee also hosted a jazz music show on the campus radio station, and he wrote for the student newspaper. Though he lived on campus, Lee ate his meals at his grandmother's house.

When he graduated in 1979, Lee interned at Columbia Pictures, and then won entry to the prestigious film school at New York University. Being one of just a handful of black students, he felt the invisible currents of elitism and racism. During his first year, Lee encountered problems with his teachers and the administrators for his adamant opinions. He was labeled a "militant" after submitting an assignment film about an African American screenwriter who has been hired to shoot a remake of *Birth of a Nation*, the classic,

A scene with Lee, John Canada Terrell, and Redmond Hicks from the 1986 film *She's Gotta Have It*, the first full-length film written, directed, edited, and produced by Lee.

but controversial, 1915 silent film by D. W. Griffith that portrays African Americans in a negative light. Lee resisted "suggestions" that he pursue his education elsewhere, and after several semesters, he managed to strike a balance between his political beliefs and his artistic vision. This came to fruition with the 1982 short *Joe's Bed-Stuy Barbershop: We Cut Heads.* His grandmother, who put up some money for the film, was listed as producer in the credits. Set in the Brooklyn neighborhood of Bedford-Stuyvestant that he knew intimately, Lee was able to call people he knew to request use of their homes or stores for locations. Its lead, Monty Ross, was a friend of Lee's from Morehouse, who held a number of other production jobs on the film. Ross plays a Brooklyn barber whose establishment is also an illegal numbers joint. Lee won the N.Y.U. student award for *Joe's Bed-Stuy Barbershop* that year, a peer-group honor that is not bestowed haphazardly.

Because of this success, talent agencies began courting him, but none seemed interested in expanding the themes of *Joe's Bed-Stuy* into a larger project. Undeterred, Lee wrote the script for an all-black film he called "Homecoming." The story is set at a college, not unlike Morehouse, around the festive atmosphere of its homecoming weekend. It was subject matter that Lee knew about first-hand; he had served as pageant coordinator during his student years for the annual football-season parades. None of the talent agencies that courted him were interested in the script, and so Lee realized then that he would have to fly solo if he wanted to pursue a career as a commercial filmmaker.

"A definite case of racism"

After graduation, Lee found work in a movie distribution warehouse, applied for arts grants for production money, and networked around New York. In Greenwich Village he met actor Lawrence Fishburne, who had appeared in the Francis Ford Coppola film *Apocalypse Now* and the 1975 flick *Cornbread, Earl and Me;* Lee simply approached him on the street and told him he liked his work. Fishburne agreed to star in Lee's first planned feature film, the tale of a Brooklyn bike messenger and his family. But Fishburne and some of the others were Screen Actors Guild (SAG) members, and Lee would be compelled to pay them union rates. He applied for an "experimental film"

waiver designed to help young directors only after he had won one grant and committed other funds to the production budget for *The Messenger,* but the SAG rates committee declined; Lee then tried to recast with unknowns, but abandoned the project and tried to have his one main grant from the American Film Institute transferred to another script. That group also rejected his plan. "I got a list of ten films that had been given a waiver within the [previous] year," Lee wrote in *Spike Lee's "Gotta Have It".* "All of them were done by white independent filmmakers. All of them worked with a whole lot more money than I had. Yet they said my film was too commercial. . . . That was a definite case of racism."

Finally Lee won a grant from a New York-area arts council and shot his first feature film, *She's Gotta Have It,* in just twelve days. It starred Tracy Camilla Johns as Nola Darling, an African American woman who enjoys three beaus—one of whom, Mars Blackmon, was played by Lee—but cannot choose between the trio, and does not want to have to choose. In the end, one sexually assaults her, and she abandons all three. Lee edited the film in his studio apartment—a huge editing machine wedged next to his bed—took it to the 1986 Cannes Film Festival, and won the Prix de Jeunesse. At the time, he was sharing a Cannes apartment with seven other people, unable to even pay for a hotel room. Then *She's Gotta Have It* was picked up for distribution and became a massive art-house hit across the United States, grossing $8 million. The film, opined Charles Derry in an essay on Lee for *International Directory of Films and Filmmakers,* "reflects the sensibilities of an already sophisticated filmmaker and harkens back to the early French New Wave in its exuberant embracing of bravura technique . . . wedded nevertheless to serious philosophical/sociological examination."

The buzz on Lee described him as "the black Woody Allen," but Derry disparaged the comparisons, instead likening the upstart filmmaker in "his work's energy, style, eclecticism, and social commitment" to Martin Scorsese, also an N.Y.U. film-school graduate. By now, the Hollywood studios were now enthusiastically courting Lee and were more than willing to make a film about African American life after seeing how well audiences responded to *She's Gotta Have It* and its absence of poverty, misery, violence, or drugs. Island Pictures offered Lee a deal to put the

Danny Aiello and Lee star in Lee's explosive 1989 film *Do the Right Thing.*

"Homecoming" script into production, then changed their minds; he turned to Columbia Pictures and began shooting what would become the 1988 musical *School Daze* after receiving permission from the Atlanta University Center to film on campus. The Atlanta University Center was the administrative body that controlled Morehouse, Spelman, and three other black colleges whose campuses were almost adjacent to one another.

The cast of *School Daze* included Vanessa Williams, Tyra Banks, and Lawrence Fishburne; Lee cast himself in the role of Half Pint, a student who hopes to achieve social success by pledging the top fraternity at Mission College. Half Pint served as a symbol of the conflict faced by many African American students at elite black colleges, who could boast such prominent alumni as Alice Walker and the late Dr. Martin Luther King, Jr. Such institutions had long served as a training ground for the black middle class in America, but also made their educational opportunities open to

students who often were the first in their family to graduate from high school. In his script, Lee constructed this tension around two groups of students he called "wannabes"—light-skinned students from affluent families who dressed conservatively, straightened their hair and even wore blue contact lenses—and "jigaboos," dark skinned students who possessed a distinct street credibility or a rural Southern accent, and returned the sense of contempt they received from the wannabes.

Exploring such sensitive themes in a musical comedy landed Lee in hot water. Halfway through the filming, an attorney for the Atlanta University Center administrators, who feared that Morehouse and the historic black college experience in general would be tarnished, sent Lee a letter requesting to review the script. He refused, and they banned the film crew, forcing him to re-shoot several weeks worth of footage. *New York Times Magazine* writer Stuart Mieher visited Lee on the set

Lee's 1990 film *Mo' Better Blues,* which stars Denzel Washington, is loosely based on the life of Lee's father.

before and after this fracas, and explained that inside the African American community, "even the thought of such color lines is controversial." The reporter quoted Morehouse College president Hugh Morris Glosser as saying, "I don't see anyone around here wanting to be white."

Lee also detailed the controversy in his companion book to the film, *Uplift the Race: The Construction of "School Daze,"* co-authored with Lisa Jones. He saw the colleges' attitudes as dovetailing perfectly with the issues he was trying to raise. Lee also described in the book how he deliberately engineered tension among cast and extras by segregating them according to their roles, and the infighting that arose surprised even him. He housed "jigaboo" cast members at a Ramada Inn, for instance, and put their rivals at a posher hotel. "It was brilliant," Fishburne told Mieher in the *New York Times Magazine.* "He knew a director just cannot tell a group of eight actors, 'I want you

all to be as one.' So he sets you up in a situation where you're going to be together 24 hours a day."

"Who's gonna do the right thing?"

Human nature's need to divide and do battle against itself was again the theme of his next film, 1989's *Do the Right Thing.* Again, controversy erupted over the film even before its release. Lee let the film's theme song set viewers up in the first few minutes—Public Enemy's "Fight the Power." Lee again starred as Mookie, a pizza deliverer for a Bedford-Stuyvestant pizzeria run by Sal, an Italian-American played by Danny Aiello. Sal and his sons are the last vestiges of Bed-Stuy's once-populous Italian community, and their resentment of this changing world simmers below the surface. The action in *Do the Right Thing* takes place on the hottest day of the year, when Bugin'

Out, an Afrocentric-minded black customer, tells Sal he needs to include some photographs of African Americans on the pizzeria's Wall of Fame, which is Sal's way of taking pride in his Italian-American heritage. He refuses, so Bugin' Out tries to organize a boycott of Sal's establishment, which is unsuccessful, and then recruits the ominous-looking Radio Raheem. A racial slur escapes from Sal, and the summer heat and sociological tensions escalate to a terrible moment when Raheem becomes a casualty of police brutality in front of the pizzeria. Mookie's toss of a garbage can through the window of his employer's business is the spark that incites a riot.

Lee later recalled that the scene was "my most pressured moment as an actor on this film," he wrote in the companion book, again written with Jones, *"Do the Right Thing": The New Spike Lee Joint*. "No one thought about this beforehand, but the window glass was almost one-quarter inch

thick. Breaking glass that thick is no easy feat. . . . I was on the spot: We were filming with a special crane that had to be sent back to the rental house the next day, and the sun was coming up." Lee's sister, Joie Lee, played his sister Jade on-camera, and called the film's riots scenes harrowing to watch, as did Richard Edson, who played one of Sal's sons. "You'd stop and see the pizza parlor burning, 200 extras running out in the street, and you'd think, 'This could be the real thing. . .,'" Edson told *Rolling Stone* reporter David Handelman. "The question is, why do these things keep happening?," Edson continued. "Who's gonna do the right thing? Would I? And what is the right thing, at the moment of truth?"

Lee chose to end *Do the Right Thing* with quotes from both Malcolm X and Martin Luther King—one who, during a period in his political career, advocated violence as a means to an end; the other who built a political career by eschewing

Denzel Washington was also assigned the lead role in the 1992 film *Malcolm X.*

it. This time Lee's efforts were shunned at the Cannes Festival; the controversy surrounding the film was just as heated as the New York City summer day it chronicled. Universal Pictures chose to release the film during the summer, and there had already been several notorious racially-motivated murders or incidents in and around New York in recent years. At a press conference that Handelman chronicled for the *Rolling Stone* article, *USA Today* journalist Jeannie Williams fumed, "I live in New York. I don't need this movie in New York this summer!" Lee, however, rejoindered to the assembled journalists, "If anything happens, it'll be because the cops killed somebody else with no reason, but it won't be because of *Do the Right Thing.*"

Lee was also criticized for making his first true film about urban culture and depicting an impoverished American neighborhood in which illegal drugs were all but nonexistent. To this he retorted at the same conference, "How many of you went and saw *Working Girl* or *Rain Man* and asked, 'Where are the drugs?' Nobody. But the minute we have a black film that takes place in the ghetto, people want to know where the drugs are . . . because that's the way you think of black people," Handelman quoted Lee as saying. The filmmaker declared that he could not make drugs a casual subplot in a story about larger issues, that the topic deserved its own film.

With his successful track record, Lee was able to create his own production company; Forty Acres and a Mule borrowed its name from the never-realized promise to America's slaves at the end of the Civil War. *Mo' Better Blues* was the first of his films under this banner, a lushly photographed work that starred Denzel Washington as a jazz musician in Harlem in the 1940s. The film was also a reflection of Lee's own upbringing in a music-loving household, his father's career, the dangerous lure of artistic obligation, and whether it is compatible with stable, middle-class aspirations and a family life. Though Lee did not make narcotics an element in his narrative about trumpeter Bleek Gilliam, as most jazz films were wont to do, the action does not flinch from the seamy underside of the nightclub world and includes subplots involving gambling and mobsters. Gilliam's own personal cross is his infidelity, and in the end, after realizing the limitations of his talent, he returns to one woman and marries her. The film concludes with the father giving his son

Clockers, a 1995 film based on a novel by Richard Price, examines the drug trade in a New York housing project.

rigorous music lessons in a vintage Brooklyn apartment as his friends on the street call up to him to come outside and play.

A Stand against Interracial Romance

Lee touched upon more than one controversial theme in another film that was released in 1991: *Jungle Fever*. The screenplay, written by Lee, tracks the start-to-finish tale of an interracial romance between Wesley Snipes, in the role of architect Flipper Purify, and an Italian-American woman played by Annabella Sciorra whom he meets in the workplace. Purify is happily married and has a young daughter, and lives on one of Harlem's grandest addresses that retains the charm of decades past. At his firm, he has requested an African American secretary and is incensed when Sciorra's "temp" character is sent instead; his white bosses are portrayed as smug and condescending. A mutually wary respect leads to friendship between boss and assistant, and late nights at work give way to an affair. Purify confesses his transgression to his best friend, played by Lee, who then tells his wife, played by Veronica Webb (Lee's real-life paramour at the time). Webb's character then spills the beans to Flipper's wife, who throws him out of the house. Angie, Sciorra's character, is also ejected from her Bensonhurst home by her racist father.

Flipper and Angie move into a shared Greenwich Village apartment together, but the relationship is clearly doomed, accentuated by a terrible dinner experience at the home of his parents. Lee cast Ossie Davis as his somewhat unbalanced minister father, with Ruby Dee as his long-suffering wife who secretly gives money to their other son, Gator, a crackhead played with gruesome comedy by Samuel L. Jackson. The film clearly takes a stand against interracial romance. As Lee told Janice Mosier Richolson in an interview in *Cineaste,* after his mother's death in 1977, his father remarried a white woman; he granted that it was a successful love match, but when prodded by Richolson admitted, "We don't get along, but it's not because she's white," Lee said. "I was my mother's first child, so my stepmother's never going to be my mother." Lee said his father and stepmother had not yet seen *Jungle Fever.* "It might be hard for him to look at," he told Richolson. "She ain't gonna like it."

Up until this point in his career, Lee's works had usually been met with some reproach from the film-critic community for what some viewed as their flashy camera work. *Film Comment*'s Kent Jones explained some of the technical or artistic criticisms leveled at Lee's films in a 1997 article, citing one as his reliance on the actor-on-dolly shot (borrowed from Scorsese) which made it appear that the actors were ambling along on moving sidewalks. Lee has also been accused of keeping his actors so tightly directed that they never really seem to take on their roles, and for portraying whites in very heavy-handed terms. Jones granted that "there are appalling things in *Jungle Fever,* but it remains his most devastating film." The critic likened Anthony Quinn's racist dinner-table railing at Sciorra's character to "an industrial disaster in an olive oil factory," but declared that in the end, "Lee achieves something rare in American cinema, which is an illustration of the degree to which people are products of their environment, a far cry from the bogus individualism of so much American cinema."

Lee's 1992 opus *Malcolm X* marked a turning point in his career. He had a substantial, larger-than-life martyr as the subject, a large studio budget, and a screenplay written by James Baldwin. Lee, however, chose to make the biopic his own way, rewriting the screenplay when he found historical inaccuracies in the speeches that Baldwin had included. He also gave more emphasis to a crucial turning point in Malcolm's life by fleshing out the ideological breech that caused him to sunder ties with the Nation of Islam and its leader,

Elijah Muhammad. He hired Betty Shabazz, Malcolm's widow, as a consultant, and also worked on the screenplay with Denzel Washington, cast as the lead. Lee told Gary Crowdus and Dan Georgakas in an interview for *Cineaste* that the actor "has a good story sense. We both knew a lot was riding on this film," Lee said. "We did not want to live in another country for the rest of our lives. We could not go anywhere without being reminded by black folks, '. . . don't mess this one up.' We were under tremendous pressure on this film."

Lee also ran into budget problems with *Malcolm X.* Warner had provided Lee with $20 million. He asked for more. Refused, he sold the foreign rights to raise more, but still ran short. Lee then went to the media and declared that the studio suffered from a "plantation" mentality. By soliciting large sums from supportive figures in the entertainment industry like Oprah Winfrey and Bill Cosby, he was able to complete the film. Still, even the production was wrought with tension; once Lee and the crew were filming an exterior scene in Harlem when a empty car began careening toward them, Lee told Harry Waters of *Newsweek.* They got out of the way, and discovered that "someone had tied a brick to the accelerator and gunned it in our direction," Lee said. Though the movie was marketed as a civil-rights biography, Warner nevertheless gave advance screenings of *Malcolm X* to police departments across the country, which Lee termed "inappropriate," as he said in the *Cineaste* interview. "I mean, if they do that to us, they should do it to *Terminator.* How many cops got killed in those films?"

Malcolm X established Lee as a significant and respected figure in American cinema. The three-plus hour film was both a commercial success—earning more than two million dollars on the day it opened—and a critical achievement. "Spike Lee has accomplished something historic in movies: a rousing, full-sized epic about a defiantly idealistic black hero whose humanitarianism never extends to turning the other cheek," noted Peter Travers in *Rolling Stone.* David Ansen, reviewing it for *Newsweek,* remarked that with Lee's "first foray into the epic mode . . . he takes hold of the form with verve and confidence," and despite its length, *Malcolm X* "passes swiftly with only a few lulls."

Perhaps even more telling than box-office receipts and the ubiquitous "X" baseball caps—sold by

Lee's company in a profitable tie-in venture that was met with some criticism—was the fact that *The Autobiography of Malcolm X* zoomed to the top of the *New York Times* bestseller list thirty years after its initial publication. Lee titled his companion book *By Any Means Necessary: The Trials and Tribulations of the Making of Malcolm X.* Perhaps no other of his works were so fraught with controversy before its debut, and for this reason the *Chicago Tribune*'s Clarence Petersen called Lee's book "extraordinary reading." Petersen also noted that the chronicle of his struggle to make it is as "full of the contentiousness Lee is known for."

Contention and controversy were distinctly absent from Lee's next film, a bittersweet 1994 look at life in the Brooklyn of his youth. He made *Crooklyn* from a screenplay written with his sister Joie and brother Cinque. The story follows the five children of the Carmichael family, a household headed by a jazz-musician father and school-

teacher mother. Despite the similarities with his own upbringing, Lee remained adamant in the press that it was a work of fiction. "Those who know the Lees say Spike has a painful, personal reason for insisting this," explained Sellers in *Entertainment Weekly*. "He and his siblings, who all still live in Brooklyn, are apparently concerned about their father's reaction to *Crooklyn*. Bill Lee scored most of his son's movies until *Malcolm X* but has fallen from Spike's graces, an estrangement that Bill's 1991 arrest for heroin possession didn't help," Sellers wrote.

Alfre Woodard and Delroy Lindo portrayed *Crooklyn's* on-screen parents, and three of the five children cast as the Carmichaels had never acted before. To prepare them for playing kids mired in the culture of the late 1960s and early 1970s, he banned Nintendo in their lives and showed them reruns of the television shows of the era such as *The Partridge Family.* Lee had said once

A prison inmate (Denzel Washington) is paroled for a week to convince his son Jesus Shuttleworth (Ray Allen) to play basketball for a politician's alma mater in the 1998 film *He Got Game.*

before he would never again work with children, that he found them too difficult to direct after this first, albeit brief, encounter with using them in the family scenes in *Mo' Better Blues*. "This movie was tough," Lee told *Premiere*'s Martha Southgate about the making of *Crooklyn*. "We had kids and animals," he pointed out, to which Joie Lee added, "At least the animals were trained."

One impetus Lee had with the gentleness and lack of controversy in *Crooklyn* was to show cinemagoers another side of urban youth, not one rife with the violence and gore of most contemporary films set in rough American cities. "We were able to have childhoods," Lee told Sellers in *Entertainment Weekly*, and Sellers noted that indeed, "innocence is evident in almost every scene of *Crooklyn*; the Carmichael kids spend their summer watching TV, eating junk food, and making mostly benign mischief." Lee himself plays the only true bad guy in the movie, a diminutive glue-sniffer. Still, it is a film not without sadness, as the children come to grips with their mother's illness and death. "There is a moment at the end of Crooklyn when three of the children are walking up a public staircase," wrote Jones in *Film Comment*, when they stop singsonging a tune as they speculate about what they are going to wear to their mother's funeral. "The heartbreak—and the moment is heartbreaking like few moments in recent cinema—is in the high oblique angle that places the kids in a vast expanse of concrete," Jones ruminated, "a detail that feels as if it comes straight from the filmmaker's memory."

Lee did tackle the subjects of drugs, crime, and the city in his next film, *Clockers*. He adapted the screenplay from the Richard Price novel of the same name about young crack dealers. The 1995 film starred an unknown, Mekhi Phifer, as Strike, the Brooklyn crack dealer "torn between the demands of a veteran police detective (Harvey Keitel) and a local drug lord (Delroy Lindo)," wrote a contributor in *Premiere*, "and in Lee's hands it has become an epic African-American tragedy, as morally complex as it is moving and powerful." During filming in New York, Lee cast non-actors as the extras; when Anna Deavere Smith interviewed Lee for *Premiere*, she asked him about the two expectant mothers shown in one scene. Lee admitted they, too, had been pulled off the street, and "it crushed the whole crew to see these two black women pregnant—showing—who were on the pipe," Lee told Smith.

If you enjoy the works of Spike Lee, you may also want to check out the following films:

Boyz N the Hood, a film by John Singleton, 1991.
The Five Heartbeats, a film starring Robert Townsend, 1991.
Hoop Dreams, an acclaimed documentary, 1994.

Whether breaking or reiterating stereotypes, Lee remained adamant about his vision as a filmmaker. "White America, they just want black men to always be smiling," he said in the *Premiere* interview with Smith. "So, if you don't do that all the time, then they label you the Angry Black Man. As if we had nothing to be angry about, anyway! I mean, a lot of people's attitude is, 'Look, you're successful, you have money—what do you have to be angry about?' . . . I was one of the lucky ones," he pointed out.

Inspired to Strive Harder

Universal Studios offered to finance his next project, *Get on the Bus*, but Lee rejected the funding and instead put together a budget from a number of African American entertainment personalities, including Snipes, Will Smith, and Danny Glover. The 1996 film relives the fictional experiences of a group of men journeying to Washington, D.C., for the Million Man March in the fall of 1995. The characters include a black Muslim, a cop, a Republican, a juvenile delinquent son and his father—handcuffed to one another by court order—and a gay couple. Like *Crooklyn* and *Clockers*, it was met with relative indifference by critics and the public alike. "*Bus* disappeared from theaters with ruthless speed," remarked Jones in *Film Comment*, opining that Spike Lee is "slowly [losing] his audience in the increasingly foul atmosphere of corporate culture."

The same fate befell Lee's 1998 film, *He Got Game*. The first of his movies to take on the theme of African Americans and the cult of professional athletics in America, it tracks a hotshot young player and the college athletics world in its look at "the dilemma athletes face when confronted with the choice between college or the cash and flash of the NBA," noted a contributor to *Premiere*. The protagonist, Jesus Shuttleworth, was played by Milwaukee Bucks guard Ray Allen, and Lee's screenplay follows one week in the life of the number-one high school player in the nation as competing forces vie for his talent. Denzel Washington plays his father, a prison inmate who is paroled for a week by the state's governor on a mission to convince Shuttleworth to sign with the politician's alma mater.

Despite his disappointments, Lee continued to work on a variety of projects. He made a 1997 documentary about the bombing of a Birmingham, Alabama church during the civil rights era, *4 Little Girls*. He also explored a longtime passion in his 1997 book, *The Best Seat in the House*, a basketball memoir in which he chronicles his life through the prism of his fanaticism for the New York Knicks. Lee was a teenager when the team last won a league championship. It includes interviews with his heroes—Walt Frazier, Michael Jordan, and even fellow Knicks fan Woody Allen—but Lee also discusses the increasing popularity of pro basketball, once largely ignored by mainstream America as an African American sport. In her critique of *Best Seat in the House* for the *New York Times Book Review*, Lena Williams found that "too much of the book sounds like a play-by-play television commentary," but *Booklist* reviewer Bonnie Smothers termed it "the sweetest book about sports to be published in a long time." Smothers found Lee's endless trove of sports trivia charming—"like the true, dyed-in-the-wool, fan, he can not mention a player without giving pertinent stats," noted Smothers.

Lee, who once filmed a series of hilarious commercials for Nike that starred Michael Jordan as himself and Lee as Mars Blackmon, is the principle of his own agency, Spike DDB. In 1994 he married an attorney, Tonya Lee, with whom he has two children. They live in apartments in both Brooklyn and TriBeCa. "A true New Yorker, Spike Lee is learning to drive at 41," wrote Barbara Lippert in *New York* magazine. "My wife is teaching me," Lee told Lippert. The filmmaker remains close to his siblings, and retains a strong sense of family. He knows the Lee genealogy dating back to the slave era and a couple named Mike and Phoebe. "They were married in Virginia and she was sold off to another plantation owner in Alabama," Lee told Smith in the *Premiere* interview.

"And Mike worked for three or four years and bought his freedom and walked from Virginia to Alabama to reunited with his wife. . . . I'm not trying to say that it's a Kunta Kinte-Alex Haley thing, but this is not something that is special to the Lee family. If we all knew our history, there would be a story like that in every African-American family, and if you knew the hardships and the great heroic deeds that our ancestors did, you could be inspired to strive harder."

■ Works Cited

Ansen, David, review of *Malcolm X, Newsweek,* November 16, 1992, p. 74.

Crowdus, Gary, and Dan Georgakas, "Our Film Is Only a Starting Point: An Interview with Spike Lee," *Cineaste*, Volume 19, number 4, 1993, pp. 20-24.

Derry, Charles, "Spike Lee," in *International Directory of Films and Filmmakers*, Volume 2: *Directors*, edited by Nicholas Thomas, St. James Press, 1991.

Handelman, David, "Insight to Riot," *Rolling Stone*, July 13, 1989, pp. 104, 107, 109, 174.

Jones, Kent, "Invisible Man: Spike Lee," *Film Comment*, January/February, 1997, p. 42.

Lee, Spike, *Spike Lee's "Gotta Have It": Inside Guerrilla Filmmaking*, Simon & Schuster, 1987.

Lee, Spike, and Lisa Jones, *"Do the Right Thing": The New Spike Lee Joint*, Fireside Press, 1989.

Lippert, Barbara, "He's Gotta Have It (All)," *New York*, May 11, 1998, pp. 20-21

Mieher, Stuart, "Spike Lee's Gotta Have It," *New York Times Magazine*, August 9, 1987, pp. 26, 29, 39, 41.

Petersen, Clarence, *Chicago Tribune*, December 27, 1992, section 14, p. 2.

Richolson, Janice Mosier, "He's Gotta Have It: An Interview with Spike Lee," *Cineaste*, Volume 18, number 4, 1991, pp. 12-15.

Sellers, Patricia, "Do the Light Thing," *Entertainment Weekly*, May 20, 1994, p. 22.

Smith, Anna Deavere, "Spike: The Filmmaker Series" *Premiere*, October, 1995, pp. 104-8.

Smothers, Bonnie, review of *The Best Seat in the House, Booklist*, April 1, 1997, p. 1267.

Southgate, Martha, "FamiLee," *Premiere*, June, 1994, pp. 64-65.

"Spike Lee's Hoop Dreams," *Premiere*, January 1998, pp. 27-28.

Travers, Peter, "Insight to Riot," *Rolling Stone*, December 10, 1992, pp. 192-93.

Waters, Harry, "Spike's Mo Better Moviemaking," *Newsweek*, November 16, 1992, p. 71.

Williams, Lena, review of *The Best Seat in the House, New York Times Book Review,* June 8, 1997, p. 24.

■ For More Information See

BOOKS

Chapman, Kathleen Ferguson, *Spike Lee*, Creative Education, 1997.

Five for Five: The Films of Spike Lee, Stewart, Tabori, 1991.

Hardy, James Earl, *Spike Lee*, Chelsea House, 1996.

Haskins, Jim, *Spike Lee: By Any Means Necessary,* Walker and Co., 1997.

Jones, Maurice K., *Spike Lee and the African American Filmmakers; A Choice of Colors*, Millbrook Press, 1996.

Reid, Mark A., editor, *Spike Lee's Do the Right Thing,* Cambridge University Press, 1997.

PERIODICALS

Advocate, October 31, 1995, p. 49.

American Film, September, 1986; January-February, 1988; July-August, 1989.

Black Scholar, winter, 1993, p. 35.

Ebony, January, 1987; September, 1987; May, 1994, p. 28.

Entertainment Weekly, October 14, 1994, p. 70; November 17, 1995, p. 91; March 15, 1996, p. 74; April 5, 1996, p. 55; October 25, 1996, p. 92; May 22, 1998, p. 46.

Essence, September, 1986; February, 1988; July, 1988.

Film Comment, October, 1986.

Film Quarterly, winter, 1986-87.

London Review of Books, March 25, 1993, p. 24.

Los Angeles Times, August 21, 1986; February 11, 1988; February 12, 1988.

Ms., September-October, 1991, p. 78.

Nation, June 20, 1994, p. 882; April 29, 1996, p. 35.

New Republic, April 29, 1996, p. 26.

New Yorker, October 6, 1986, pp. 128-30; July 24, 1989, pp. 78-81; August 13, 1990, pp. 82-84; June 17, 1991, p. 99; November 30, 1992, pp. 160-62; May 23, 1994, p. 95.

New York Review of Books, September 28, 1989, p. 37.

New York Times, March 27, 1983; April 10, 1986; August 8, 1986; September 7, 1986; November 14, 1986; August 9, 1987; February 12, 1988; February 20, 1989; October 29, 1992, p. C22; November 15, 1992, p. H1, H23; November 18, 1992, pp. C19, C23; November 19, 1992, p. B4; April 7, 1996, p. H13.

New York Times Book Review, December 13, 1987, p. 14; November 29, 1992, p. 3.

People, May 23, 1994, p. 128.

Publishers Weekly, November 16, 1992, pp. 56-57; April 28, 1997, p. 61.

Rolling Stone, December 1980; April 21, 1988, p. 32; June 30, 1988, p. 21; December 1, 1988, p. 31; June 29, 1989, p. 27; June 27, 1991, p. 75; July 11, 1991, p. 63; June 2, 1994, p. 75; April, 18, 1996, p. 77.

Time, October 6, 1986, p. 94; July 3, 1989, p. 62; July 17, 1989, p. 92; August 20, 1990, p. 62; June 17, 1991, pp. 64-66, 68; March 16, 1992, p. 71; November 23, 1992, pp. 64-65; November 30, 1992; December 19, 1994, p. 29; September 18, 1995; February 26, 1996, p. 71.

Village Voice, February 16, 1988; March 22, 1988.

Wall Street Journal, November 16, 1992; April 2, 1996, p. A12.

Washington Post, August 22, 1986; August 24, 1986; August 29, 1986; March 20, 1987; February 19, 1988.*

—Sketch by Carol Brennan

Morgan Llywelyn

■ Personal

Born December 3, 1937, in New York, NY; surname legally changed to Llywelyn, August, 1981; daughter of Joseph John (an attorney) and Henri Llywelyn (a secretary; maiden name, Price) Snyder (changed from the original Shannon); married Charles Winter (a professional pilot), January 1, 1957 (died March 25, 1985); children: John Joseph. *Education:* Attended high school in Dallas, TX.

■ Addresses

Agent—Richard Curtis Associates, 171 East 74th St., New York, NY, 10021; Abner Stein, 10 Roland Gardens, London SW7 3PH, England. *E-mail*—Boru@celt.net.

■ Career

Fashion model and dance instructor in Dallas, TX, 1954-56; secretary in Denver, CO, 1956-59; riding instructor in Denver, 1959-61; amateur equestrian, training and showing her own horses, 1961-76; writer, 1974—. *Member:* National League of American Penwomen, Authors League of America, Authors Guild, Fantasy and Science Fiction Writers Association, Gaelic Arts League, St. Brendan Society, Irish Society of Pittsburgh, National Geographic Society.

■ Awards, Honors

Women's U.S. equestrian high jump record, 1953; Cultural Heritage Award, and Award of Merit, Texas Booksellers Association, both for *Lion of Ireland: The Legend of Brian Boru;* Best Novel, National League of American Penwomen, 1983, Best Book for Young Adults citation, American Library Association, and Historical Novel of the Year, RT Times Awards, all for *The Horse Goddess;* Poetry in Prose award, Galician Society, University of Santiago de Compostela, and Award of Merit, Celtic League, both for *Bard: The Odyssey of the Irish;* Bisto Award for Excellence in Children's Literature, for *Brian Boru;* Bisto Award for Excellence in Children's Literature, and winner of Reading Association of Ireland Biennial Award for Best Book for Children, both for *Strongbow;* Nebula Award nomination, for short story "Fletcher Found"; Stafford Prize, for short story "The Man Who Killed the Last Great Auk."

■ Writings

The Wind from Hastings, Houghton, 1978.
Lion of Ireland: The Legend of Brian Boru, Houghton, 1979.
The Horse Goddess, Houghton, 1982.

(Under the pseudonym Shannon Lewis) *Personal Habits*, Doubleday, 1982.

Bard: The Odyssey of the Irish, Houghton, 1984.

Grania: She-King of the Irish Seas, Houghton, 1986.

Xerxes, Chelsea House, 1988.

Isles of the Blest, Ace Books, 1989.

Red Branch, Morrow, 1989, published as *On Raven's Wing*, Heinemann (United Kingdom), 1990.

Brian Boru, Tor, 1990, O'Brien Press (Ireland), 1990.

Druids, Morrow, 1991, Heinemann, 1991.

The Last Prince of Ireland, Morrow, 1992, published as *O'Sullivan's March*, Heinemann, 1992.

Strongbow, Tor, 1992, O'Brien Press, 1992.

The Elementals, Tor, 1993.

Star Dancer, O'Brien Press, 1993.

Finn MacCool, Tor, 1994, Heinemann, 1994.

(With Michael Scott) *Silverhand: Volume I of The Arcana*, Baen, 1995.

(With Michael Scott) *Ireland: A Graphic History*, Element (United Kingdom), 1995.

Cold Places, Poolberg Press (Ireland), 1995.

Pride of Lions, Tor, 1996, Poolberg Press, 1997.

(With Michael Scott) *Silverlight: Volume II of The Arcana*, Baen, 1996.

(With Michael Scott) *19 Railway Street*, Poolberg Press, 1996.

Vikings in Ireland, O'Brien Press, 1996.

1916: A Novel of the Irish Rebellion, Forge, 1998.

The Essential Library for Irish Americans, Forge/St. Martin's Press, 1999.

Author of novella *Galway Bay*, included in *Irish Magic*, Kensington Press, 1995. Also author of numerous nonfiction articles for various publications, and of short stories, which have been published in anthologies.

Llywelyn has a manuscript collection at the University of Maryland, College Park.

■ Work in Progress

Whom the Gods Love, a historical fantasy co-authored with Michael Scott; *1921*, a sequel to *1916: A Novel of the Irish Rebellion*, tentatively scheduled for publication in 2001.

■ Sidelights

With more than forty million of her books in print, New York-born author Morgan Llywelyn is one of the world's leading popular chroniclers of Celtic culture and history. A prolific storyteller, she has written more than twenty books over the past two decades. In the words of Judith A. Gifford of the reference publication *Twentieth-Century Romance and Historical Writers,* "Drawing on the history and lore that are part of her own heritage, the works of Morgan Llywelyn concern themselves with Celtic heroes and heroines, both real and mythical, bringing them and the times they inhabited to life with stunning clarity." Pauline Morgan, writing in the *St. James Guide to Fantasy Writers*, has explained, "[t]he majority of Morgan Llywelyn's books may be regarded as fictional biographies. Each book takes a person, often historical or legendary, and relates the story of their life. Most of the novels with a fantasy connection rely heavily on Celtic mythology, particularly that of the Irish. Each book is complete in itself."

Morgan Llywelyn was born December 3, 1937, in New York City. While neither of her parents was a writer, words and storytelling were certainly in their blood. Llywelyn recalled in a 1999 interview with *Artists and Authors for Young Adults* (*AAYA*) that "a lot of related influences were brought to bear" on her during her childhood. Her father Joe Snyder, an attorney by profession, was by inclination "an Irish *seanchai,* (storyteller) in the classic sense"; her mother Henri was a university professor, whose own father was a newspaper publisher and printing company owner. Young Morgan grew up in a house that was filled with books, and being extremely bright (she is a lapsed member of Mensa) and precocious, she read "voraciously and omnivorously." As she told *AAYA*, "I began with adult books because my family had an immense library—the only so-called 'children's books' I remember reading were *Wind in the Willows, Winnie the Pooh,* and *Black Beauty.* I always loved animal stories. My early favorite authors were Enid Bagnold, Ray Bradbury, Joseph Conrad, and John Steinbeck. Come to think of it, I would still classify them among my favorites."

Blessed with striking good looks and exceptional athletic ability, Llywelyn was employed as a fashion model and a dance instructor from 1954 to 1956 in Dallas, Texas, where she had attended high school. In late 1956, Llywelyn moved to Denver, Colorado, where she worked as a secretary and riding instructor. There she married and got seriously involved in equestrian training and the showing of horses. To this point in her life, Llywelyn recalls she had never even thought of becoming a writer, although in a way she already was one. "I was the sort of person who always wrote thirty-five page letters to her friends," she recalled in an interview with Jean W. Ross of *Contemporary Authors* (*CA*).

It was her involvement with horses that spurred Llywelyn to take the next step toward becoming a writer. To help pay the costs of trying to make the U.S. Olympic equestrian team, she began writing articles about horse training, selling them to such publications as *Classic, Western Horseman,* and *Horse Lover.* Llywelyn failed to earn a spot on the Olympic team, but two good things came of her journalistic efforts. For one, as Llywelyn told Jean Ross of *CA,* she found that she "enjoyed the sculpting of the words, putting them together, the assimilation of facts and then transmitting those facts." For another, Llywelyn began working on her first novel in an attempt to ease the frustrations that she was feeling and to "distract . . . [and] entertain myself."

Tracing Family History

Llywelyn began delving into her own family's history, and it was while doing so that she came across a story that intrigued her. When she related the details to her husband, her enthusiasm proved infectious. "Before I knew what I had done, he had insisted I write it down," Llywelyn told Jean Ross. "I had about two hundred pages written, and good heavens, it was almost a book." Llywelyn also found that the genealogical research she had done piqued her curiosity. "I became interested in the family of man, in everybody's family and where we all came from. So I moved out of that earlier, narrow focus into all of Western Europe," she added.

Although she knew nothing about how to write a novel, Llywelyn forged ahead. "I operated from a position of ignorance, in that I did not know it couldn't be done—which I think is always an advantage," she recalled in the *CA* interview with Jean Ross. From the beginning, Llywelyn (she adopted her mother's middle name) relied heavily on the meticulous historical research that has become her trademark. She thinks and reads extensively about whatever period she is writing about. The early fruit of Llywelyn's labors was her first novel, which appeared in 1978. *The Wind from Hastings* is a historical romance set in England around the time of the Battle of Hastings, the 1066 encounter in which the invading Normans conquered England by defeating the Saxons. The book is a fictionalized account of the story of Aldith of Mercia, the real-life wife of the vanquished King Harold. "[Aldith] was an interesting person," Llywelyn told Ross. "Her life was very vivid. The thing that made her difficult to write about in some ways was that she was not a catalyst in any sense of the word. She was just an observer. But what she observed was historic and important." Reviews for *The Wind from Hastings* were mixed. Ellen Kaye Stoppel of *Library Journal* wrote that Llywelyn "describes [this period of British

Set in tenth-century Ireland, this work tells the tale of Brian Boru, one of Ireland's greatest heroes.

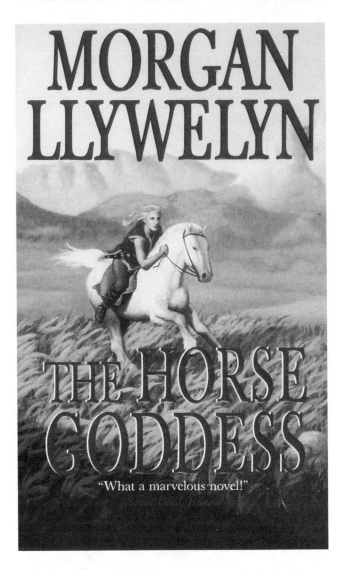

Epona and her Scythian warrior and lover Prince Kazhak traverse eighth-century Europe to escape the druid priest Kernunnos in this 1982 historical novel.

history] as seen by a woman participating in it, an unusual and interesting approach." However, a reviewer from *Publishers Weekly* commented, "The author's considerable style and rich sense of English history" does not offset "the absence of a strong plot."

Llywelyn had little time to ponder her first reviews; she was too busy to do so, already being hard at work on her next novel. That book, *Lion of Ireland: The Legend of Brian Boru,* is a fictional portrait of one of Ireland's greatest heroes, a legendary tenth-century king and warrior who laid the foundations for Irish nationhood by defeating the invading Vikings. The book received almost universal praise. *Library Journal*'s reviewer W. Keith McCoy lauded Llywelyn for her "vivid portrait" of Brian Boru and for "battle scenes and court life as colorful as the central character." A reviewer from *Booklist* agreed, praising *Lion of Ireland* as a "spellbinding tale . . . with style and passion."

Relating Celtic History

Llywelyn continued to win legions of fans (among them the then-president Ronald Reagan) as she mined the rich mother lode of Celtic folklore history with her next three novels: *The Horse Goddess, Bard: The Odyssey of the Irish,* and *Grania: She-King of the Irish Seas. The Horse Goddess* is another ambitious effort set not in medieval England or Ireland, but rather in central Europe, prior to the Celts' emigration from the British Isles. The central character in the work is a young woman named Epona, who falls in love with Kazhak, a Scythian warrior from the Russian steppes, and runs off with him in order to escape a lecherous and evil Druid priest. Llywelyn tells the story of Epona's adventures and of how she eventually returns to her people to become a high priestess among them. Calling *The Horse Goddess* "Epic in character and vivid in its descriptions," Nancy Chapin of *School Library Journal* declared that "the novel does for Celtic mythology something of what Mary Renault's [1958 novel] *The King Must Die* did for that of the Greeks."

Bard: The Odyssey of the Irish is similarly steeped in history. The story deals with Amergin, a real-life fourth-century Celtic bard who is said to have inspired his warrior clan, the Gaels, to cross the sea from the Iberian Peninsula to conquer Irene—the present-day Ireland. "I studied the ancient Celtic poets, trying to pick up the alliterations, to get the appropriate style for that book," Llywelyn told Jean Ross. Her efforts met with mixed success. A reviewer for *Publishers Weekly* decried Llywelyn's efforts, writing that "this novel delivers neither the punch nor the bawdy humor of the old sagas it tries to create." A *Booklist* critic disagreed, stating that this "full-bodied historical novel" is "rich in color and a sense of druidic mystery," with "characters [who] . . . come to life as individuals."

Llywelyn's next book, *Grania: She-King of the Irish Seas* is about a legendary sixteenth-century Irish

If you enjoy the works of Morgan Llywelyn, you may also want to check out the following books and films:

Marion Zimmer Bradley, *The Forest House*, 1994.
Cecelia Holland, *The Kings in Winter*, 1967.
Mary Stolz, *Pangur Ban*, 1988.
The Secret of Roan Inish, a film directed by John Sayles, 1994.

chieftain. Llywelyn "has pillaged Irish history and Celtic mythology," to create "an epic-length historical romance" with a tale that is engaging "despite a prose style that can make reading as treacherous as walking on a stony shore," reviewer Sherie Posesorski wrote in the *New York Times Book Review*. W. Keith McCoy of *Library Journal* observed, "The reader gets more action but less understanding of this unique historical character."

Llywelyn has continued to win fans and enjoy enormous popular success in recent years, with more novels rooted in Celtic history, and with works of historical nonfiction such as *Xerxes*, a commissioned biography of the ancient Persian king, and *Vikings in Ireland*, which is—as the title suggests—a history of the Viking experience in Ireland. Included in Llywelyn's literary output have been novels that present unadulterated historical facts, as well as others that venture into the realm of mythology, melding fantasy with reality. "Novels such as *Grania* and *The Last Prince of Ireland* are straight and very gritty history," Llywelyn explains in an interview that appears on her Web page. Other novels such as *Druids*, which examines the druidic culture of ancient Gaul, and *Strongbow*, a fictionalized biography of two twelfth-century historical figures, feature the strong spiritual—or "fantasy"—element that lies at the root of much of Llywelyn's fiction. "Since the Otherworld was very real to the Celts, actually an alternate reality, it is impossible to attempt an accurate recreation of the Celtic past without including their view of that Otherworld," she adds. "Magical realism and elevated reality, those current literary catch-phrases, had serious meaning for the Celts. The same holds true for the Celtic Irish." Llywelyn novels that reflect this theme include *Red Branch* and *Finn MacCool*. "[They] are

retellings of two of the great mythic hero-tales of Ireland. In each case, I have attempted to depict the protagonists as real men living in a real time," she writes.

Research, Research, and More Research

While much of what Llywelyn writes is what she terms "speculative history," her books have found favor and been widely praised by academics and other experts, who admire the realism and attention to detail that she pours into them. Llywelyn reads Gaelic and some Welsh, has accumulated an

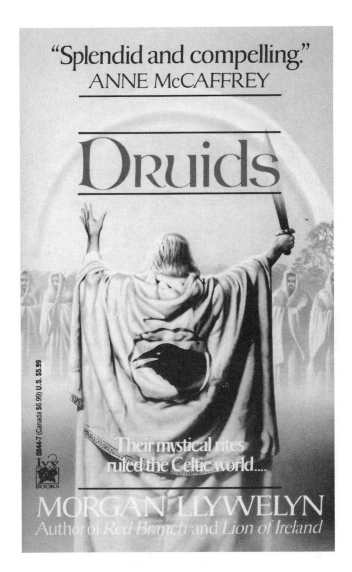

In this 1991 novel, a young orphan named Ainvar is taken in by the chief druid of the Carnutes and learns the secrets of the druids' magical powers.

extensive library on Celtic history, and whenever possible she spends time in the areas she is writing about; according to her Web page, she is "the only woman to have walked the breadth and length of Ireland"—all 427 miles of it. "I try to nail everything down concretely first that can be nailed down. I deal with anthropologists and archaeologists, with all the tangible artifacts that we know, and the current level . . . of scientific knowledge about an era," Llywelyn told Jean Ross.

Llywelyn has tried her hand at writing pure fantasy with *The Elementals*, a series of four linked

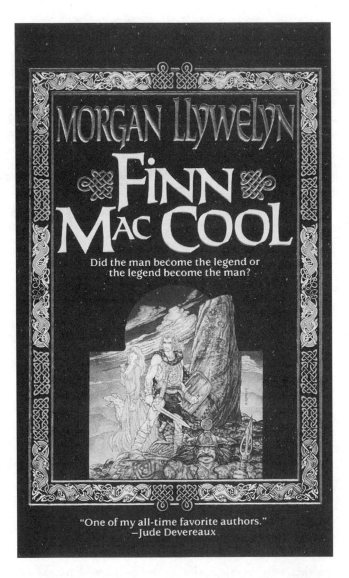

Llywelyn delves into the life of a legendary Irish hero in her 1994 fictional biography.

novellas, each of which focuses on a story about one of the classical elements—earth, air, water, and fire. Llywelyn told *AAYA* that the book "explores man's troubled relationship with the planet, beginning with the ancient Irish post-Deluge story, going from there to Thera and the explosion which may have been the destruction of Atlantic, thence to modern America, a story set in the State of New Hampshire, and finally to a conclusion somewhere in the American southwest, a century or so in the future."

Llywelyn has also collaborated with Michael Scott, an author whom the *Irish Times* newspaper has hailed as "the king of fantasy in these Isles." One project the pair have teamed up to write is a two-book series called *The Arcana*. The first volume in the series, *Silverhand: The Arcana, Book I*, appeared in 1995. This epic, action-filled saga is about a teenage superhero named Caeled who battles a pair of evil magician twins. Caeled loses an arm in an attack by a savage creature known as a weredog, but friendly monks use long-dormant technologies to build him a powerful prosthetic silver replacement limb. Thus "re-armed," Caeled sets out in search of the magical implements of the Arcana. "This rich tale shows how good fantasy can be when its authors" do not deny their reader's "intelligence nor obscure their ideas with overwrought language and overblown symbologies," a *Publishers Weekly* reviewer wrote. A second volume in the *Silverhand* series appeared in 1996. In addition, Llywelyn and Scott have coauthored *19 Railway Street*, a 1996 ghost novel for young adults, an adult novel entitled *Ireland: A Graphic History*, and an historical fantasy about Etruscan culture, *Whom the Gods Love*.

In a completely different vein, Llywelyn has written *1916: A Novel of the Irish Rebellion*. A *Publishers Weekly* reviewer described it as having an "easy, gripping style [that] will enthrall casual readers with what is Llywelyn's best work yet." A. J. Anderson of *Library Journal* also had high praise for the novel, writing that Llywelyn "has succeeded in capturing and vivifying one of the most critical moments in Ireland's troubled history."

Llywelyn was particularly pleased to receive such positive reviews, for she says she regards *1916* as the first step in a fresh direction for her career. She notes that it is the first book she has done in which the subject matter is not rooted in ancient history or mythology, but rather on contemporary events with powerful political undertones. "[It] is the book I have been 'working up to' writing for many years," Llywelyn told *AAYA*. "It is a departure in several ways. Firstly, it is set in this century. Secondly, it explores an Ireland which no longer has any recognizable elements of the ancient Druid culture, but is desperately struggling to carve a new identify for itself. Thirdly, my own grandfather, Henry Mooney Price, is one of the major characters. It is straight history in the purest sense, with no event altered in any degree to produce a more dramatic structure. The story itself is so dramatic it didn't need any help from me! All my previous historical novels about Ireland have been laying a background for *1916* and the . . . books which will follow it."

■ Works Cited

Anderson, A. J., review of *1916: A Novel of the Irish Rebellion, Library Journal*, February 15, 1998, pp. 170-71.

Review of *Bard: The Odyssey of the Irish, Booklist*, September 1, 1984, p. 3.

Review of *Bard: The Odyssey of the Irish, Publishers Weekly*, August 17, 1984, p. 45.

Chapin, Nancy, review of *The Horse Goddess, School Library Journal*, December, 1982, p. 87.

Gifford, Judith A., "Morgan Llywelyn," *Twentieth-Century Romance and Historical Writers*, St. James Press, 1990, pp. 400-1.

Review of *Lion of Ireland, Booklist*, February 1, 1980, p. 757.

Llywelyn, Morgan, interview with Ken Cuthbertson for *Artists and Authors for Young Adults*, January 7, 1999.

Llywelyn, Morgan, author's Web site located at http://celt.net/Boru.

McCoy, W. Keith, review of *Lion of Ireland: The Legend of Brian Boru, Library Journal*, January 15, 1980, p. 225.

McCoy, W. Keith, review of *Grania: She-King of the Irish Seas, Library School Journal*, March 1, 1986, p. 110.

Morgan, Pauline, "Morgan Llywelyn," *St. James Guide to Fantasy Writers*, St. James Press, 1996, pp. 370-71.

Review of *1916: A Novel of the Irish Rebellion, Publishers Weekly*, February 16, 1998, p. 204.

Posesorski, Sherie, review of *Grania: She-King of the Irish Seas, New York Times Book Review*, March 2, 1986, p. 24.

Ross, Jean, interview with Morgan Llywelyn, *Contemporary Authors, New Revision Series*, Volume 16, Gale, 1986, pp. 226-30.

Review of *Silverhand: The Arcana, Book I, Publishers Weekly*, March 13, 1995, p. 64.

Stoppel, Ellen Kaye, review of *The Wind from Hastings, Library Journal*, June 1, 1978, pp. 1196-97.

Review of *The Wind from Hastings, Publishers Weekly*, April 3, 1978, p. 69.

■ For More Information See

PERIODICALS

Analog, December 15, 1993, p. 162.

Booklist, December 1, 1990, p. 692; August, 1992, pp. 1995-96; May 15, 1993, pp. 1678, 1682; February 1, 1994, p. 979; February 15, 1995, pp. 1059, 1067; March 15, 1995, p. 1315; March 1, 1996, p. 1227.

Kirkus Reviews, June 1, 1995, p. 782; January 1, 1996, p. 16; April 1, 1996, p. 533; February 15, 1998, p. 216.

Library Journal, September 15, 1982, p. 1770.

Locus, March, 1990, p. 64; January, 1991, p. 25; July, 1993, p. 44; April, 1994, p. 31.

New York Times Book Review, July 16, 1989, p. 24.

Publishers Weekly, December 10, 1979, pp. 58-59; March 9, 1992, p. 48; February 28, 1994, p. 74; February 6, 1996, p. 77.

School Library Journal, July, 1991, p. 97; December, 1994, p. 144.

Washington Post Book World, October 7, 1984, p. 10; June 21, 1992, p. 12.

Voice of Youth Advocates, December, 1993, p. 311; August, 1996, p. 157.

—Sketch by Ken Cuthbertson

Jess Mowry

■ Personal

Born March 27, 1960, in Starkville, MS; son of Jessup Willys Mowry (a scrap iron collector); partner of Markita Brown (a social worker); children: Jeremy, Weylen, Shara, Keeja. *Education:* Attended elementary school in Oakland, CA. *Politics:* "Survival."

■ Addresses

Home—Oakland, CA.

■ Career

Works with inner city street children at drop-in center; cartoonist; writer, 1988—. Has also worked as a mechanic, truck driver, tugboat engineer, and scrap metal collector.

■ Awards, Honors

PEN-Oakland Josephine Miles Award, 1990, for *Rats in the Trees*; American Library Association Best Book for Young Adults Award, 1993, for *Way Past Cool*; Pushcart Anthology Prize, 1993.

■ Writings

Rats in the Trees (stories), John Daniel & Co., 1990.
Children of the Night, Holloway House, 1991.
Way Past Cool, Farrar, Straus and Giroux, 1992.
Six Out Seven, Anchor, 1993.
Ghost Train, Henry Holt, 1996.
Babylon Boyz, illustrated by Eric Dinger, Simon & Schuster, 1997.
(With Yule Caise) *Way Past Cool* (screenplay based on novel of same name), Redeemable Features, 1998.
Bones Become Flowers, Pride and Imprints, 1999.

Also author of stage play, *Skeleton Key.* Contributor to various anthologies and to periodicals, including *Writer's Digest, Alchemy, Obsidian, Sequoia, Santa Clara Review, Nation, Los Angeles Times, Might Magazine, Buzz Magazine,* and *San Francisco Examiner.*

■ Work in Progress

Burma Jeep, a novel "about kids exploited via the Internet for 'kiddie porn'"; *The Black Gang,* a novel about caring for the world's children versus caring for animals; a novel based on Mowry's stage play entitled *Skeleton Key;* a screenplay based on the novel *Six Out Seven.*

■ Sidelights

Most people who have lived the kind of life that Jess Mowry did in his youth are in jail, dead, or

ISBN 0-87067-575-3 $3.95

CHILDREN *of the* **NIGHT**

BY JESS MOWRY

THEY WERE GOOD KIDS, DIRT POOR AND THE ONLY WAY OUT WAS TO DEAL DRUGS TO KIDS EVEN YOUNGER. OR WAS IT?

In this 1991 novel, thirteen-year-old Ryo must reconsider his decision to sell crack to younger kids in his neighborhood after his friend Chipmunk is killed during a drug run.

are fated to a life of hardship and poverty. Yet Mowry, at age thirty-eight, has defied the odds to become both an accomplished author and a role model for the young black street kids whom he works with and writes about. Mowry is such a powerful, visceral writer that the editor of one of his books has likened him to Charles Dickens. The comparison is not far-fetched, for Mowry's talent and his gift for articulating the searing rage and frustrations of the black youth is nothing short of remarkable. According to Cathi Dunn MacRae of the *Wilson Library Bulletin,* the writer's "own life is so solidly enmeshed in his work that perhaps

we need a new word for it. Such social commentary is actually 'docufiction.'" In a *Nation* review of *Way Past Cool,* Mowry's 1992 novel about rival Oakland street gangs, Ishmael Reed echoed that idea, hailing Mowry as "the Homer of inner-city youth."

With seven books, two movie screenplays, a stage play, and numerous short stories to his credit, Jess Mowry has emerged during the 1990s as one of America's most original and important—yet relatively unheralded—black writers. His low profile is as much a matter of personal preference as of any lack of merit or of public interest in his writing. Mowry has declined to take "the easy way," refusing to be seduced by fame or money, or to play the role of "angry black man," which America's mainstream media seem intent on ascribing to him. Instead, Mowry remains socially committed and aware; he prefers doing things his way as he works to improve the lives and self-image of black street kids. To that end, Mowry continues to live in his old neighborhood, and to work at a youth drop-in center. He also tries to advise young writers of color and to encourage them to follow his lead in breaking down the stereotypes that he feels have become so harmful to young blacks in America's inner cities. Mowry is as frank about his own role in that process as he is realistic. "The 'powers that be'—in this case meaning the 'mainstream' publishing industry (also film, music, and American society in general) WANT to see these stereotypes," Mowry told *Authors and Artists for Young Adults* (*AAYA*) in a recent interview. "Stereotypes are very reassuring to them (yes, these kids are not really 'human,' so we don't have to feel bad about how we're treating them), but I'm only one man. I can't 'save' the world, or all the kids in it; I can only do the best I can with what I've got."

Everything that Jess Mowry has, he's worked hard for. His early life was a hardscrabble existence, filled with the kind of pain and struggle that breaks—or hopelessly embitters—most people. Mowry was born on March 27, 1960, near the town of Starkville, Mississippi, the product of an interracial relationship; his father was black, his mother white. "One has only to read about the social mores (or lack of same) in Mississippi in that era to know that this was 'not a good thing,'" Mowry told *AAYA.* "My mother 'disappeared,' and has not been heard of to this day, though I haven't been interested enough . . . to try to find her. Nor do I care to." Mowry's father, Jessup, moved west with his infant son to Oakland, California, about three months later. It was there that young Jess was raised, learning the ways of the street early on. Yet Mowry recalls a childhood filled "with much love and fun," although he does point out that his upbringing was anything but conventional "by today's white middle-class American standards."

It was from his father that Mowry inherited his passion for words. Jessup Mowry was "a voracious, eclectic reader," as Mowry explained in his *AAYA* interview. "When one grows up surrounded by books of all sorts—even if they be mostly junk-shop paperbacks—then reading is a very natural thing." Like his dad, Mowry read anything that was at hand. While the environment made it dif-

NATIONAL BESTSELLER
WAY PAST COOL
A NOVEL
JESS MOWRY

"A STELLAR LITERARY DEBUT THAT SHOULD BE READ BY ALL OF MAINSTREAM AMERICA."—TERRY McMILLAN, author of WAITING TO EXHALE

Mowry addresses black gang life in this suspenseful 1992 novel set in Oakland.

ficult for him to succeed in school, Mowry was precocious, and this sometimes put him in conflict with "the system." He angered his fourth-grade teacher, for instance, by reading ahead in assigned books. Mowry read the Herman Melville classic *Moby Dick* when his teacher had criticized him by saying that someone his age could never understand such a serious novel. Mowry didn't stop with Melville; he went on to read books by John Steinbeck (whose 1947 novel *The Wayward Bus* remains Mowry's favorite book), by black novelist Ralph Ellison, and horror and fantasy writers such as H. P. Lovecraft and J. R. R. Tolkien, among others.

Escapes Life on the Street

Despite his love of reading, the siren call of the streets proved irresistible. Mowry dropped out of school in grade eight to become a drug dealer's bodyguard. He survived for nine years in this tough, kill-or-be-killed world. However, by the still-young age of seventeen, he had seen enough violence and death; Mowry decided to go straight. He worked by times as a mechanic, a truck driver, a tugboat engineer (in Alaska), and a scrap metal collector. In 1976, Mowry and his partner, Markita Brown, gave birth to the first of their four children. The family set up housekeeping in an abandoned Greyhound bus, and soon the vehicle also began to serve as an ersatz drop-in center for neighborhood youths. It was Mowry's involvement with street kids that eventually moved him to become a writer.

"I began writing stories for and about the kids at a West Oakland youth center in 1988," he told *AAYA*. "I sent one of those stories to *Zyzzvya* (a San Francisco literary magazine). They published it. The rest, as they say, is history." Using money he'd earned by collecting aluminum cans, Mowry bought an old 1923 model Underwood typewriter for eight dollars. To help dispel negative media stereotypes and to offer positive messages these same kids could relate to, he began writing down some of the stories he had been creating about street kids. The product of Mowry's efforts was *Rats in the Trees*, a 1990 collection of nine related stories about a thirteen-year-old Oakland street kid named Robby. "*Rats* reflects the inner-city conditions for kids during the late 1980s, which was when crack-cocaine was starting to flood into U.S. 'ghettoes,'" Mowry explains in an essay about his writing, which appears on his Web page. The book, which is written in the gritty lingo of the streets, was published in paperback by a small Santa Barbara publisher, and distribution was limited. However, what little critical reaction there was to Mowry's literary debut in the United States was highly positive, and the book was also published overseas in the United Kingdom, Germany, and Japan. A *Publishers Weekly* reviewer wrote that *Rats in the Trees* "at once saddens, overwhelms and charms as it explores a realm unto itself—urban gangs." Cathi Dunn MacRae of the *Wilson Library Journal* observed, "Rarely has street life been so encapsulated in its own language."

It is with no sense of satisfaction that Mowry points out on his Web page how the grim predictions he made in 1990 in *Rats in the Trees* have come to pass. "Sadly, all [of them] have come true . . .," he writes, "the ever-increasing and senseless Black-on-Black crime, the 'guns, gangs, drugs, and violence' in U.S. inner cities, the kids killing kids, and the decline in the quality of public education. . . . It was also predicted in *Rats* that 'guns, gangs, drugs and violence' would move into 'white suburbia,' too—as Chuck (an older white teenager in *Rats*) said: 'Coming soon to a neighborhood near YOU!'—and they have."

Despite favorable reviews and positive word-of-mouth for *Rats in the Trees,* mainstream publishers failed to take note of Jess Mowry or of his writing. As a result, when his second book, a novel called *Children of the Night,* was published in 1991 by Holloway House, another small West Coast publisher, again it was as an inexpensive paperback. The book is the story of Ryo, a thirteen-year-old West Oakland youth and his "homey" Chipmunk, who go to work for a neighborhood crack dealer named Big Bird. When Chipmunk is killed in a drug run, Ryo reevaluates the life that he has chosen and then sets out to save himself and destroy Big Bird.

Children of the Night was gritty, vivid, and uncompromising in its condemnation of the parasitic drug lords and the systemic racism which confines young black street kids to lives of poverty, crime, and hardship. As Mowry, speaking through Brownie, one of the characters in the book points out, a big problem is "[white] people not believin' what's goin' on in places like this . . . as long as they can keep it in places like this." Despite Mowry's hopes, *Children of the Night* attracted little

Corbitt Wainwright, a thirteen-year-old from Mississippi, moves to Oakland to escape his past but finds more trouble after joining a local street gang.

media attention. However, the few reviews there were again hailing Mowry as an important new black literary voice; for example, Cathi Dunn MacRae praised his novel as a "vibrant, mesmerizing evocation . . . of an underworld that the classes above ignore." "Mowry," she added "captures that world with descriptions of ugly places and desperate people so lyrical that they force us to really see what we would rather not."

Major Publishers Take Note

With two critically acclaimed books to his credit, in 1992 Mowry suddenly won the kind of literary success that he had never dared to dream about. The street-kid-turned-author's next book, another novel about black youth gangs—"Little Rascals with Uzis," he termed them—was published by Farrar, Straus and Giroux, a major New York-based national publisher. Farrar, Straus and Giroux made *Way Past Cool* its lead fiction title in its spring catalog. According to Bronwen Hruska writing in the *Voice Literary Supplement,* Mowry received a $30,000 advance. What's more, according to Hruska, the "Disney studios optioned the film rights to the book for another $75,000." That money, more than Mowry had ever earned before in his life, enabled him to move his family into an apartment. He spent what was left on worthwhile projects in his own neighborhood. Hruska explained, Mowry "didn't write *Cool* for profits. . . . He wrote it for the kids it's about— even though they won't be the ones laying down the $17 for the hardback edition." If conclusive proof of that was needed, it came when, as Daniel Max of the entertainment industry trade publication *Variety* reported, Mowry turned down a request to write a screenplay based on the book. He eventually did so for a company called Redeemable Features, the third company to option the rights. "The screenplay they had was such a mess I just basically said, 'Oh here, let me do the damn thing!'" Mowry told *AAYA.*

"It seems as if many writers will have one book in their careers for which they will be remembered more than for any others they write," Mowry notes on his Web page. "It seems that for me the book I will probably be most 'remembered' (if at all) for is *Way Past Cool.*" This "has been both a blessing and a curse," he adds. "A 'blessing' in that I was able to tell the truth and to show the world a view of how the U.S. treats [black street kids] . . . but a 'curse' in that I seem to be expected (by the 'mainstream' publishers) to write this kind of 'ghetto fiction' for evermore; and it has become clear to me . . . that 'they' are not about to publish anything of mine outside of or beyond this type of work—and DEFINITELY not 'just stories.'"

Unlike Mowry's first two books, *Way Past Cool* grabbed the media's attention. Novelist Robert Ward, writing in the *Los Angeles Times Book Review,* praised the work as "a gut-wrenching, heartbreaking suspense novel about black gang life in Oakland." However, reviewers for many mainstream publications were not quite as enthusiastic in their assessments. Nelson George of the *New York Times* described *Way Past Cool* as "maddeningly uneven, occasionally poetic." Reviewer Nick Kimberley, writing in *New Statesman & Society,* mused that "There's tough urgency in its street ellipses, and a pulpy cheerfulness in its sudden switches of mood and scene. . . . But its very mobility eventually drains *Way Past Cool* of its purpose." And a critic in *Kirkus Reviews* faulted the book's "very slow moving story" that was written in "overheated prose." Although Mowry concedes that he is disappointed by negative reviews, he says that he is not surprised by them. "Many are racist," he told *AAYA.* "Often, it seems, without their (white) writers being aware of it; they really want to see the stereotypes, and it angers and/or confuses them when they don't."

Undeterred, Mowry continued to write about issues that he felt were of vital concern to the black community. His next novel, *Six Out Seven* (which was actually written before *Way Past Cool,* but published after), is "basically a 'country-mouse, city-mouse,' kind of tale," according to Mowry's Web page. The story deals with Corbitt Wainwright, a thirteen-year-old black youth from rural Mississippi, who moves to Oakland to escape some trouble back home. In the novel's early chapters, Mowry juxtaposes details of Corbitt's life in the two locales. He then goes on to describe Corbitt's enforced coming of age after he joins a street gang called The Collectors; the boy becomes a foot soldier in the deadly turf war that's being fought on the streets of Oakland and other American cities—a war where to "kick" someone is to kill him, and "dirt nap" is a euphemism for death. Mowry explained on his Web site, "Unlike *Way Past Cool,* which presented a view of Black kids trapped in the inner city—knowing there was probably a way out but too caught up in day-to-day survival to try to find it—*Six Out Seven* dug deeper in to the reasons WHY these kids have to live as they do—the 'self-cleaning oven,' the fact that 'gang-violence,' and kids killing kids is actually encouraged by certain segments of white U.S. society, and that drugs are seldom if ever brought into the U.S. and poured into the 'ghettoes' by Black people."

Taking a Stand on the Issues

Such opinions are controversial, and have stirred discussion, pro and con. In the words of Bob Sipchen of the *Los Angeles Times Book Review,* in *Six Out Seven* Jess Mowry "grapple[s] angrily and

If you enjoy the works of Jess Mowry, you may also want to check out the following books and films:

Alice Hoffman, *Property Of*, 1988.
Walter Dean Myers, *Scorpions*, 1988.
Richard Wright, *Rite of Passage*, 1994.
Boyz N the Hood, a film directed by John Singleton, 1991.

honestly with the forces killing young black men; with individual and societal responsibility; with the complexities of modern racism, including drive-by shooters whom, Mowry says, roam inner cities "like the KKK's Afro-American auxiliary." Sipchen went on to praise *Six Out Seven* as a "heartfelt, beautifully written book that will make readers see that the kids (Mowry) portrays are *everyone's* kids, and to let their dreams wither unnurtured is *everyone's* shame." Clarence Petersen, writing in the Chicago *Tribune Books*, echoed those comments when he wrote, "Mowry tells us things we need to hear with a raw eloquence that both touches and enrages."

Other mainstream reviewers, obviously much less comfortable with Mowry's ideas, were also less sympathetic. David Nicholson of the *Washington Post Book World*—a self-described "middle-aged reader," who conceded that he "never found himself hanging with the homeboys," chided the author for writing a book that was "not only improbable but, in the end, flat and predictable." Similarly, a *Kirkus Reviews* critic dismissed *Six Out Seven* as a "weakly plotted" novel that "leave[s] few lasting impressions." Donna Seaman of *Booklist* wrote, "This is an interesting near miss. Mowry has burdened his fine characters with too many messages and tried, unsuccessfully, to blend mysticism with polemics." Michael Upchurch of the *New York Times* praised Mowry as "a vital and important literary voice," but he went on to chide the author for the tone as well as the substance of his message. "To a greater degree than before . . .," Upchurch wrote, "Mowry uses his fiction as a soapbox from which his characters voice their frustrations, their sense of victimization and defeat and their conspiracy theories. This creates some problems. The most disturbing theory proffered is the conviction that black-on-black violence

is a well-planned Caucasian battle plan in a brewing race war."

Mowry's next book was decidedly lighter fare and a clear change of pace for him. *Ghost Train* is a supernatural mystery story aimed at young readers. The story is about Remi DuMont, a young Haitian immigrant, who with help from his new American friend Niya, sets out to solve a fifty-year-old murder mystery. Mowry spins a suspense-filled yarn about time travel, social issues, and Voodoo magic—the latter being a subject in which the author himself has a keen interest. Mowry says his main purpose in writing *Ghost Train* was to tell a good story, something he feels that not enough black male writers are doing, or being allowed to do by a white-dominated publishing industry that insists on turning out books about stereotypical black characters living in a world of guns, drugs, gangs, and killing, and by black intellectuals who feel writing—or reading— escapist fiction is not a worthwhile pastime. "Of course our young people should know their history and be aware of racism on all levels, and of social issues and concerns in the world around them," Mowry writes on his Web page, "but they MUST also be entertained in positive ways," and offered valid, realistic role models.

Mowry apparently succeeded on all counts with *Ghost Train*. Although reviewer Ann C. Sparanese of the *Voice of Youth Advocates* faulted the "dialog['s] stilted quality" that intercepts the story's flow, she asserted that "the novel's strength is in its plot." From the start of the novel, "the suspense pulls the reader along to the climactic last chapter, where danger gives way to a satisfying resolution." Susan L. Rogers of *School Library Journal* praised *Ghost Train* as a "short, easy-to-read, and very successful mystery."

Mowry returned to familiar turf with *Babylon Boyz*, a 1997 novel about three teenage friends named Dante, Pook, and Wyatt, who live in a run-down inner-city Oakland neighborhood called Babylon. Mowry tells the story of what happens when the youths find a suitcase full of drugs, which has been discarded by a white drug dealer on the run. Dante, Pook, and Wyatt are suddenly confronted with gut-wrenching decisions about whether or not to try to sell the drugs. *Babylon Boyz* is a tough, hard-hitting story with earthy dialogue, violence, and some graphic sex scenes. "While it's sometimes difficult to read about this subject matter, toning it down would have sadly compromised the story's realism," reviewer Florence Munat of *Voice of Youth Advocates* allowed. "Instead, Mowry has delivered a realistic, tenacious tale of urban hopes and dreams." Bill Ott of *Booklist* agreed. "Each of the boys rises above the stereotypical aspects of his character to become, not emblems of hard life in the ghetto, but vivid reminders that we are all more than the sum of our situations," he wrote. Reviewer Beth Wright of *School Library Journal* observed that *Babylon Boyz* offers a view of "family, friendship, love, and . . . kids living in poverty and victimized by drugs still trying to make the right choices in their lives."

In addition to his novels and short stories, Mowry has shown his versatility by writing a stage play

In this 1997 novel three teenage friends find a discarded suitcase filled with drugs and contemplate whether to sell them.

called *Skeleton Key*, which was staged at a private school in Berkeley, and by collaborating on the screenplay for a film based on his novel *Way Past Cool*. Nonetheless, Mowry feels that he still faces an uphill struggle to succeed as a writer, even if he does concede that he is still learning, about writing and about life. "One radio talk-show host gave me a left-handed compliment on the air by saying how 'well I expressed myself, considering that I'd only completed seventh grade,'" Mowry said in his *AAYA* interview. "I replied that I'd always thought life was a learning process that never stopped, as opposed to those who had finished high school and perhaps college and so felt they had learned everything they needed to know."

Mowry's own independence of mind (he has been with four literary agents in his brief career and is now representing himself), which is one of his strengths, has also been one of the biggest obstacles he has had to overcome. However, he insists that an even greater difficulty is the racism that he—and other blacks—face on a daily basis in American society. "In the case of [black] writers, musicians, or filmmakers it's very hard because 'they' (and you should know who 'they' are) control everything," Mowry explained to *AAYA*. "A 'black book' that does not please a white editor will not be published. . . . A white writer with my track record—ALL of my books still in print after almost ten years (in eight languages), a film, and a play—would have no problem finding a publisher for their next work. With me, it's a case of back to square-one every time and start all over again. It's very tiring to say the least."

Following His Own Plan

Despite this, and despite the hostility of some mainstream book reviewers, Jess Mowry continues to pursue his art as truthfully and honestly as he knows how; he insists on having it no other way. After all, Mowry feels strongly that every successful black man or woman has a duty to serve as a role model for young people in their communities. Part and parcel with that, Mowry says he feels obliged to continue speaking out against the social injustices that he sees, and to do all he can to help smash the harmful black stereotypes that are depicted in the media. "I'd be less than human if I didn't [get angry]. Although I try to temper my anger with the 'I used to be disgusted, now I'm just amused' philosophy," Mowry told *AAYA*.

Mowry's stories have been included in various anthologies, and he has also written two more novels. One, which is based on the play *Skeleton Key*, is unpublished; the other, called *Bones Become Flowers*. "I consider [this] to be the BEST writing I have done to date," Mowry explains on his Web page. The novel, which is set in Haiti, is an entertaining story about children, Voodoo, a search for God, and the exploitation of poor nations by rich nations. "*Bones Become Flowers* may turn out to be my last try at writing. It will certainly prove to me whether I am right or wrong in thinking that Black readers of all ages want more than just 'guns, gangs, drugs, and violence.'"

■ Works Cited

George, Nelson, "Boyz Against the Hoods," *New York Times*, May 24, 1992, p. 21.

Hruska, Bronwen, "Goodbye, Cool World," *Voice Literary Supplement*, May, 1992, p. 31.

Kimberley, Nick, "Unhappy Days," *New Statesman & Society*, July 17, 1992, pp. 46-47.

MacRae, Cathi Dunn, "Young Adult Perplex," *Wilson Library Bulletin*, March, 1991, pp. 112-13.

MacRae, Cathi Dunn, "The Young Adult Perplex," *Wilson Library Bulletin*, September, 1992, pp. 96-97, 126-27.

Max, Daniel, "Will Hollywood get serious about black lit?" *Variety*, January 27, 1992, p. 68.

Mowry, Jess, author's Web page at http://members.tripod.com/~Timoun/index-7.htm.

Mowry, Jess, interviews with Ken Cuthbertson for *Authors and Artists for Young Adults*, December 23, 1998, and January 8, 1999.

Munat, Florence, review of *Babylon Boyz, Voice of Youth Advocates*, June, 1997, p. 112.

Nicholson, David, "Mean Streetz and Lost Boyz," *Washington Post Book World*, November 2, 1993, p. E-2.

Ott, Bill, review of *Babylon Boyz, Booklist*, February 15, 1997, p. 1020.

Petersen, Clarence, "Paperbacks," *Tribune Books* (Chicago), September 18, 1994, p. 8.

Review of *Rats in the Trees, Publishers Weekly*, March 2, 1990, p. 78.

Reed, Ishmael, "The Activist Library: A Symposium," *Nation*, September 21, 1992, pp. 293-294.

Rogers, Susan L., review of *Ghost Train, School Library Journal*, December, 1996, p. 139.

Seaman, Donna, review of *Six Out Seven, Booklist*, September 15, 1993, p. 128.

Sipchen, Bob, "What the Use in Dreamin?" *Los Angeles Times Book Review*, November 7, 1993, pp. 2, 9.

Review of *Six Out Seven, Kirkus Reviews*, August 1, 1993, p. 960.

Sparanese, Ann C., review of *Ghost Train, Voice of Youth Advocates*, February, 1997, p. 330.

Upchurch, Michael, "Where Death is a Dirt-Nap," *New York Times Book Review*, October 31, 1993.

Ward, Robert, "Dispatch From the Hood," *Los Angeles Times Book Review*, April 19, 1992.

Wright, Beth, review of *Babylon Boyz, School Library Journal*, September, 1997, p. 222.

■ For More Information See

BOOKS

Contemporary Black Biography, Volume 7, Gale, 1994.

PERIODICALS

Booklist, February 15, 1997.
Kirkus Reviews, April 15, 1997.
People, June 22, 1992, p. 66.
Publishers Weekly, February 3, 1997, p. 107.

—Sketch by Ken Cuthbertson

Edvard Munch

■ Personal

Born December 12, 1863, in Loten, Norway; died January 23, 1944, in Oslo, Norway; son of Laura Catherine (Bjolstad) and Christian Munch (a military doctor). *Education:* Attended Royal School of Drawing; studied under Christian Krohg; studied with Leon Bonnat in Paris, c. 1889.

■ Career

Painter, living and working primarily in Paris, France, and Berlin, Germany, from 1889 to 1908, and near Oslo, Norway, after 1908. First traveled to Paris, 1885; mounted first solo show of his own work in Kristiania (now Oslo), 1889; settled in Berlin, 1890; show at the Verein Berliner Kuenstler (Association of Berlin Artists) in 1892 closed by scandal; work included in the Armory Show, New York City, 1913; awarded commission for murals of the Aula of the University of Oslo, 1910. *Exhibitions:* Major collections of Munch's work are housed in two museums in Oslo, Norway, the National Gallery, and the Munch Museum. The artist exhibited at the annual Autumn Exhibitions

in Kristiania, Norway, during the 1890s, and was invited to participate in the Sonderbund Internationale, Cologne, Germany, in 1912, and in the Berlin Autumn Exhibition, 1913. Many European museums hosted retrospectives of his work beginning in the 1920s, and continuing after his death well toward the end of the century on an international spectrum.

■ Awards, Honors

Awarded Order of St. Olav, 1908, government of Norway, and the Grand Cross of St. Olav, 1933.

■ Sidelights

Rather fortunately for Norwegian painter and printmaker Edvard Munch, he found expression for his bouts of physical and spiritual turmoil in his art, and during his lifetime enjoyed an estimable reputation with many critics and collectors; he also was an eminent figure to a generation of younger European artists and lent a profound impact to the direction of their work. He is widely considered Scandinavia's most famous and influential visual artist. But to the general public and those who did not know him personally, Munch was assumed to be mentally unstable. "My art is rooted in a single reflection," Munch once declared, according to Michael Gibson's 1997 book *Symbolism.* "Why am I not as others are? Why was there a curse on my cradle? Why did I come into the world without any choice?" Munch further noted that "my art gives meaning to my life."

Munch's personal and professional career were marked by controversy, and almost all of his work before 1909 is infused with despair—he painted not the sunny landscapes of Claude Monet's Giverny, nor even the fields of humming wildflowers depicted by a certifiably unsound Vincent Van Gogh—both artists whose work a young Munch looked toward for technical and thematic inspiration. Instead Munch painted images of sickness, death, jealousy, and sexual dread, and it is a single painting that stands as a marker of his enduring power. It was also a work that caused many to assume that anyone who could imagine, then depict, such a scene of psychic terror must surely be himself deranged: 1893's *The Scream*. Since the day it was first shown in public, *The*

Scream has become one of the most ubiquitous images of modern art and popular culture.

Munch was born on December 12, 1863, in Loten, a suburb of Oslo, Norway's major city that was then known as Christiania (the name was changed to Kristiania in 1877, and finally to its present name in 1925). He was one of five children of Christian Munch, a military physician and a deeply religious man. The elder Munch was the descendant of a well-known painter, Jacob Munch (1776-1839), and brother to a distinguished historian; the family also boasted a long line of academics and even clergy. Still, Munch came to feel that he had inherited his forebears' susceptibility toward both consumption, also known as tuberculosis, and mental illness. His mother, Laura, died from the deadly respiratory disease when he was just five, and a fifteen-year-old sister later succumbed to it when he was in his early teens.

Painted between 1899 and 1900, *The Dance of Life* exemplifies Munch's desire to encompass the entire range of human existence.

Another sister suffered from mental problems early in her childhood.

Munch himself was sickly as a child, often ill with bronchitis, and feared death was imminent for him as well. Even the fact that his father was a doctor brought him little comfort. Poverty and close living quarters played a role in the spread of tuberculosis, and the Munch family were poor despite their reputable name, living in tenement apartments outside the city. It was a household rife with tension and guilt. The death of Laura Munch plunged his father into periods of depression and only increased his religious fervor. Dr. Munch, plagued by occasional hallucinations and a violent temper, saw the deaths in his family as a punishment from God.

Artistic Talent Emerges

Early in adolescence, Munch became interested in art and began to display a talent for it. Not surprisingly, his father initially tried to discourage him from pursuing it as a career, and for a time Munch acquiesced to his wishes and took engineering courses in school. Finally he was allowed to enroll at the Royal School of Drawing in Kristiania around 1880, where he was able to meet and learn from other young people in the city who shared his interests and ideas. For a time he studied under Christian Krohg, then one of the most esteemed painters in Norway.

As he entered his twenties, Munch yearned to see the capital of European culture and wellspring of the avant-garde: Paris. In 1885 he arrived there on funds from a government grant and began painting landscapes. One recurring subject, which would hold an important thematic interest for Munch for most of his life, was the Norway resort Aasgaardstrand. In particular he loved its long Arctic summer nights and the special, almost eerie light these warmer months brought to its sky.

Munch took his canvases back to Norway and began exhibiting in the annual autumn salons in Kristiania. One of his earliest efforts from this period, which he had begun in Paris, was *The Sick Child*, a work commemorating the death of his sister. He showed this emotionally searing work, with its somber blue, green, and gray tones capturing a tragic interior scene of a woman bent in

grief over a bedridden child, in the 1886 Exhibition, and was vilified by critics for it. "Most of my later work had its origin in this picture," Munch later said, typically undaunted by criticism.

In Kristiania, Munch moved in its more bohemian circles and counted radical anarchists and free-love enthusiasts among his friends. He also began writing, feeling the need to express in words what it was he was attempting to formulate in his art. After 1889, he began spending more time away from Kristiania. He went back to Paris, studied under Leon Bonnat for a spell, and there learned that his father had died. His 1890 painting *Night* is emblematic of the sadness and loneliness he felt upon receiving this news so far from home. A figure stands alone at a window, bathed in shades of blue.

Though Munch's art was infused with a particularly dour Scandinavian mysticism—pagan traditions thrived in these northern lands until the establishment of Christianity in Sweden around the ninth century, and in Norway two centuries later—his works were also indebted to Van Gogh and the French painter Paul Gauguin, both of whom employed vibrant colors and gave great emphasis to pattern and line. Gauguin was closely associated with Synthetism, a movement then thriving in France whose hallmarks were the use of intense shades of paint upon simplified, curvilinear forms.

Synthetism grew out of the French Symbolism of the 1870s and 1880s, and much of this new direction was a backlash of sorts resulting from the invention of the camera—a magical and much heralded innovation of the day. Munch once famously offered his opinion of the argument then raging between the opposing philosophical adherents of photography versus painting: "The camera will never compete with the brush and the palette," Munch wrote, "until such time as photographs can be taken in Heaven or Hell."

Disturbing, Disquieting Work

Many of Munch's most disturbing yet significant works emerged from his studio during the 1890s. These include *Melancholy,* sometimes called *The Yellow Boat* or *Jealousy,* which shows human figures against bleak landscape at Aasgaardstrand; a man in the foreground—probably Munch's art-

The Scream, painted in 1893 and one of Munch most famous paintings, is generally regarded as the catalyst for German expressionism.

critic friend Jappe Nilssen—cannot conceal despair as a woman and a man depart on a boat in the distance behind him. The ominous rocks and oppressive sky were Munch's way of using the physical world to echo the human soul's agony. It was first exhibited in the Autumn Exhibition of 1891 in Kristiania.

In 1892 Munch went to Berlin after an invitation by the Verein Berliner Kuenstler (Association of Berlin Artists) to mount a retrospective of his work there. The public was outraged at many of the works—*Vampire* was considered especially lurid—and it closed after just a few days. Because of the sensation, the Verein members voted on whether to shut it down, and the older, more conservative artists held the majority. The younger dissenting ones then broke with the Verein to launch the Neue Berlin Sezession (New Berlin Secession) movement, a stylistic and interpretative direction that became integral to the establishment of German Expressionism.

Yet the Berlin show and its attendant publicity helped boost Munch's reputation in Germany even more. He remained there for the next few years, and came to know Swedish dramatist August Strindberg, also in temporary artistic exile. Strindberg's bleak plays were characterized by tense interpersonal relationships, in many ways the stage equivalent of Munch's art. Munch later came to know another well-known Scandinavian dramatist and fellow Norwegian, Henrik Ibsen, and designed the sets for a staging of Ibsen's *Peer Gynt* in Paris. His contemporaries began calling Munch's work "psychological realism," a term used by Polish poet Stanislaw Przybyszewski in the book *Das Werk des Edvard Munch*, co-authored with German art historian Julius Meier-Graefe and published in Berlin in 1894. These two, plus Munch and Strindberg, established a convivial social set of intellectuals and artists who made a Berlin bierkeller called Zum schwarzen Ferkel their meeting place.

Munch began working more in the graphic arts around this time, but continued to work towards completing a cycle of paintings he called the *Frieze of Life: A Poem about Life, Love, and Death.* The first of the works in the series—which included the aforementioned *Melancholy*—were exhibited at a space on Unter den Linden, the fashionable Berlin avenue, in December of 1893. *Death in the Sickroom* (1893), another work commemorating the death of his older sister, was included. The following year *Anxiety, Ashes,* and the controversial *Madonna,* a nude in ecstasy, also joined the cycle.

The Scream

The Scream, sometimes called *The Cry,* also emerged from this fruitful period of Munch's career. It has been termed the work that sired German Expressionism, for it was one of the first to impact upon the viewer not the traditional artistic depiction of a specific moment in time or space, but rather a state of mind. Its expression of inner angst also reflected the late nineteenth century's increasing concern with the self and the burgeoning field of psychiatry. In the painting, a skeletal figure standing on a bridge covers its ears while the mouth is agape in an agonizing scream, a sound that does not appear to disturb in the slightest the two people in the background who are walking away. The screaming figure is in the foreground of the picture, but appears rushing toward viewer, increasing the feeling of anxiety. Surrounding this Munch painted ominous fjord and sky in thick, undulating blue-black tones and the red of blood. The tempera version of *The Scream* dates from 1893, but he also did a lithograph of it 1895. When first exhibited, it was disparaged by some as the work of an unsound mind. Munch himself wrote on its frame: "Could only have been painted by a madman."

Munch showed the completed *Frieze of Life* for the first time in its entirety in the Berlin Secession show of 1902. From this moment onward, Munch came to be a great influence upon some German artists working in Dresden around the years 1905 to 1908 who called themselves "Die Bruecke," or "The Bridge"; Emil Nolde was among them. Later, a few headed south to Munich and came to be known as the "Der Blaue Reiter" ("The Blue Rider") group, among them Wassily Kandinsky and Max Beckmann, and their works are considered the most faultless and dramatic images of pre-World War I German Expressionism.

Until about 1908 Munch alternated his time between Paris and Berlin, though he spent summers in Aasgaardstrand after he bought a small place there in 1897. Yet he had become embroiled in a desperate love affair—with incidents of blackmail and threats of suicide—that finally ended in Aasgaardstrand in a crisis involving a gun. The

The 1892 work *Death in the Sickroom,* also known as *The Death Chamber,* portrays Munch's family's response to his sister's early death.

artist permanently damaged a finger trying to wrest the weapon away from his paramour, a woman who probably appears in his 1907 work *Death of Marat.* He had also begun to drink and smoke quite heavily, and from a combination of these factors he suffered a nervous collapse in 1908. He returned to Scandinavia, first to Denmark and eight months in a Copenhagen sanitarium, where he occupied his days by sketching the doctors and nurses. Later he returned to the Oslo area, and would remain in his homeland for the rest of his life.

Earns Honors

Oddly enough, Munch recovered relatively quickly from his breakdown and entered into a period of psychic peace and artistic renewal. (He would later say that he simply abandoned his twin vices of women and alcohol.) Settling near Oslo on the coast, he set up an outdoor studio for the warm months and from this point onward painted more pleasant, far less morbid scenes in gentle, subdued tones. He also took up portraiture in earnest, executing full- or three-quarter-length works depicting his friends and some of the best known names of the era, such as his portrait of the philosopher Frederic Nietzsche (1908). Munch was knighted with his country's Order of St. Olav in 1908, and the following year its Nasjonalgalleriet in Oslo began purchasing his work in earnest for their collection. At the time, the curators' first 1909 acquisition was the museum's largest purchase in its history of work by a living artist. He also won a large commission for murals that decorate the

If you enjoy the works of Edvard Munch, you may also want to check out the following:

The plays of Henrik Ibsen, including *A Doll's House,* 1889, and *Ghosts,* 1890.

The prints and drawings of Käthe Kollwitz, including *Weaver's Riot,* 1897, and *Death Seizing a Woman,* 1934.

The paintings of Vincent van Gogh, including *Potato Eaters,* 1885, and *The Starry Night,* 1889.

Aula of the University of Oslo, which he worked on from 1910 to 1916. There was some controversy about installing them, but those at the college who recognized Munch's status won out, and they were put in place and he was paid. With the proceeds he bought a place in Ekely, also near Oslo.

In 1912 Munch was feted at the Sonderbund Internationale Exhibition in Cologne, Germany, which placed his works in the realm of all the pioneers of modern art. He and Pablo Picasso were the only two living artists given their own gallery rooms. Munch became interested in the burgeoning trade union movement in Scandinavia, and painted *Workers on Their Way Home* (1913-15) as a reflection of this liberal bent. During the 1920s, he was honored with numerous exhibitions throughout Europe, and in 1933 he was bestowed with the Grand Cross of St. Olav in honor of his seventieth birthday. That same year the first of several biographies of Munch appeared in print. But seven years later Norway was occupied by Nazi Germany, and Munch lived out his final years in Ekely under foreign rule. His works that were in German and Norwegian museums were condemned, along with the art of the German Ex-

pressionists, as "degenerate" by the German chancellor Adolf Hitler and removed from public view. During the winter of 1943-44, an explosion at a nearby munitions factory shattered the windows of Munch's house. As a result he became gravely ill, and died in January of 1944 at the age of eighty.

Munch's will bequeathed all of the works in his estate to city of Oslo, and over the next few decades curators worked to acquire other paintings by the artist that had been sold to private collectors through his dealers during his lifetime. Finally in 1963 his legacy was formally christened with the opening of the Munch Museet in Oslo. The Nasjonalgalleriet is home to the remainder of Munch's work in Norway.

Works Cited

Gibson, Michael, *Symbolism,* Taschen America, 1997.

Mildner, Stormy, "The Scream: Still Heard a Century Later," *Imprint,* March 21, 1997.

For More Information See

BOOKS

Hodin, Josef Paul, *Edvard Munch,* Thames and Hudson, 1985.

Messer, Thomas M., *Edvard Munch,* Abrams, 1986.

Munch, Edvard, and Uwe M. Schneede, *Edvard Munch: The Early Masterpieces,* Norton, 1991.

Prelinger, Elizabeth, and Michael Parke-Taylor, *The Symbolist Prints of Edvard Munch: The Vivian and David Campbell Collection,* Yale University Press, 1996.

Turner, Jane, editor, *Dictionary of Art,* Volume 22, Macmillan, 1996.

—Sketch by Carol Brennan

Phyllis Reynolds Naylor

DC, editorial assistant with *NEA Journal*, 1959-60; full-time writer, 1960—. Active in civil rights and peace organizations. *Member:* Society of Children's Book Writers and Illustrators, Authors Guild, Authors League of America, Children's Book Guild (president, 1974-75, 1983-84).

■ Personal

Born January 4, 1933, in Anderson, IN; daughter of Eugene S. and Lura (Schield) Reynolds; married second husband, Rex V. Naylor (a speech pathologist), May 26, 1960; children: Jeffrey Alan, Michael Scott. *Education:* Joliet Junior College, diploma, 1953; American University, B.A., 1963. *Politics:* Independent. *Religion:* Unitarian Universalist. *Hobbies and other interests:* Music, drama, hiking, swimming.

■ Addresses

Home—9910 Holmhurst Rd., Bethesda, MD 20817. *Agent*—John Hawkins and Associates, Inc., 71 West 23rd St., Suite 1600, New York, NY 10010.

■ Career

Elementary school teacher in Hazel Crest, IL, 1956; Montgomery County Education Association, Rockville, MD, assistant executive secretary, 1958-59; National Education Association, Washington,

■ Awards, Honors

Children's Book of the Year, Child Study Association of America, 1971, for *Wrestle the Mountain;* Golden Kite Award for nonfiction, Society of Children's Book Authors, 1978, and International Reading Association (IRA) Children's Choice citation, 1979, both for *How I Came to Be a Writer;* Children's Book of the Year, Child Study Association of America, 1979, and IRA Children's Choice citation, 1980, for *How Lazy Can You Get?;* American Library Association (ALA) Young Adult Services Division (YASD) Best Book for Young Adults citation, and Notable Children's Book in the Field of Social Studies citation, National Council for Social Studies, both 1982, and, South Carolina Young Adult Book Award, 1985-86, all for *A String of Chances;* Child Study Award, Bank Street College, 1983, for *The Solomon System;* ALA Notable Book citation, 1985, and IRA Children's Choice Citation, 1986, both for *The Agony of Alice;* Edgar Allan Poe Award, Mystery Writers of America, 1985, for *Night Cry;* Notable Children's Book in the Field of Social Studies citation, 1985, for *The Dark of the Tunnel;* ALA YASD Best Book for

Young Adults Citation, 1986, for *The Keeper;* creative writing fellowship, grant, National Endowment for the Arts, 1987; ALA YASD Best Book for Young Adults citation, 1987, and Best Young Adult Book of the Year, Michigan Library Association, 1988, both for *Year of the Gopher;* Society of School Librarians International Book Award, 1988, for *Maudie in the Middle;* Christopher Award, 1989, for *Keeping a Christmas Secret;* ALA Notable Book for Young Adults Citation, 1989, for *Send No Blessings.*

Hedda Seisler Mason Award, Enoch Pratt Free Library, 1991, for *Alice in Rapture, Sort Of;* Newbery Medal, 1992, for *Shiloh;* Dorothy Canfield Fisher Award, 1993; Kerlan Award, University of Minnesota Kerlan Collection, 1995, for her body of work; Appalachian Medallion, University of Charleston, 1997, for distinguished writing. Several of Naylor's books have been named selections of the Literary and Junior Literary Guilds and the Weekly Reader Book Club; she has also received numerous several state and child-selected awards (twenty-six for *Shiloh* alone).

■ **Writings**

PICTURE BOOKS

Jennifer Jean, the Cross-Eyed Queen, illustrated by Harold K. Lamson, Lerner, 1967.
The New Schoolmaster, illustrated by Mamoru Funai, Silver Burdett, 1967.
A New Year's Surprise, by Jack Endewelt, Silver Burdett, 1967.
Meet Murdock, illustrated by Gioia Fiammenghi, Follett, 1969.
The Boy with the Helium Head, illustrated by Kay Chorao, Atheneum, 1982.
Old Sadie and the Christmas Bear, illustrated by Patricia Montgomery, Atheneum, 1984.
The Baby, the Bed, and the Rose, illustrated by Mary Stilagyi, Atheneum, 1987.
Keeping a Christmas Secret, illustrated by Lena Shiffman, Atheneum, 1989.
King of the Playground, illustrated by Nola Langner Malone, Atheneum, 1991.
Ducks Disappearing, illustrated by Tony Maddox, Atheneum, 1996.
I Can't Take You Anywhere, illustrated by Jef Kaminsky, Atheneum, 1997.
Sweet Strawberries, illustrated by Rosalind Charney Kaye, Atheneum, 1999.

FICTION

What the Gulls Were Singing, illustrated by Jack Smith, Follett, 1967.
To Shake a Shadow, Abingdon, 1967.
When Rivers Meet, Friendship, 1968.
To Make a Wee Moon, Follett, 1969.
Making It Happen, Follett, 1970.
Wrestle the Mountain, Follett, 1971.
No Easy Circle, Follett, 1972.
To Walk the Sky Path, Follett, 1973.
Walking through the Dark, Atheneum, 1976.
How Lazy Can You Get?, illustrated by Alan Daniel, Atheneum, 1979.
Eddie, Incorporated, illustrated by Blanche Sims, Atheneum, 1980.
All Because I'm Older, illustrated by Leslie Morrill, Atheneum, 1981.
A String of Chances, Atheneum, 1982.
The Solomon System, Atheneum, 1983.
Night Cry, Atheneum, 1984.
The Dark of the Tunnel, Atheneum, 1985.
The Keeper, Atheneum, 1986.
The Year of the Gopher, Atheneum, 1987.
Beetles, Lightly Toasted, Atheneum, 1987.
(With mother, Lura Schield Reynolds) *Maudie in the Middle,* illustrated by Judith Gwyn Brown, Atheneum, 1988.
One of the Third Grade Thonkers, illustrated by Walter Gaffney-Kessell, Atheneum, 1988.
Send No Blessings, Atheneum, 1990.
Josie's Troubles, illustrated by Shelley Matheis, Atheneum, 1992.
The Grand Escape, illustrated by Alan Daniel, Atheneum, 1993.
The Fear Place, Atheneum, 1994.
Being Danny's Dog, Atheneum, 1995.
Ice, Atheneum, 1996.
The Healing of Texas Jake (sequel to *The Grand Escape*), illustrated by Alan Daniel, Atheneum, 1997.
Danny's Desert Rats (sequel to *Being Danny's Dog*), Atheneum, 1998.
Sang Spell, Atheneum, 1998.
Walker's Crossing, Atheneum, 1999.

"WITCH" SERIES

Witch's Sister, illustrated by Gail Owens, Atheneum, 1975.
Witch Water, illustrated by Gail Owens, Atheneum, 1977.
The Witch Herself, illustrated by Gale Owens, Atheneum, 1978.

The Witch's Eye, illustrated by Joe Burleson, Delacorte, 1990.

Witch Weed, illustrated by Joe Burleson, Delacorte, 1991.

The Witch Returns, illustrated by Joe Burleson, Delacorte, 1992.

"YORK" SERIES

Shadows on the Wall, Atheneum, 1980.
Faces in the Water, Atheneum, 1981.
Footprints at the Window, Atheneum, 1981.

"BESSLEDORF" SERIES

The Mad Gasser of Bessledorf Street, Atheneum, 1983.
The Bodies in the Bessledorf Hotel, Atheneum, 1986.
Bernie and the Bessledorf Ghost, Atheneum, 1990.
The Face in the Bessledorf Funeral Parlor, Atheneum, 1993.
The Bomb in the Bessledorf Bus Depot, Atheneum, 1996.
The Treasure of Bessledorf Hill, Atheneum, 1998.

"ALICE" SERIES

The Agony of Alice, Atheneum, 1985.
Alice in Rapture, Sort Of, Atheneum, 1989.
Reluctantly Alice, Atheneum, 1991.
All but Alice, Atheneum, 1992.
Alice in April, Atheneum, 1993.
Alice In-Between, Atheneum, 1994.
Alice the Brave, Atheneum, 1995.
Alice in Lace, Atheneum, 1996.
Outrageously Alice, Atheneum, 1997.
Achingly Alice, Atheneum, 1998.
Alice on the Outside, Atheneum, 1999.

"SHILOH" SERIES

Shiloh, Atheneum, 1991.
Shiloh Season, Atheneum, 1996.
Saving Shiloh, Atheneum, 1997.

"BOYS AND GIRLS" SERIES

The Boys Start the War, Delacorte, 1993.
The Girls Get Even, Delacorte, 1993.
Boys Against Girls, Delacorte, 1994.
The Girls' Revenge, Delacorte, 1998.
A Traitor among the Boys, Delacorte, 1999.

SHORT STORIES

The Galloping Goat and Other Stories, illustrated by Robert L. Jefferson, Abingdon, 1965.

Grasshoppers in the Soup: Short Stories for Teen-agers, Fortress, 1965.
Knee-Deep in Ice Cream and Other Stories, Fortress, 1967.
The Dark Side of the Moon, Fortress, 1969.
The Private I and Other Stories, Fortress, 1969.
Ships in the Night, Fortress, 1970.
A Change in the Wind, Augsburg Press, 1980.
Never Born a Hero, Augsburg Press, 1982.
A Triangle Has Four Sides, Augsburg Press, 1984.

JUVENILE NONFICTION

How to Find Your Wonderful Someone, How to Keep Him/Her if You Do, How to Survive if You Don't, Fortress, 1972.
An Amish Family, illustrated by George Armstrong, J. Philip O'Hara, 1974.
Getting Along in Your Family, illustrated by Rick Cooley, Abingdon, 1976.
How I Came to Be a Writer, Atheneum, 1978, revised edition, Aladdin Books, 1987.
Getting Along with Your Friends, illustrated by Rick Cooley, Abingdon, 1980.
Getting Along with Your Teachers, illustrated by Rick Cooley, Abingdon, 1981.

FOR ADULTS; FICTION AND NONFICTION

Crazy Love: An Autobiographical Account of Marriage and Madness (nonfiction), Morrow, 1977.
In Small Doses (essays), Atheneum, 1979.
Revelations (novel), St. Martin's, 1979.
Unexpected Pleasures (novel), Putnam, 1986.
The Craft of Writing the Novel (nonfiction), The Writer, 1989.

Author of weekly columns for church magazines. Contributor to numerous newspapers and magazines. Naylor's papers are housed at the de Grummond Collection, University of Southern Mississippi, and the Kerlan Collection, University of Minnesota.

■ Adaptations

The Keeper was adapted into the ABC Afterschool Special *My Dad Can't Be Crazy; Shiloh* was adapted into a feature film and released in 1997. Audio recordings of *Shiloh* and *Shiloh Season* were released by Bantam Doubleday Dell Audio Publishing in 1992 and 1997, respectively; unabridged sound recordings were made of *Alice the Brave* and

The Fear Place in 1996 by Recorded Books. Sound recordings by the American Audio Prose Library have been made of Naylor reading from her own works: excerpts from *The Agony of Alice* and *The Keeper* were released on one cassette in 1987, and excerpts from *Unexpected Pleasures* were released on another cassette in the same year. An interview with Naylor by Kay Bonetti was released as a sound recording by American Audio Prose Library in 1987.

■ Work in Progress

Percy's Picnic, a picture book illustrated by Lynne Munsinger, for Atheneum, 2000; *Jade Green: A Ghost Story*, a novel for Atheneum, 2000; *Peril in the Bessledorf Parachute Factory*, for Atheneum, 2000.

■ Sidelights

A prolific author who is often celebrated both for her versatility and for the diversity of her works, Phyllis Reynolds Naylor has written well-received books for children and young adults in a number of genres and styles. She is the creator of novels, short stories, picture books, and nonfiction for children as well as fiction and nonfiction for adults. As a writer for young people, Naylor has written books for children from preschool through high school in such genres as historical fiction, the gothic novel, the mystery story, the time-travel fantasy, and the problem novel; her works range from young adult novels that sensitively treat serious issues to humorous, lighthearted stories for younger children. She is perhaps best known as the author of *Shiloh*, a story for middle graders about a West Virginia boy and an abused dog that won the Newbery Medal in 1992.

As an author of nonfiction, Naylor writes instructional books about such subjects as relationships and writing as a profession; in the former category, Naylor provides techniques for effective interaction with parents, siblings, teachers, and friends while stressing communication, tolerance, and self-understanding. Naylor's fiction usually features young people who face adverse situations and inner fears to find personal strength and grow toward maturity. Addressing moral, religious, psychological, and family issues, she writes about such subjects as mental and physical illness, loss of faith, crib death, war, and sex; consequently,

Eleven-year-old Marty Preston take things into his own hands to save a dog from its abusive owner in this award-winning 1991 novel.

some of her books have been regarded as controversial. Although she often writes about the difficulties of living, Naylor presents young readers with a positive, optimistic view of life and a philosophy that stresses acceptance of both self and others.

Praised for her acute observations of human nature as well as for her sympathetic understanding of the young, Naylor is noted for her appealing characterizations, nondidactic approach, and evocation of place. Although initially her prose was often considered crisp but pedestrian, she is now regarded as a craftsmanlike writer with a distinctive voice. In *Twentieth-Century Children's Writers*, John D. Stahl commented, "From comedy to tragedy, from books for younger children to books for older young adults, in novels with rural settings or urban landscapes, from fantasy to realism, she reveals a fine sense of the unexpected difficulties and rewards of life." The critic concluded, "Symptomatic of Naylor's vision is her willingness to present religious, ethical, and psychological issues without a hidden—or, for that matter, obvious—agenda, but simply with honesty and sensitivity." And Deborah Stevenson of *Bulletin of the Center for Children's Books* wrote that Naylor is "still one of our best writers of everyday junior-high life."

Naylor has often included autobiographical elements in her works. Writing in *Horn Book,* her husband Rex commented, "Life-affirming and positive, Phyllis has nevertheless used writing to work through all manner of vexing concerns about herself, her work, family, and friends." Born in Anderson, Indiana, Naylor grew up in a home that treasured the arts; her parents, a traveling salesman and a religious education teacher, had met at Anderson College, where they were involved in school plays and musical productions. "My sister, brother, and I," Naylor remembered in her essay in *Something about the Author Autobiography Series* (SAAS), "grew up surrounded by stories. Since these were the Depression years in Indiana, we did not have much of anything, but we did have a few books." The family's collection included two volumes of Grimm's fairy tales, Egermeier's *Bible Story Book, Child-Rhymes* by James Whitcomb Riley, *Missionary Stories for Little Folks,* a set of Sherlock Holmes detective stories, the complete works of Mark Twain, a set of Collier's encyclopedias, and, wrote the author, "a book about righteous living, which had pictures showing what would happen if you lived any other way—devils chopping people in two. I did not read this book, but I spent a lot of time worrying about the pictures." In addition, Naylor's parents told stories to their children and sang long epic songs to them. "My mother, and sometimes my father, read to us each night till we were well into our teens, though I would never have admitted it to anyone," Naylor once recalled.

Early Efforts at Writing

In 1988, Naylor collaborated with her mother on *Maudie in the Middle,* a story about an eight-year-old in the early 1900s that is based on her mother's reminiscences about her own childhood.

The author wrote in *SAAS* that the "excitement my parents had kindled over stories read, recited, or sung began to grow, and when I entered fourth grade, I started writing my own books." Naylor filled boxes with the books she wrote, both fiction and nonfiction; she wrote in *SAAS* about an example of the latter: "When my mother told me how babies were born, I was eager to show off my new knowledge, and promptly wrote a book called 'Manual for Pregnant Women,' with illustrations by the author. Mother read my books and liked them, but it wasn't for the audience that I wrote: it was for the excitement it engendered in me."

As a young girl, Naylor became known in school for her writing talent; for example, in fifth grade

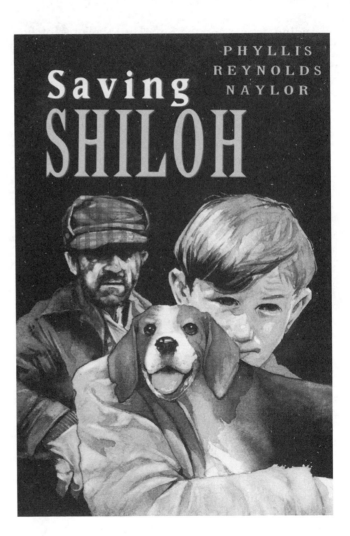

Life turns around for Shiloh in this third novel in the series when Judd, the dog's abusive owner, saves Shiloh from drowning.

she was called upon to write a poem in twenty minutes that would be read aloud at a school assembly in honor of her principal's birthday. However, the author later wrote in *How I Came to Be a Writer*, "I never considered myself 'bookish.'" An active child, Naylor liked arts and crafts and playing with her friends. She began going to revival meetings at the age of about nine or ten, and later explored this subject in several of her books. By the time she reached high school, Naylor had published her first story, a tale about baseball—"my first and only sports story," the author noted in *SAAS*—that was printed in a church school paper edited by one of her former Sunday School teachers. "Send me more, my teacher-turned-editor said," Naylor recalled, and the young author obliged, turning out holiday poems, adventure stories, and morality tales.

Deciding to expand her market, Naylor sent her writings to youth magazines such as *Highlights*, *Seventeen*, and *Jack and Jill*; after two years of rejection letters, she received what she called "a new respect for the business of writing." However, a weekly column that Naylor wrote for a church paper—humor for teenagers written from the viewpoint of a fifteen-year-old boy—lasted twenty-five years and appeared in church magazines throughout the United States. In her senior year, Naylor was selected as class poet; writing in *SAAS*, Naylor commented, "[I] am convinced that I won because no one else wanted the job."

Although Naylor loved writing, she considered it merely a hobby and pondered full-time careers in music, dance, teaching, and missionary work. At the age of eighteen, she married a young man from her hometown who was eight years her senior; after graduating from junior college, she moved to Chicago with her husband, who was working on his Ph.D. While he was in school, Naylor worked as a clinical secretary in a university hospital and then as a third-grade teacher. She also began reading the plays of Shakespeare and books by such authors as Dickens, Tolstoy, Chaucer, Dostoevski, Steinbeck, Faulkner, and Freud. "But always," the author noted in *How I Came to Be a Writer*, "when I wasn't working and wasn't reading, I wrote."

When Naylor was twenty-three, her husband began showing signs of severe mental illness. For the next three years, Naylor noted, "while we moved from state to state, hospital to hospital, I wrote in earnest and in panic to support us. . . . Not all of the ideas were workable, of course, but I was able to use enough of them to pay the rent and buy our food." In retrospect, the author realized that this period "is still very sad to me, but it also made me think, you know, I'm really stronger that I thought. . . . And sometimes when I'm facing something difficult I have to say to myself 'Hey, I went through that, I can go through this.' And so, there is something to be said for weathering storms and becoming stronger." After hospitalizing her husband at a sanitarium in Maryland, it became clear to Naylor that his paranoid schizophrenia was incurable; after their divorce became final, Naylor went back to college with the intention of becoming a clinical psychologist.

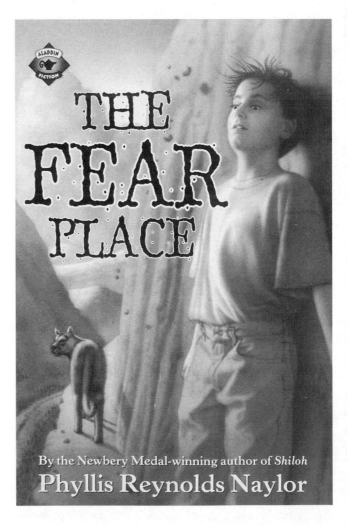

In this 1994 novel, Doug summons up all his courage to overcome his fear of crossing a narrow ledge in order to rescue his brother, Gordie.

In 1977, she published *Crazy Love: An Autobiographical Account of Marriage and Madness,* an adult nonfiction title about her experience.

New Life

In 1960, the author married Dr. Rex Naylor, a speech pathologist; the couple has two children, Jeffrey and Michael. In 1965, Naylor published her first book, *The Galloping Goat and Other Stories,* a collection of stories originally published in magazines; she has now published approximately one hundred books and two thousand stories and articles. Her first novel for children, *What the Gulls Were Singing,* was published in 1967 and describes how a ten-year-old middle child learns about the love of her family and community during a beach holiday; after its publication, Naylor began to write an average of two books per year. Settling with her husband in Bethesda, Maryland, she was not far from Marbury, Maryland, an area familiar to Naylor from childhood visits to her paternal grandparents. The author used Marbury as the setting for one of her most popular—and controversial—books, *A String of Chances.*

Published in 1982, *A String of Chances* features sixteen-year-old Evie Hutchins, the daughter of a small-town fundamentalist preacher. Evie begins to question her faith, and her doubts are intensified when her cousin's baby dies of SIDS; eventually, Evie comes to grips with his death and embarks upon, in the words of Sally Estes of *Booklist,* "a search for a God in whom she can believe." Estes concluded that the specific scenes and themes "all smoothly converge and interlock to give vivid dimension to the story and to delineate the individuals within it. The effect is totally involving and moving." Writing in *School Library Journal,* Roger Sutton called Naylor's style "sensible and warm, but not florid," and added that her "handling of a large cast of characters is skillful, and her depiction of contemporary small-town life is exact and evocative, without sentimentality." In *SAAS,* Naylor wrote, "[Coming] from a deeply religious background in which many things are accepted on faith, I also understand the need for answers. Caught in the middle of this push and pull, I know what it is like for those who dare to question, or to choose a different church that speaks more specifically to their concerns. My novel *A String of Chances* was my attempt to grapple with such a situation." Naylor also used

Naylor's 1998 novel from her popular "Alice" series features the trials and triumphs of junior high school student Alice McKinley.

her grandparents as the models for the parents in her story.

Another of Naylor's most distinguished books is *Night Cry,* a mystery that won the Edgar Allan Poe Award in 1985. In this novel, thirteen-year-old Ellen Stump, a motherless girl living on a backwoods farm in Mississippi, faces her fears to rescue a small boy from a husband-and-wife team of kidnappers. Writing in *Booklist,* Carolyn Phelan noted, "So skillful is Naylor's portrayal of Ellen that aspects of the background and plot are convincing, seen through the girl's eyes," while Charlotte W. Draper of *Horn Book* commented that the "sense of place integral to the author's fiction provides the backdrop for Ellen's suspenseful struggle."

The Keeper, a young adult novel published two years after *Night Cry*, is also considered one of Naylor's best. Based loosely on the author's adult nonfiction book *Crazy Love*, *The Keeper* depicts the struggles of teenager Nick Karpinski as he watches his father's descent into mental illness. Mr. Karpinski refuses to get help while Mrs. Karpinski refuses to acknowledge her husband's symptoms; although Nick feels helpless and is filled with anguish, he recognizes his father's problem and, despite his difficulties at home, makes friends and even goes on a successful first date. At the end of the novel, Mr. Karpinski's condition deteriorates to a point where hospitalization is the only alternative. Writing in *Booklist*, Denise M. Wilms commented that *The Keeper* "is a sensitively wrought novel with no happy ending but certainly with an affirmation of individual strength and emotional survival in the face of adversity." A reviewer in *Bulletin of the Center for Children's Books* noted that Naylor's "focus on the problem is unrelenting, but the story is grippingly detailed, with characters emerging full-dimensional rather than being cast into roles of typical reactions." Ann A. Flowers of *Horn Book* concluded that the author is "extremely adept at showing us the destruction of comfort and happiness and the horror and misery of having someone we know and love turn into a frightening, suspicious stranger. [This is a] book of considerable power."

Writing in *SAAS*, Naylor outlined the genesis of *The Keeper*. Ten years after writing *Crazy Love*, she began to think about how a teenager would have handled the situation that she went through with her husband: "If I, as a young wife, could scarcely cope, what would a teenager have done? What if he were a *young* teenager, still awkward and ill at ease? What if, in his vulnerability, he suddenly found himself the keeper of a secret that his mother, in all her anguish, simply could not share with anyone outside the family, as I could not do for a while? It seemed to speak to the problem of how you can rely on a loved and familiar person who is suddenly no longer to be trusted. So I wrote *The Keeper* because I felt I must."

Throughout her career, Naylor has written several well-regarded series. The "Bessledorf" stories are humorous mysteries that center around the adventures of young Bernie Magruder, whose father is the manager of the Bessledorf Hotel in Middleburg, Indiana. The "Witch" gothic fiction series features Lynn Morley, a brave young girl who,

Hitchhiking his way to Dallas, Josh is badly beaten, then rescued by a kind woman belonging to the Melungeons, a band of people from a forgotten culture, in this 1998 work.

with her best friend Marjorie (nicknamed Mouse), battles the evil Mrs. Tuggle, a witch who threatens their peaceful Indiana neighborhood. The "York" trilogy is made of supernatural fantasies for young adults in which fifteen-year-old Dan Roberts becomes involved with several generations of gypsies, a family he meets in York, England, who may hold the key to the possibility that he and his father have the genes for Huntington's disease. Perhaps Naylor's most popular series are the multivolume set of titles about Alice McKinley, a motherless girl whom Naylor depicts as a sixth, seventh, and eighth grader, and the "Shiloh" series, which features young Marty Preston and his beagle Shiloh and is set in modern rural West Virginia.

In the "Alice" books, the protagonist longs for a female role model, learns about relationships with boys, tries to establish her popularity in junior high, conquers her fear of swimming, learns about her changing body, deals with the suicide of a classmate, and grows into a thoughtful and mature young woman. Reviewers have appreciated both the humor and poignancy of the series, have acknowledged Alice as an especially charming character, and have favorably compared Naylor to Betsy Byars for the freshness and authenticity of her series, which is noted for growing in sophistication as its heroine progresses. In fact, claimed Hazel Rochman in her review of *Alice In-Between* in *Booklist*, "Naylor's books about Alice get better and better." In her review of *Alice the Brave*, Deborah Stevenson of *Bulletin of the Center for Children's Books* added, "There's nobody quite like Alice, yet she's like everybody"; Stevenson concluded her review of *Achingly Alice* by stating, "Alice fans will be grateful that, aching or not, Alice is everlastingly Alice."

Popular "Shiloh" Series

After the success of her novel *Shiloh*, Naylor wrote two sequels, *Shiloh Season* and *Saving Shiloh*. In the "Shiloh" stories, Marty rescues the runaway dog and hides him from his abusive owner Judd Travers, blackmails Judd and makes a deal with him to keep the dog, faces the consequences of his bargain, makes peace with Judd after an accident, and ends up defending the man against accusations of murder and robbery. At the conclusion of *Saving Shiloh*, a novel published in 1997, Judd saves Shiloh—the dog he formerly abused—from drowning. In assessing the first novel in the series, reviewers noted the ethical questions that Naylor explores in the book, such as the nature of truth, and praised the suspenseful plot and rounded characterizations. In her review in *Horn Book*, Elizabeth S. Watson commented that the adventures of a boy and his dog almost always make an appealing story, but "when the boy faces a very difficult decision and takes a giant step toward maturity, the story acquires depth and importance." The critic ended her review by quoting Marty: "I saved Shiloh and opened my eyes some. Now that ain't bad for eleven."

In her assessment in the *New York Times Book Review*, Jane Langton questioned the suitability of *Shiloh* as the winner of the Newbery Medal and

If you enjoy the works of Phyllis Reynolds Naylor, you may also want to check out the following books:

Paula Danziger, *The Cat Ate My Gymsuit*, 1974.
Vicki Grove, *The Fastest Friend in the West*, 1990.
Carolyn Meyer, *This Stranger, My Father*, 1988.
Susan Beth Pfeffer, *Dear Dad, Love Laurie*, 1989.
Rachel Vail, *Wonder*, 1991.

commented, "Did *Shiloh* really deserve the prize? Surely there must have been a book more important than this agreeable but slight story." In conclusion, Langton deemed *Shiloh* a "good book, not a great book." However, other reviewers found the work to be more noteworthy. For example, a critic in *Kirkus Reviews* called the book a "gripping account" and declared that "young readers will rejoice that Shiloh and Marty end up together," while Betsy Hearne of *Bulletin of the Center for Children's Books* commented that young readers will be "absorbed by the suspenseful plot, which will leave them with some memorable characterizations as well as several intriguing questions."

Writing in *Horn Book* about *Shiloh Season*, the 1996 sequel to *Shiloh*, Elizabeth S. Watson noted that Marty's voice "is consistently strong and true" and that fans of the first book "will be well served by the sequel." A reviewer in *Publishers Weekly* concluded, "The author's sympathy for her characters . . . communicates itself almost invisibly to the reader, who may well come away hoping for a full-fledged Shiloh series." Although the story's focus blurs and the dialogue "sounds right out of made-for-TV movies," a critic in *Kirkus Reviews* wrote that readers "will find Marty's anxiety, and his love for Shiloh, engrossingly genuine." Ellen Mandel of *Booklist* called the third volume of the series, *Saving Shiloh*, a "masterfully written conclusion to a sterling trilogy." Roger Sutton of *Horn Book* wrote, "Although the plotting is lackadaisical here, Naylor's writing has its customary ease and generosity," adding that the strongest virtue of the book is "its sure evocation, without quaintness or sentimentality, of contemporary rural life."

Naylor has often written about her career as an author and about the process of writing; in 1978 she published an informational book for young adults, *How I Came to Be a Writer*, that combines these two subjects. In this title, the author demonstrates the development of a literary work from inception to publication while including personal examples and career advice. Writing in *Horn Book*, Karen M. Klockner noted that though the integration "of all these parts is not as fluid as it might have been and the number of sample pieces seems a bit too profuse, the book presents an interesting personal account of what it is like to be a professional writer." In 1989, Naylor published *The Craft of Writing the Novel*, an informational book for adults. Throughout her career, Naylor has commented on the satisfaction she has received from her profession. She once told *SATA*, "Writing, for me, is the best occupation I can think of, and there is the nothing in the world I would rather do."

In *How I Came to Be a Writer*, Naylor stated, "I already know what my next five books will be, and this is probably the way it will be for the rest of my life. On my deathbed, I am sure, I will gasp, 'But I still have five more books to write!'. . . I am happy and miserable and excited and devastated and encouraged and depressed all at the same time. But accepted or rejected, I will go on writing, because an idea in the head is like a rock in the shoe; I just can't wait to get it out." Naylor noted in her essay in *SAAS*, "No matter what type of characters I write about, . . . I am a part of each one—even the ugly, the foolish, and the evil. How else can I make them real on paper?" The author concluded by saying that she is lucky "to have the troop of noisy, chattering characters who travel with me inside my head. As long as they are poking, prodding, demanding a place in a book, I have things to do and stories to tell."

■ Works Cited

Draper, Charlotte W., review of *Night Cry, Horn Book*, June, 1984, p. 331.

Estes, Sally, review of *A String of Chances, Booklist*, August, 1982, p. 1518.

Flowers, Ann A., review of *The Keeper, Horn Book*, September-October, 1986, pp. 598-99.

Hearne, Betsy, review of *Shiloh, Bulletin of the Center for Children's Books*, October, 1991, p. 45.

Review of *The Keeper, Bulletin of the Center for Children's Books*, May, 1986, pp. 175-76.

Klockner, Karen M., review of *How I Came to Be a Writer, Horn Book*, August, 1978, pp. 410-11.

Langton, Jane, review of *Shiloh, New York Times Book Review*, May 10, 1992, p. 21.

Mandel, Ellen, review of *Saving Shiloh, Booklist*, September 1, 1997, p. 118.

Naylor, Phyllis Reynolds, *How I Came to Be a Writer*, Atheneum, 1978, revised edition, Aladdin Books, 1987.

Naylor, Phyllis Reynolds, essay in *Something about the Author Autobiography Series*, Volume 10, Gale, 1990.

Naylor, Rex, "Phyllis Reynolds Naylor," *Horn Book*, July-August, 1992, pp. 412-15.

Phelan, Carolyn, review of *Night Cry, Booklist*, July, 1984, p. 1550.

Rochman, Hazel, review of *Alice In-Between, Booklist*, May 1, 1994, p. 1601.

Review of *Shiloh, Kirkus Reviews*, September 1, 1991, p. 1163.

Review of *Shiloh Season, Kirkus Reviews*, July 15, 1995, p. 1053.

Review of *Shiloh Season, Publishers Weekly*, July 1, 1996, p. 60.

Stahl, John D., essay on Naylor in *Twentieth-Century Children's Writers*, 4th edition, edited by Laura Standley Berger, St. James Press, 1996.

Stevenson, Deborah, review of *Alice the Brave, Bulletin of the Center for Children's Books*, April, 1995, p. 283.

Stevenson, Deborah, review of *Alice in Lace, Bulletin of the Center for Children's Books*, April, 1996.

Stevenson, Deborah, review of *Achingly Alice, Bulletin of the Center for Children's Books*, April, 1998, pp. 290-91.

Sutton, Roger, review of *A String of Chances, School Library Journal*, September, 1982, p. 142.

Sutton, Roger, review of *Saving Shiloh, Horn Book*, September-October, 1997, p. 576.

Watson, Elizabeth S., review of *Shiloh, Horn Book*, January-February, 1992, pp. 78-79.

Watson, Elizabeth S., review of *Shiloh Season, Horn Book*, December, 1996, pp. 737-38.

Wilms, Denise M., review of *The Keeper, Booklist*, April 1, 1986, p. 1144.

■ For More Information See

BOOKS

Children's Literature Review, Volume 17, Gale, 1989.

Helbig, Alethea K., and Agnes Regan Perkins, *Dictionary of American Children's Fiction*, Greenwood Press, 2nd edition, 1990.

Holtze, Sally Holmes, editor, *Fifth Book of Junior Authors and Illustrators*, H. W. Wilson, 1983.

Silvey, Anita, editor, *Children's Books and Their Creators*, Houghton, 1995.

Twentieth-Century Young Adult Writers, St. James Press, 1994.

PERIODICALS

Bulletin of the Center for Children's Books, June, 1989, p. 261; January, 1999, pp. 176-77.

Horn Book, November-December, 1998, pp. 737-38.

Kirkus Reviews, September 15, 1998, p. 1387; February 1, 1999, p. 226.

Lion and the Unicorn, fall, 1977, pp. 1111-15.

Publishers Weekly, July 12, 1991, pp. 66-67; August 17, 1992, p. 501; October 17, 1994, p. 82; March 4, 1996, p. 67; October 5, 1998, p. 92.

Quill and Quire, January, 1996, p. 45.

School Library Journal, May, 1996, p. 114.

Voice of Youth Advocates, February, 1999, p. 446.

Washington Post, January 28, 1992, section E, p. 1.

Washington Post Book World, January 7, 1996, p. 10.

Washington Post Magazine, August 13, 1995, p. 14.

—*Sketch by Gerard J. Senick*

Mary Stewart

■ Personal

Born September 17, 1916, in Sunderland, Durham, England; daughter of Frederick Albert (a Church of England clergyman) and Mary Edith (Matthews) Rainbow; married Frederick Henry Stewart, 1945. *Education:* University of Durham, B.A. (first class honours), 1938, M.A., 1941. *Hobbies and other interests:* Music, painting, the theatre, gardening.

■ Addresses

Agent—c/o William Morrow & Co., 105 Madison Ave., New York, NY 10016.

■ Career

University of Durham, Durham, England, lecturer, 1941-45, part-time lecturer, 1948-55; writer, 1954—. *Wartime Service:* Royal Observer Corps, World War II. *Member:* PEN, Royal Society of Arts (fellow).

■ Awards, Honors

British Crime Writers Association Silver Dagger Award, 1961, for *My Brother Michael;* Mystery Writers of America Edgar Award, 1964, for *This Rough Magic;* Frederick Niven Literary Award, 1971, for *The Crystal Cave;* Scottish Arts Council Award, 1975, for *Ludo and the Star Horse;* fellow, Newnham College, Cambridge, 1986.

■ Writings

Madam, Will You Talk? (also see below), Hodder & Stoughton (London), 1955.

Wildfire at Midnight (also see below), Appleton (New York City), 1956.

Thunder on the Right, Hodder & Stoughton, 1957.

Nine Coaches Waiting (also see below), Hodder & Stoughton, 1958.

My Brother Michael (also see below), Hodder & Stoughton, 1960.

The Ivy Tree (also see below), Hodder & Stoughton, 1961, Mill (New York City), 1962.

The Moon-Spinners (also see below), Hodder & Stoughton, 1962.

Three Novels of Suspense (contains *Madam, Will You Talk?, Nine Coaches Waiting,* and *My Brother Michael*), Mill, 1963.

This Rough Magic (Literary Guild selection; also see below), Mill, 1964.

Airs above the Ground (also see below), Mill, 1965.

The Gabriel Hounds (Doubleday Book Club selection; Reader's Digest Condensed Book Club selection; Literary Guild alternate selection; also see below), Mill, 1967.

The Wind Off the Small Isles, Hodder & Stoughton, 1968.

The Spell of Mary Stewart (contains *This Rough Magic, The Ivy Tree,* and *Wildfire at Midnight*), Doubleday (New York City), 1968.

Mary Stewart Omnibus (contains *Madam, Will You Talk?, Wildfire at Midnight,* and *Nine Coaches Waiting*), Hodder & Stoughton, 1969.

The Crystal Cave (Literary Guild selection; also see below), Morrow (New York City), 1970.

The Little Broomstick (juvenile), Brockhampton Press (Leicester, England), 1971.

The Hollow Hills (also see below), Morrow, 1973.

Ludo and the Star Horse (juvenile), Brockhampton Press, 1974.

Touch Not the Cat (also see below), Morrow, 1976.

Triple Jeopardy (contains *My Brother Michael, The Moon-Spinners,* and *This Rough Magic*), Hodder & Stoughton, 1978.

Selected Works (contains *The Crystal Cave, The Hollow Hills, Wildfire at Midnight,* and *Airs above the Ground*), Heinemann (London), 1978.

The Last Enchantment (Literary Guild selection; also see below), Morrow, 1979.

A Walk in Wolf Wood, Morrow, 1980.

Mary Stewart's Merlin Trilogy (contains *The Crystal Cave, The Hollow Hills,* and *The Last Enchantment*), Morrow, 1980.

The Wicked Day, Morrow, 1983.

Mary Stewart—Four Complete Novels (contains *Touch Not the Cat, The Gabriel Hounds, This Rough Magic,* and *My Brother Michael*), Avenel Books (New York City), 1983.

Thornyhold, Morrow, 1988.

Frost on the Window and Other Poems, Morrow, 1990.

The Stormy Petrel, Morrow, 1991.

The Prince and the Pilgrim, Morrow, 1995.

Rose Cottage, Morrow, 1997.

Also author of radio plays, *Lift from a Stranger, Call Me at Ten-Thirty, The Crime of Mr. Merry* and *The Lord of Langdale,* produced by British Broadcasting Corporation, 1957-58. Stewart's works have been translated into sixteen languages, including Hebrew, Icelandic, and Slovak. The National Library of Scotland houses Stewart's manuscript collection.

■ Adaptations

The Moon-Spinners was filmed by Walt Disney in 1964.

■ Sidelights

Mary Stewart's writing career divides into two distinct parts. In her first period, according to Kay Mussell in the *St. James Guide to Crime and Mystery Writers,* Stewart "wrote a remarkable series of 10 popular novels of romantic suspense. . . . In her later phase, beginning in the late 1960s, Stewart's novels have been concerned with history and frequently with the occult. Her best-known work from this period is her four-volume series about King Arthur and Merlin." In the words of a *National Observer* critic, Stewart writes "like a magician, she conjures exotic moods and mysteries from mere words, her only aim to entertain."

Stewart explains in an article for *Writer* magazine: "I am first and foremost a teller of tales, but I am also a serious-minded woman who accepts the responsibilities of her job, and that job, if I am to be true to what is in me, is to say with every voice at my command: 'We must love and imitate the beautiful and the good.' It is a comment on our age that one hesitates to stand up and say this aloud."

While "predictability" is not a quality most authors would strive for, a *Christian Science Monitor* reviewer feels that this very trait is the secret of Stewart's success. Prior to 1970, for example, her plots followed a fairly consistent pattern of romance and suspense set in vividly depicted locales such as Provence, the Isle of Skye, the Pyrenees, Delphi, and Lebanon. Furthermore, notes the *Christian Science Monitor* reviewer, "Mrs. Stewart doesn't pull any tricks or introduce uncomfortable issues. Attractive, well-brought-up girls pair off with clean, confident young men, always on the side of the angels. And when the villains are finally rounded up, no doubts disturb us—it is clear that the best men have won again." The heroine of these stories is always "a girl displaying just the right combination of strengths and weaknesses. She may blunder into traps and misread most of the signals, but she will—feminine intuition being what it is—stumble onto something important. She will also need rescuing in a cliffhanging finale." In short, the reviewer concludes, "it all makes excellent escape fiction."

"One of Stewart's finest qualities as a writer," Mussell writes, "is her extraordinary descriptive prose. Stewart's ability to evoke a highly specific time and place, through sensuous descriptions of locale, character, and food, provides an immediacy that is often lacking in mystery fiction." Anthony Boucher in the *New York Times Book Review,* discussing *Airs above the Ground,* states that "nobody set forth the romantic feminine thriller with such grace and humor and vigor as Mary Stewart. . . . This is one of [her] best—which means escape fiction at its most enchanting."

Other critics have noted the same qualities in Stewart's writing. James Sandoe of the *New York Herald Tribune Book Review* calls *Madam, Will You*

In this 1973 novel Stewart describes how the prophetic Merlin aids Arthur in his quest to become king.

Talk? "a distinctly charming, romantic thriller . . . [that is] intelligently soft-boiled, pittypat and a good deal of fun." *My Brother Michael,* according to Francis Iles of the *Guardian,* is "the contemporary thriller at its very best." Speaking of the same novel, Christopher Pym of the *Spectator* comments: "Mary Stewart gives each of her admirable novels an exotically handsome (if somewhat rather travel-folderish) setting. . . . The Greek landscape and—much more subtle—the Greek character are splendidly done, in a long, charmingly written, highly evocative, imperative piece of required reading for an Hellenic cruise." Boucher, too, finds the book worthy of praise: "This detective adventure, rich in action and suspense, is seen through the eyes of a characteristic Stewart heroine; and surely there are few more attractive young women in today's popular fiction. . . . These girls are as far removed as you can imagine from the Idiot Heroine who disfigures (at least for men) so much romantic fiction."

Historical Sagas Focus on Merlin

In 1970, Stewart turned to historical fiction. The main focus of this new interest was Arthurian England, especially as seen through the eyes of Merlin the magician. Liz Holliday in the *St. James Guide to Fantasy Writers* believes Stewart's Merlin character "is an intriguing mixture of pragmatist and fey, believer and agnostic. He has visions, true dreams in which he sees what is and what is to come. These, he believes, come from a god. . . . At the same time he is portrayed as a polymath, dedicated to understanding the world through scholarship in the fields of science, mathematics and engineering."

Unlike most other authors who have written about the legends of Camelot in terms of the Middle Ages, Stewart places her story in more historically accurate fifth-century Britain. Reviewing *The Crystal Cave,* the first of three books on Merlin, a *Best Sellers* critic writes: "Fifth century Britain and Brittany come to life in Miss Stewart's vigorous imagination. . . . Those who have read and enjoyed the many novels of Mary Stewart will not need to be told this is an expertly fashioned continually absorbing story, with a facile imagination fleshing out the legend of the parentage of the future King Arthur—and, too, of Merlin himself." A *Books and Bookmen* critic calls it "a highly plotted and rattling good yarn. Mary Stewart's evo-

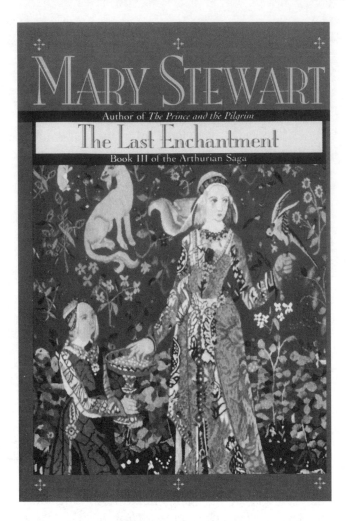

Now king, Arthur seeks Merlin's help to retain his position in Camelot in this 1979 novel.

cation of an era of magic, as well as of bloodletting, is magnificently done. Her writing is virile, and of a very high quality indeed. Her descriptions of the countryside are often moving, also poetical."

Martin Levin of the *New York Times Book Review,* after reminding readers that little is actually known of Merlin's life, notes that "the author obligingly expands [Merlin's] myth into a first person history. . . . Cheerfully disclaiming authenticity, Miss Stewart . . . lightens the Dark Ages with legend, pure invention and a lively sense of history." A *Christian Science Monitor* reviewer, however, finds this type of "history" to be somewhat compromised by the author's emphasis on Merlin's magical powers. "There really is little 'magic' in the story," the reviewer begins, "and what there

is rarely exceeds the familiar 'knowing before the event.' But the very uncertainty of its inclusion lends a certain falseness to an otherwise absorbing story, which has been carefully researched historically so that it is peripherally authentic." At any rate, the reviewer concludes, "*The Crystal Cave*

If you enjoy the works of Mary Stewart, you may also want to check out the following books and films:

Mike Ashley, *The Pendragon Chronicles,* 1990.
Stephen R. Lawhead, the "Pendragon Cycle," including *Merlin,* 1988.
Morgan Llywelyn, *Lion of Ireland: The Legend of Brian Boru,* 1979.
Excalibur, a film about the life of King Arthur, 1981.

---

evokes an England long gone and could prove an interesting guidebook to some of the less touristy attractions of the Cornish and Welsh countryside." *The Hollow Hills,* a continuation of Merlin's story in which he helps Arthur become king of all Britain, was also fairly well-received. A *Publishers Weekly* critic calls it "romantic, refreshing and most pleasant reading. . . . Mrs. Stewart has steeped herself well in the folklore and known history of fifth century Britain and she makes of her feuding, fighting warlords lively and intriguing subjects." A *Best Sellers* critic writes: "All in all, this makes a smashing good tale. The suspense is superb and the reader is kept involved in the unwinding of the plot. Miss Stewart has taken the main lines of the Arthurian legend and has developed the basic elements in a plausible way."

Joseph McLellan of the *Washington Post Book World* finds the third Merlin book, *The Last Enchantment,* to be somewhat anti-climactic. "Having used two long, exciting novels to get Arthur on the throne," he writes, "Miss Stewart has reached the final volume of her trilogy and we can settle back expecting to hear the old stories told again with her unique touch. There is only one trouble with this expectation: Mary Stewart does not fulfill it, and she quite clearly never had any intentions of fulfilling it. Her story is not strictly about Arthur but about Merlin. . . . Strictly speaking, once

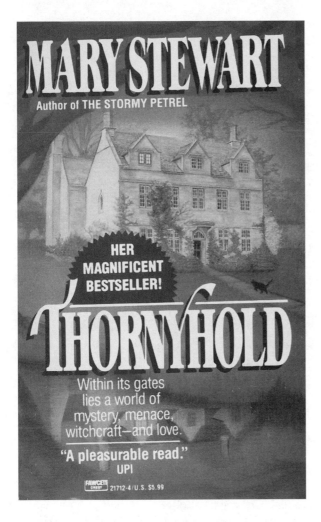

MARY STEWART
Author of THE STORMY PETREL

HER MAGNIFICENT BESTSELLER!

THORNYHOLD

Within its gates lies a world of mystery, menace, witchcraft—and love.

"A pleasurable read."
UPI

21712-4 / U.S. $5.99

Gilly is unprepared for the strange and mysterious happenings surrounding the cottage she recently inherited from her beloved godmother in this 1988 work.

Arthur is safely on the throne . . . Merlin's life work is over. He spends most of *The Last Enchantment* fading away as gracefully as he can manage. . . . [As a result of this shift in emphasis,] the role of Arthur in this volume is fitful and erratic; he is a powerful presence but not the central character."

Very much aware of the difficulties involved in gathering and making sense out of the confusing source material available on Merlin's life, McLellan praises Stewart for "the ingenuity of [her] effort," though he feels that the story's ultimate plausibility is somewhat in doubt. "She gives us . . . traditional materials," he notes, "but the treatment is her own, the emphasis shifted for her purpose,

which is not simply to recast old material but to bring alive a long-dead historical epoch—not the Middle Ages of Malory but the Dark Ages of the original Arthur. This she does splendidly. Fifth-century Britain is caught in these pages, and while it may lack some of the exotic glitter of the imaginary 12th-century Britain that Arthur usually inhabits, it is a fascinating place."

Arthurian Drama

Stewart followed her Merlin Trilogy with one last book based on the Arthurian legends, *The Wicked Day*, a tale told by Arthur's bastard son Mordred. According to Arthurian tradition, Mordred is the cause of Arthur's eventual downfall. He has a "bad reputation as Arthur's mean-spirited, traitorous, regicidal son," as Roy Hoffman explains in the *New York Times Book Review*.

But in Stewart's version of the story, Mordred is more a tragic figure in the drama than a conscious agent of destruction. "Stewart," Hoffman writes, "attempts to resurrect him as a compassionate young man who is helpless before fate." M. Jean Greenlaw in the *Journal of Reading* finds that "Stewart shapes a sense of the inevitable doom of Camelot, not by Mordred's desire but by the fateful actions of many men and women." Mary Mills in *School Library Journal* concludes that "Stewart has created flesh and blood characters out of legends, and in doing so has crafted a well-plotted and passionate drama." Holliday believes that "telling the tale from Mordred's point of view works splendidly. It allows his character to emerge as much more complex and sympathetic than it might otherwise have done. Here, Mordred is clearly as much a victim . . . as Arthur ever was, and his attempts to overcome the weakness of character that leads him to his final clash with his father make him an engaging, if not wholly likeable, character."

In an article for *Philological Quarterly*, Maureen Fries compares Stewart's treatment of Arthurian legend with that of T. H. White, the author of *The Once and Future King*. "Of all literary genres," Fries begins, "romance is perhaps the most irrational, focusing as it does upon the strange, the marvelous, and the supernatural. And of all the 'matters' of romance, that of Britain contains the most irrationalities." But Fries concludes that "in making over medieval romance into modern novels, T. H. White and Mary Stewart have not only coped, mostly successfully, with the irrationality of the Matter of Britain. They have also grasped and translated into a convincing modern, if diverse, idiom that rational core of truth about human psychology, and the human condition, which constitutes not only the greatness of the Arthurian legend but also its enduring appeal to readers of all centuries and all countries, and to writers of every time and every literary persuasion."

In the early 1980s Stewart continued writing medieval tales. *A Walk in Wolf Wood* concerns two modern-day children who are thrust backwards in time to the Middle Ages. "The eerie events that overtake [the children] become the vehicle for an incisive exploration of magic, savagery and the mis-uses of power," observes Mary Cadogan in the *Times Literary Supplement*. "The trappings of another time like jousts and hunts, terraces and towers, are vivid and atmospheric but not overdone."

Explaining her decision to switch from writing thrillers to historical fiction, Stewart once commented: "I always planned that some day I would write a historical novel, and I intended to use Roman Britain as the setting. This is a period that I have studied over many years. But then, quite by chance, I came across a passage in Geoffrey of Monmouth's *History of the Kings of Britain*, which described the first appearance of Merlin, the Arthurian 'enchanter.' Here was a new story, offering a new approach to a dark and difficult period, with nothing known about the 'hero' except scraps of legend. The story would have to come purely from imagination, pitched somewhere between legend and truth and fairy-tale and known history. The setting would be imaginary, too, a Dark Age Britain in the unrecorded aftermath of the Roman withdrawal. I had originally no intention of writing more than one volume, but the story seized my imagination. . . . It has been a tough job and a rewarding one. I have learned a lot, not least that the powerful themes of the Arthurian 'Matter of Britain' are as cogent and real today as they were fourteen centuries ago. And Merlin's story has allowed me to return to my first avocation of all, that of poet."

■ Works Cited

Best Sellers, July 15, 1970.

Best Sellers, July 15, 1973.

Books and Bookmen, August, 1970.

Boucher, Anthony, review of *My Brother Michael*, *New York Times Book Review*, April 10, 1960.

Boucher, Anthony, review of *Airs above the Ground*, *New York Times Book Review*, October 24, 1965.

Cadogan, Mary, *Times Literary Supplement*, July 18, 1980, p. 806.

Christian Science Monitor, September 28, 1967.

Christian Science Monitor, September 3, 1970.

Fries, Maureen, *Philological Quarterly*, spring, 1977, pp. 259-265.

Greenlaw, M. Jean, *Journal of Reading*, May, 1984, p. 741.

Hoffman, Roy, *New York Times Book Review*, January 1, 1984, p. 20.

Holliday, Liz, *St. James Guide to Fantasy Writers*, St. James Press, 1996.

Review of *The Hollow Hills*, *Publishers Weekly*, May 28, 1973.

Iles, Frances, review of *My Brother Michael*, *Guardian*, February 26, 1960.

Levin, Martin, *New York Times Book Review*, August 9, 1970.

McLellan, Joseph, *Washington Post Book World*, July 22, 1979.

Mills, Mary, *School Library Journal*, March, 1984, p. 178.

Mussell, Kay, *St. James Guide to Crime and Mystery Writers*, 4th edition, St. James Press, 1996.

National Observer, October 23, 1967.

Pym, Christopher, review of *My Brother Michael*, *Spectator*, March 18, 1960.

Sandoe, James, review of *Madam, Will You Talk?*, *New York Herald Tribune Book Review*, May 27, 1956.

Writer, May, 1970, pp. 9-12, 46.

■ For More Information See

BOOKS

Contemporary Literary Criticism, Gale (Detroit), Volume 7, 1977; Volume 35, 1985.

Friedman, Lenemaja, *Mary Stewart*, Twayne (Boston), 1990.

Newquist, Roy, *Counterpoint*, Rand McNally, 1964.

PERIODICALS

Arthurian Interpretations, spring, 1987, pp. 70-83.

Best Sellers, October 1, 1967; November, 1976.

Booklist, April 15, 1992, p. 1547.

Book Week, November 21, 1965.

Harper's, September, 1970.

Kirkus Reviews, August 1, 1983, p. 840; July 15, 1991, p. 887.

Library Journal, June 15, 1973.

New Statesman, November 5, 1965.

New York Herald Tribune Book Review, October 5, 1958; March 8, 1959; March 4, 1962.

New York Times, March 18, 1956; September 9, 1956; May 18, 1958; January 18, 1959.

New York Times Book Review, January 7, 1962; October 15, 1967; July 29, 1973; September 2, 1979.

Publishers Weekly, September 16, 1988; July 12, 1991.

San Francisco Chronicle, October 21, 1956; May 22, 1960.

Sunday Times Colour Supplement, June 13, 1976.

Time, January 5, 1968.

Times Educational Supplement, February 5, 1982, p. 28.

Washington Post Book World, March 31, 1968; September 15, 1976.*

—Sketch by Stanley Olson

Vincent van Gogh

Major collections of van Gogh's work are located in Otterlo and at the Rijksmuseum Vincent Van Gogh in Amsterdam. Masterworks include *Bearers of the Burden*, 1880; *Potato Eaters*, 1885; *Père Tanguy*, 1887; *Orchard*, 1888; *Sailing Boats at Les Saintes Maries*, 1888; *Postman Roulin*, 1888; *Sunflowers*, 1888; *The Night Café*, 1888; *The Arlesienne*, 1888; *Starry Night*, 1889; *Portrait of Dr. Gachet*, 1890; *Wheatfield with Crows*, 1890.

■ Writings

Verzamelde Brieven, edited by J. Van Gogh-Bonger, four volumes, 1952-54, and two volumes, 1955, published as *Complete Letters*, [Greenwich, CT], three volumes, 1958.

Correspondance complete, enrichie de tous les dessins originaux, edited by Georges Charensol, three volumes, [Paris], 1960.

Van Gogh: A Self-Portrait, edited by W. H. Auden, [Greenwich, CT], 1961.

Letters, edited by Mark Roskill, [London], 1963, [New York], 1967.

Dagboek, edited by Jan Hulsker, [Amsterdam], 1970, published as *Diary*, [New York], 1971.

■ Sidelights

"What I'm trying to do is not to faithfully imitate on canvas what I see before me but rather to use color in the most arbitrary way to express myself better."

—*Vincent van Gogh*

■ Personal

Born March 30, 1853 in Zundert, Netherlands; committed suicide July 29, 1890, in Auvers-sur-Oise, France; son of Theodorus (a church pastor) and Anna Cornelia (a homemaker; maiden name, Carbentus) van Gogh. *Education:* Attended schools in Zundert, Zevenbergen, and Tilburg, Netherlands, to age fifteen.

■ Career

Worked as apprentice for the Goupil Gallery picture dealers in The Hague, 1869-74, London, 1874-75, and Paris, 1875-76; taught in English schools in Ramsgate and Isleworth, 1876; worked in a bookshop, Dordrecht, 1877; prepared for theology study, then took an evangelist course in Brussels, and worked as a missionary in the coal-mining Borinage district of Belgium, 1879; focused attention on his drawing from 1880, living with his family off and on, and in other Dutch towns until 1886 (attended Antwerp Academy briefly, 1885-86); lived in Paris, 1886-88; institutionalized as epileptic in Arles, 1889, Saint-Remy, 1889-90, and Auvers-sur-Oise, 1890.

Vincent van Gogh's troubled life and tragic death have fascinated people since he committed suicide over hundred years ago. The paintings and drawings he left have appreciated considerably in that time and are now among the most valuable and popular in the world. The unmistakable intensity of his work—his color sense, use of pigments, and above all, his emotional expression—has influenced many of the greatest artists of the twentieth century. And the indelible images he created, including numerous self-portraits, raucous sunflowers, and the swirling blues of the night sky, are some of the most copied in history.

Born in Zundert, Netherlands, on March 30, 1853, Vincent Willem van Gogh was raised in a small Netherlands town where his father, the Reverend Theodorus van Gogh, was the pastor of the town's Calvinist church. Van Gogh's mother, Anna Cornelia Carbentus, was a woman of formidable character who busied herself with local charity work and shouldered the lion's share of responsibility for bringing up her six children, of whom Vincent was the oldest. Beginning in early childhood, van Gogh struggled with the demands of society. He was unusually shy and spent a lot of time by himself. He also had a very quick temper and sometimes became violent. Yet he loved to wander in the countryside collecting flowers and insects, observing the colors of the sunset or watching the wind move the leaves. The only person close to van Gogh was his younger brother Theo, who was able to draw him out and get him to talk about his problems. Throughout their lives,

Van Gogh painted *La chambre de Vincent à Arles* ("The Artist's Bedroom at Arles") in 1889, during his stay in the small French town of Arles.

Theo consistently supported his brother emotionally and financially. Much is known about the artist's life from the many letters exchanged by the two over the years.

Van Gogh's school years were not particularly notable. He was uninterested and often unruly, but he did spend time reading the many books in his father's library and seemed truly inspired by his father's Sunday sermons. His parents were at a loss to handle this child, though his mother was sympathetic and encouraged the boy in his early attempts to express himself through drawing.

When van Gogh was sixteen, his father arranged for him to work in an art gallery with his uncle in The Hague. The family hoped that his interest in art would lead him to a successful career in the gallery world. He did well at first and enjoyed being around the sculptures and paintings that came through the gallery. After a few years van Gogh was sent to work in a branch office in London. There he was able to visit several world-renowned museums and view works by British artists. But his happiness in London did not last long. He fell in love with a young woman who rejected him; the artist was deeply wounded and returned to his sullen, often volatile behavior.

Religious Mission

Still seeking answers to the questions about himself that had plagued him as a boy, van Gogh turned to religion. He became fervently involved in religious ideas and missionary work over the next few years. By the time he was twenty-five, he was working as a missionary in the coal-mining region of Belgium. He had given away most of his belongings and lived in a shack. But his fanaticism, manifested by an overzealous devotion to his work, actually led to his termination by the missionary organization for which he worked.

All along he continued to draw. His work from this period features miners and peasants living in the most dire of circumstances, in dingy huts with little food. He drew groups of women staggering under huge loads of coal on their backs. His most famous work inspired by this time—though it was painted several years after he left the area—is the *Potato Eaters.* The family of peasants gathered around the table in their dark hovel have only a plate of potatoes to share. Their weathered hands

If you enjoy the works of Vincent van Gogh, you may also want to check out the following:

The paintings of Paul Gaugin, including *Tahitian Landscape,* 1891.
The works of Claude Monet, including *Impression: Sunrise,* 1872, and *Water Lilies,* 1916-23.
The art of Pierre-Auguste Renoir, including *le Moulin de la Galette,* 1876.

indicate hard labor, their faces fatigue and despair. The colors in the painting, mostly black, brown, and gray, are typical of van Gogh's work in these days. The artist shows with great sympathy the wretched condition of the people he was trying to help and his own sadness as well. "Life has the color of dishwater," he wrote to Theo. Still, despite his uncertainties, van Gogh was increasingly convinced that he was destined to become an artist.

The next few years found van Gogh wandering both physically and psychologically. He lived for a time in Brussels, Belgium, and in The Hague, where he studied with several artists. He also resided with his parents on several occasions, but these episodes always ended with him leaving in anger. In a pattern that would plague him throughout his life, he forged weak relationships with women that ended badly. Spells of depression and illness, a regular occurrence when he lived in cold apartments with little to eat, were common in these years, relieved only by van Gogh's work. Theo faithfully wrote to him from Paris, where he was working in a gallery, sending money and words of encouragement.

In the fall of 1885, van Gogh moved to Antwerp, Belgium. He seemed to be functioning more fully, socializing with other painters and visiting galleries and museums. He was especially fascinated by the works of Flemish painter Peter Paul Rubens. The active figures, unrestrained emotion, and rich colors bewitched van Gogh, who began to use some of these elements in his work. At the port of Antwerp, he came across woodblock prints from Japan and China, which caught his eye for their brightness and flat, clear colors.

Meets Impressionists in Paris

In the winter of 1886, van Gogh once again became ill. After several weeks of recovery, he decided to join Theo in Paris. The reunited brothers shared an apartment. Van Gogh's two years in Paris were very stimulating. Theo introduced him to the young, struggling artists of the day, including Claude Monet, Pierre-Auguste Renoir, Henri Toulouse-Lautrec, Georges Seurat, Edgar Degas, and Camille Pissarro. Van Gogh spent many hours at Paris cafés with these painters, most of whom would come to be called impressionists, discussing the newest notions concerning color, light, and nature. The effects on van Gogh's work were immediate; his colors became lighter and more vivid and his subjects less disturbed.

During his second winter in Paris, van Gogh met Paul Gauguin, another painter who was searching for purpose and expression in his art. They became friends, and van Gogh was able to exhibit some of his paintings in a shop owned by

Fascinated with the color yellow and sunflowers, van Gogh painted this version of *Sunflowers* in 1888.

Gauguin's father. But he did not sell anything. In fact, he had never sold a single piece.

While in Paris van Gogh began using himself as a model more frequently; over fifteen self-portraits from a three-year period, 1887-90, have survived. Other artists, among them the German Albrecht Dürer and van Gogh's countryman Rembrandt, left a series of self-portraits, so one can see their stylistic development as well as the process of aging. But van Gogh's self-portraits are different; there is little movement in time but an incredible range of emotions and psychological states. In those three years, one can see van Gogh as a dapper gentleman of Paris, a rail-thin, ghostly painter clutching his palette and brushes, a seemingly cruel, sunken-cheeked creature, and a doomed and pathetic figure, the space encircling him filled with tense and disorienting swirls. What ties the self-portraits together is the ability of the artist to illustrate the force of his experiences through his use of color, distortion of form, and control of brush strokes. These are the techniques that would lead art critics to label van Gogh's style expressionism.

By the winter of 1888, van Gogh's mental condition had begun to deteriorate; perhaps the gloomy weather and lack of financial success were too much. The painter also began to feel that he was becoming a burden on his brother. One day he packed his case, left a note for Theo, and took the train to Arles, a town in the south of France near the Mediterranean Sea. The impact of the warm, sunny climate and beautiful surroundings was enormous. Van Gogh began painting with remarkable vigor. With his brush, he captured orchards, riverbanks, bridges, flowers, haystacks, wheat fields, and sailboats, and with each painting his colors got lighter and brighter until he was using pure color right out of the paint tubes, often applying it in thick splotches. This creative energy, much of it expelled in extreme heat and heavy exposure to sunlight, eventually exhausted him. At the same time, van Gogh seemed to become obsessed with the color yellow; for several weeks he painted nothing but sunflowers. These would one day become some of his most beloved work.

His letters to and from Theo brought van Gogh into close contact with the local postman, who, along with his family, befriended the painter and often served as his model. Arguably his most fa-

The Starry Night, **painted in 1889, is considered one of van Gogh's most powerful night pictures.**

mous portraits from this period are *Postman Roulin* and *La Berceuse,* a painting of the postman's wife. Also from this time emerged scenes of the local café and of van Gogh's room. In the fall of 1888, Gauguin came to Arles to live with van Gogh and for a while, the two supported each other and lived together peacefully. Van Gogh hoped other artists from Paris would join them and start an artists' community in Arles. But Gauguin did not find Arles as inspiring as had his colleague, nor did he find it easy to live in such close proximity to van Gogh's frenzied working style. Increasingly violent quarrels ensued until finally, Gauguin announced in December 1888 that he was leaving. This abandonment was beyond van Gogh's fragile coping skills; he suffered a severe mental breakdown during which he cut off part of his earlobe. When he recovered enough to leave the hospital, he painted two self-portraits showing his bandaged head underneath a fur cap.

Months after his break with Gauguin, van Gogh entered an asylum, where he hoped to find some peace. He was able to paint there, but the wild brush strokes and severe irregularity of the forms depicted in these works suggest that peace was nowhere to be found. The artist did regain some stability by the fall of 1889, but he worried constantly about his future and his continuing dependence on Theo.

Makes His Only Sale

In early 1890 van Gogh was given a boost by the news that Theo had sold one of his paintings. It was the first and only painting sold during his lifetime. This led to such now-prized works as *Cornfield with Reaper* and the *Starry Night,* which illuminates the sparkling, spiraling starlight over Arles. Still, the twisted, rigid shapes of these efforts hint that van Gogh was not past his mental infirmities.

By the spring of 1890, van Gogh felt the need to return to Paris to be near Theo, who set him up in a room in a small town near Paris under the care of a specialist. The doctor was also an art lover and encouraged van Gogh to continue painting, even sitting as a model for him. Van Gogh attacked his canvases as a man possessed in these spring months, producing over sixty paintings, among them *Wheatfield with Crows.* But black days began to bury the artist, and soon a severe depression overcame him. On July 27, 1890, he shot himself in the abdomen. He survived for two days, Theo ever by his side, his death occurring in Auvers-sur-Oise, France.

Like many artists before him, van Gogh was keenly intent on uncovering the beauty of nature and the extent of his feelings. What sets him apart from the artists who preceded him and also links him to modern artists, was his ability to do away with "accuracy" of shape and color in order to graphically express his emotions. The colors he

employed, while perhaps not "realistic," depicted the life of his subjects; his bold brush strokes gave motion to trees, stars, flowers, and the very air. And although viewers of his time found his paintings crude and even frightening, contemporary observers have come to understand and fully appreciate van Gogh's unique and enduring artistic vision.

■ **For More Information See**

BOOKS

Crispino, Enrica, *Van Gogh,* translated by Deborah Misuri-Charkham, Peter Bedrick, 1996.

Dobrin, Arnold, *I Am a Stranger on the Earth: The Story of Vincent Van Gogh,* F. Warne, 1975.

Hammacher, Abraham Marie, *Van Gogh: A Documentary Biography,* Macmillan, 1982.

Lucas, Eileen, *Vincent Van Gogh,* Franklin Watts, 1991.

Muhlberger, Richard, *What Makes a Van Gogh a Van Gogh?,* Viking, 1993.

Sweetman, David, *Van Gogh: His Life and His Art,* Crown Publishers, 1990.

Tyson, Peter, *Vincent van Gogh: Artist,* Chelsea House, 1996.

Venezia, Mike, *Van Gogh,* Children's Press, 1988.

Robb White

■ Personal

Born June 20, 1909, in the Philippine Islands; son of Robb and Placidia (Bridgers) White; married Rosalie Mason, 1937 (divorced, 1964); married Joan Gibbs; children: Robb, Barbara, June. *Education:* U.S. Naval Academy, B.S., 1931.

■ Career

Writer. Has worked variously as book clerk, draftsman, construction engineer, and deck-hand on a sailboat. *Military service:* U.S. Navy, 1941-45; attained rank of ensign; recalled to active duty, 1947-48; served in aviation administration and public information; attained rank of captain.

■ Awards, Honors

Spring Book Festival Award for older children, *New York Herald Tribune*, 1937, for *Smuggler's Sloop*; Commonwealth Club of California, 1967, for *Silent Ship, Silent Sea*; Edgar Allan Poe Award, 1973, for *Deathwatch*.

■ Writings

The Nub, illustrated by Andrew Wyeth, Little, Brown, 1935.
Smuggler's Sloop, illustrated by Andrew Wyeth, Little, Brown, 1937.
Midshipman Lee, Little, Brown, 1938.
Run Masked, Knopf, 1938.
In Privateer's Bay, Harper, 1939.
Three Against the Sea, Harper, 1940.
Sailor in the Sun, Harper, 1941.
The Lion's Paw, Doubleday, 1946.
Secret Sea, Doubleday, 1947.
Sail Away, Doubleday, 1948.
Candy, Doubleday, 1949.
The Haunted Hound, Doubleday, 1950.
Deep Danger, Doubleday, 1952.
Our Virgin Island, Doubleday, 1953.
Midshipman Lee of the Naval Academy, Random House, 1954.
Up Periscope, Doubleday, 1956.
Flight Deck, Doubleday, 1961.
Torpedo Run, Doubleday, 1962.
The Survivor, Doubleday, 1964.
Surrender, Doubleday, 1966.
Silent Ship, Silent Sea, Doubleday, 1967.
No Man's Land, Doubleday, 1969.
Deathwatch, Doubleday, 1972.
The Frogmen, Doubleday, 1973.
The Long Way Down, Doubleday, 1977.
Fire Storm, Doubleday, 1979.
Two on the Isle: A Memory of Marina Cay, Norton, 1985.

Author of screenplays *Macabre, House on Haunted Hill, 13 Ghosts, The Tingler,* and *Homicidal.* Also author of scripts for *Silent Service, Perry Mason, Men of Annapolis,* and other television programs.

■ Sidelights

Robb White once commented: "The fact that I am a writer is not because I'm a genius, nor have a great talent, nor even that accusation of well-wishers, 'flair.' I have rigid discipline. When working for DuPont as a construction engineer in the miserable snow of New Castle, Pennsylvania, I came back every night to one dank room in a boarding house and wrote—every night—from eight until two in the morning. Even now, when I don't have to anymore, I come into this elegant office . . . at eight in the morning and go to work."

Robb White has led a life filled with adventure and mishap, as he related in his *Something about the Author Autobiography Series (SAAS)* essay. The son of an Episcopalian missionary, White was born in the Philippine Islands and lived among the Igorots, a tribe whom he describes as "a handsome and fearsome people, famed for head-hunting and instant wars, with bronze-colored skin and straight black hair; a mixture of Malay, Indonesian, and Negroid peoples." White and his parents returned to the United States in time for him to attend elementary school in Tarboro, North Carolina, where his most vivid memory is of being bullied by the other children during recess for his odd clothes and British accent. White has claimed he did not learn anything in the American public schools he attended during his childhood: "I managed to be promoted to the eighth grade without learning anything at all," he wrote in his *SAAS* essay. Finally, while living in Virginia, White was sent to the Episcopal High School at Alexandria, "a school which intended to *teach* people things. I had decided when I was thirteen that I was going to be a writer and the Episcopal High School introduced me to Latin and English literature, to history and geography. I think they tried to teach me other things such as math, chemistry, physics, but I couldn't see why a writer would need to know that sort of stuff, so I didn't pay much attention," White continued.

After high school, White was admitted to the U.S. Naval Academy where discipline was rigid and he came to regret his earlier avoidance of science

and mathematics. At the end of four years, and despite the fact that, as he wrote in his *SAAS* essay, "I really *liked* the Navy," White resigned his commission in order to be a full-time writer. When his money began to run low, he found work as a draftsman for a subsidiary of DuPont, and was eventually transferred to New Castle, Pennsylvania, where he began to write in earnest. "In New Castle I never had a date, never went to a movie, never had a drink in a saloon. All I did was try to be writer." The sale of his first short story meant the end of White's career with DuPont, as he immediately resigned and joined the crew of a small sailboat headed for the West Indies.

Literary Life Begins

After numerous mishaps at sea, White landed on Dominica, an island in the British West Indies, where he was able to write and sell enough stories to support himself. After the sale of his first book, *The Nub,* White returned to Georgia, in pursuit of Rosalie Mason, called Rodie, a girl he had met as a teenager. They eventually married and moved to the British Virgin Islands, where they bought a tiny island named Marina Cay from the government for $60. The announcement that his second book, *Smuggler's Sloop,* had won a literary prize convinced the couple to build a comfortable house on the island and make it their permanent home. Based on these years, White concluded that "life on a desert island is about as fine as you can get." Then illness, a run-in with the government, and the onset of World War II put an end to the Whites' life on Marina Cay; White was recalled to active duty in the Navy and did not return to his family for seven years. This period of his life forms the basis of *Two on the Isle: A Memory of Marina Cay,* White's well-received memoir, which a critic in *Kirkus Reviews* dubbed "bittersweet fun, laced with jolly pidgin from silver-tongued natives."

When White was finally released from the Navy, he separated from his wife and began to travel extensively throughout the world, while continuing to write primarily adventure stories for young adults, as well as becoming involved with television and film script writing. White eventually settled in Malibu, outside Hollywood, to write film scripts, and then in a suburb of Santa Barbara, where he later remarried. White once remarked: "I write [for and about young people]

Winner of an Edgar Award from the Mystery Writers of America

DEATHWATCH

In the desert without clothes, food, or water and hunted by a madman with a .358 Magnum

ROBB WHITE

Ben finds himself in a life and death situation after he is hired as a guide by a ruthless hunter in this 1972 work.

because there is some hero in every one of them—for awhile, maybe forever. And I admire a hero. I admire a man who can survive and help others to survive when conditions insist that he cannot survive. I write about children because to me they seem to have a pure courage and undoubting faith in their ability that growing old so often erodes. My people are decent and stay decent when it is to their benefit not to, because I think the young are decent and modest people. So these are the people I write to and about—good, decent, courageous and polite people."

"Robb White is an acknowledged master of the adventure yarn," wrote John W. Conner in a re-

view of White's novel *Deathwatch* in *English Journal*. Other reviewers concur, typically praising White's works for their fast-paced plots, likeable characters, and fully realized adventures. Although he is sometimes criticized for creating implausible scenarios or exaggeratedly good heroes, critics often remark that the exotic setting and fast-paced action of most White stories ensure their popularity with young people, particularly boys.

Sea Tales

Many of White's works take advantage of the author's knowledge of the sea and sailing, providing background detail and setting. In *Secret Sea*, an early effort, a young ex-naval officer goes in search of Aztec treasure reputedly sunk in the Caribbean, aided by a fifteen-year-old boy. A *Booklist* contributor remarked that despite some "unlikely" elements in the plot, "the reader has the feeling of sharing adventures firsthand." Similarly, another reviewer for *Booklist* dubbed *Candy*, in which a young boat-loving woman befriends a mysterious stranger and a homeless blind boy determined to evade institutionalization, "vastly entertaining." *New York Times Book Review* critic Margery Fisher singled out realistic dialogue and endearing characters for praise in her review of *Candy*, concluding: "This is highly recommended for girls and boys." Somewhat less successfully, White's *No Man's Land* relates the adventures of Garth, a young man sent to the Pacific by the government, who suspects an American expatriate he meets there of murder and theft. Loretta B. Jones, writing in *Library Journal*, found the plot a confusing "mishmash of incredible action."

Some of White's best-known sea adventures are set during World War II. In *Up Periscope*, a young man is sent by submarine to capture a Japanese code that is being used to relay secret information about American forces during World War II. Critics praised the tension inherent in the author's descriptions of life aboard a submarine under attack. *New York Times Book Review* contributor Henry B. Lent described *Up Periscope* as "well conceived, splendidly written." *The Survivor* also features a young American officer sent on a difficult mission against the Japanese during World War II; Jane Manthorne remarked in *Horn Book* that the plot "makes for edge-of-the-chair reading." White returned to the area where he was born for the setting of *Surrender*, which depicts the

Japanese invasion of the Philippine Islands after the attack on Pearl Harbor through the eyes of two young American naval officers and two orphaned Filipino-American children. Gerald Gottlieb described the result in *Sunday World Journal Tribune Book Week* as "a fiercely exciting tale." Though other critics did not consistently find the plot of *Surrender* realistic or its outcome original, several agreed that its themes—"the ugliness of war and the beauty of the human spirit," in the words of a *Times Literary Supplement* reviewer—along with its fast-paced action, would capture the interest of young readers.

Other White books which focus on naval action during World War II include *Silent Ship, Silent Sea*, "a taut war novel," according to E. Louise Davis

A boy is unfairly accused of setting a forest fire by a fire warden who eventually learns the truth in this fast-paced novel.

in *School Library Journal*. This work centers on young Kelsey Devereux, who is mistakenly ordered into battle aboard a destroyer during the Battle of the Solomon Islands without receiving any training. After a humiliating panic-inspired incident, Kelsey redeems himself and earns his captain's respect in what a *Publishers Weekly* contributor called "a heroic tale." White's *The Frogmen* explores similar territory in the story of a group of naval officers assigned to sneak into a Japanese-controlled harbor, disarm underwater mines they have never before encountered, and radio their success to Pearl Harbor before they escape. *New York Times Book Review* critic Robert Hood enthused: "Robb White . . . takes his characters to the limits of their endurance—and then tightens the screw one-half turn. They squirm and so will you."

Deathwatch

One of White's most enduring works, *Deathwatch*, dubbed "a classic" by Judith Druse in *Voice of Youth Advocates*, is a departure from the majority of his other novels in that it is set among hunters in the mountains. Described by *School Library Journal* reviewer Judith Higgins as an "uncomplicated good vs. raw evil" adventure, *Deathwatch* centers on an idealistic college student, Ben, who reluctantly agrees to act as a hunting guide for Madec, a wealthy businessman, in order to earn money to continue his schooling. Madec's accidental murder of another hunter sparks the novel's central conflict as Madec offers to pay for the remainder of Ben's education if he agrees to continue with the hunt. When Ben refuses, Madec strips him and sets him free to make the forty-five mile trek back to civilization without any supplies. While most critics praised those elements, such as suspenseful plot and detailed realization of setting and character, common to White's best-loved adventure stories, Elizabeth Finlayson added in her *School Librarian* review that *Deathwatch*'s "sharp, sardonic dialogue, finely orchestrated suspense and chilling evocation of atmosphere" enhance the novel.

A less successful departure from White's sea adventures is *The Long Way Down*, in which a girl joins the circus and, under the tutelage of a young man with whom she falls in love, becomes a famous trapeze artist. The greed of the circus owners endangers her life, however, allowing the

If you enjoy the works of Robb White, you may also want to check out the following books and films:

Alden R. Carter, *Between a Rock and a Hard Place*, 1995.

Brian Garfield, *Fear in a Handful of Dust*, 1979.

Walt Morey, *Death Walk*, 1991.

Farley Mowat, *Lost in the Barrens*, 1956.

Ivy Ruckman, *No Way Out*, 1988.

The Most Dangerous Game, a film based on the short story of the same name by Richard Connell, 1932.

young man to save her and both to announce their mutual love. In the *Bulletin of the Center for Children's Books*, Zena Sutherland concluded: "An unconvincing story, sugar-coated, has the circus atmosphere as its only appeal." A subsequent novel, *Fire Storm*, was more enthusiastically received. In this work, a fire warden believes he has captured the young arsonist responsible for setting the blaze that surrounds them, until the boy manages to save both their lives and an explanation of his suspicious behavior becomes apparent. Robert Unsworth wrote in *School Library Journal*: "White's descriptions of the awesome force of the fire are good," and Mary M. Burns described *Fire Storm* in *Horn Book* as "fast-moving and spare," adding that "the book could serve as bait for the reluctant reader."

White's adventure novels for young adults often pit idealistic young people against more powerful, frequently unscrupulous adults in situations that test their physical and mental courage. White has become known for his action-packed plots, well-detailed settings, likeable heroes and heroines, and suspenseful exposition. Although some critics temper their praise for the author's works by noting that they are "only" adventure stories or "thrillers," others note that White's exciting plots and admirable characters make enjoyable reading for adolescents and adults alike.

■ Works Cited

Burns, Mary M., review of *Fire Storm*, *Horn Book*, August, 1979, p. 418.

Review of *Candy*, *Booklist*, October 15, 1949.

Conner, John W., review of *Deathwatch*, *English Journal*, November, 1972.

Davis, E. Louise, review of *Silent Ship, Silent Sea*, *School Library Journal*, November 15, 1967, p. 4267.

Druse, Judith, "Easy Talking," *Voice of Youth Advocates*, December, 1992, p. 267.

Finlayson, Elizabeth, review of *Deathwatch*, *School Librarian*, August, 1989, p. 118.

Fisher, Margery, review of *Candy*, *New York Times Book Review*, February 5, 1950.

Gottlieb, Gerald, review of *Surrender*, *Sunday World Journal Tribune Book Week*, March 19, 1967.

Higgins, Judith, review of *Deathwatch*, *School Library Journal*, August, 1992, p. 90.

Hood, Robert, review of *The Frogmen*, *New York Times Book Review*, September 16, 1973, p. 12.

Jones, Loretta B., review of *No Man's Land*, *Library Journal*, January 15, 1970, p. 258.

Lent, Henry B., review of *Up Periscope*, *New York Times Book Review*, September 23, 1956.

Manthorne, Jane, review of *The Survivor*, *Horn Book*, December, 1964.

Review of *Secret Sea*, *Booklist*, December 15, 1947.

Review of *Silent Ship, Silent Sea*, *Publishers Weekly*, August 28, 1967.

Review of *Surrender*, *Times Literary Supplement*, March 14, 1968, p. 258.

Sutherland, Zena, review of *The Long Way Down*, *Bulletin of the Center for Children's Books*, May, 1978, p. 150.

Review of *Two on the Isle: A Memory of Marina Cay*, *Kirkus Reviews*, April 15, 1985, pp. 368-69.

Unsworth, Robert, review of *Fire Storm*, *School Library Journal*, May, 1979, p. 68.

White, Robb, essay in *Something about the Author Autobiography Series*, Volume 1, Gale, 1986.

■ For More Information See

BOOKS

Children's Literature Review, Volume 3, Gale, 1978.

Thornton Wilder

■ Personal

Born April 17, 1897, in Madison, WI; died of a heart attack, December 7, 1975, in Hamden, CT; son of Amos Parker (a newspaper editor and U.S. Consul to China) and Isabella Thornton (Niven) Wilder. *Education:* Attended public and private schools in the United States and in Chefoo, China; attended Oberlin College, 1915-17; Yale University, A.B., 1920; attended American Academy in Rome 1920-21; Princeton University, A.M., 1926. *Politics:* Democrat. *Religion:* Congregationalist.

■ Career

Lawrenceville School, Lawrenceville, NJ, French teacher and assistant master of Davis House, 1921-25; tutor and writer in the United States and abroad, 1925-27; Davis House, master, 1927-28; writer and cross-country lecturer, 1928-29; University of Chicago, Chicago, lecturer in comparative literature, 1930-36; writer for several motion picture studios, 1930-36; University of Hawaii, Honolulu, visiting professor, 1935; American delegate to Institut de Cooperation Intellectuelle, Paris, France, 1937; goodwill representative to Latin America for U.S. Department of State, 1941; International PEN Club Congress delegate with John Dos Passos, 1941; Harvard University, Cambridge, MA, Charles Eliot Norton Professor of poetry, 1950-51; chief of U.S. delegation to UNESCO Conference of Arts, Venice, 1952. Actor in *Our Town,* New York City and summer stock, beginning 1939, in *The Skin of Our Teeth,* stock and summer theaters. *Wartime service:* Coast Artillery Corps, Fort Adams, RI, 1918; became corporal; commissioned captain in U.S. Army Air Intelligence, and served 1942-45, advancing to lieutenant colonel; awarded Legion of Merit, Bronze Star; Legion d'Honneur, Honorary Member of the Order of the British Empire (M.B.E.). *Member:* American Academy of Arts and Letters, Modern Language Association of America (honorary member), Authors Guild, Actors Equity Association, Hispanic Society of America, Bayerische Akademie (corresponding member), Akademie der Wissenschaften und der Literatur (Mainz, West Germany), Bavarian Academy of Fine Arts (honorary member), Century Association (New York), Players (honorary member), Graduate Club, Elizabethan Club, Alpha Delta Phi.

■ Awards, Honors

Pulitzer Prize, 1928, for *The Bridge of San Luis Rey,* 1938, for *Our Town,* and 1943, for *The Skin of Our Teeth;* Chevalier, Legion of Honor, 1951; Gold

Medal for Fiction, American Academy of Arts and Letters, 1952; Friedenspreis des Deutschen Buchhandels (West Germany), 1957; Sonderpreis des Oesterreichischen Staatspreises, and Goethe-Plakette, both 1959; Brandeis University Creative Arts Award, 1959-60, for theater and film; Edward MacDowell Medal (first time presented), 1960; Century Association Art Medal; Medal of the Order of Merit (Peru); Order Pour le Merite (Bonn, West Germany); invited by President Kennedy's cabinet to present reading, 1962; Presidential Medal of Freedom, 1963; National Medal for Literature (first time presented), National Book Committee, 1965; National Book Award, 1968, for *The Eighth Day*; honorary degrees from New York University, Yale University, Kenyon College, College of Wooster, Harvard University, Northeastern University, Oberlin College, University of New Hampshire, and University of Zurich.

■ Writings

NOVELS

The Cabala (excerpt published in *Double Dealer*, September, 1922; also see below), Boni, 1926.

The Bridge of San Luis Rey (also see below), Boni, 1927, limited edition with illustrations by William Kaughan, Franklin Library, 1976.

The Woman of Andros (based on *Andria* by Terence; also see below), Boni, 1930.

Heaven's My Destination, Longmans, 1934, Harper, 1935.

The Ides of March, Harper, 1948.

The Eighth Day, Harper, 1967.

Theophilus North, Harper, 1973.

Adapter, with Jerome Kilty, of stage version of *The Ides of March*.

PLAYS

The Trumpet Shall Sound (first published in *Yale Literary Magazine*, 1919-20), produced by American Laboratory Theater, 1926.

(Adapter and translator) *Lucrece* (based on *The Rape of Lucrece* by Andre Obey; produced on Broadway, 1932), Houghton, 1933.

Our Town (three-act play; produced in Princeton, NJ, 1938; produced in New York City, 1938; produced on Broadway, 1988; also see below), Coward, 1938, acting edition, Coward, 1965, limited edition with introduction by Brooks Atkinson and illustrations by Robert J. Lee, Limited Editions Club, 1974.

(Adapter and translator) Henrik Ibsen, *A Doll's House*, produced on Broadway, 1938.

The Merchant of Yonkers: A Farce in Four Acts (based on *Einen Jux will er sich Machen* by Johann Nestroy; produced on Broadway, 1938), Harper, 1939, revised as *The Matchmaker* (produced in Edinburgh, 1954; produced on Broadway, 1955; also see below), S. French, 1957.

The Skin of Our Teeth (three-act play; produced in New Haven, CT, 1942; produced on Broadway, 1942; also see below), Harper, 1942.

Our Century (three-scene burlesque; produced in New York City, 1947), Century Association, 1947.

The Happy Journey to Trenton and Camden, produced on Broadway with *The Respectful Prostitute* by Jean Paul Sartre, 1948.

(Translator) Jean-Paul Sartre, *The Victors*, produced Off-Broadway, 1949.

A Life in the Sun (based on *Alcestis* by Euripides), produced in Edinburgh, 1955.

The Wreck of the 5:25 and Bernice, performed in West Berlin, West Germany, 1957.

The Drunken Sisters (satyr play; first appeared in centennial issue of *Atlantic Monthly*, 1957; produced as fourth act of *Die Alkestiade* [also see below], in Brooklyn Heights, NY, 1970), S. French, 1957.

Childhood (one-act; first appeared in *Atlantic Monthly*, November, 1960; also see below), S. French, 1960.

The Long Christmas Dinner (also see below), revised edition, S. French, 1960.

Plays for Bleecker Street (three volumes; includes *Infancy*, *Childhood*, and *Someone from Assisi*; produced Off-Broadway, 1962), S. French, 1960-61.

(Author of libretto) *Das Lange Weihnachtsmal* (opera; adapted from play *The Long Christmas Dinner*; produced in Mannheim, Germany, 1961), music by Paul Hindemith, translated into German by Hindemith, libretto published by Schott Music, 1961.

Infancy, A Comedy in One Act (also see below), S. French, 1961.

(Author of libretto) *Die Alkestiade* (opera; adaptation of *A Life in the Sun*), music by Louise Talma, produced in Frankfurt, West Germany, 1962.

Pullman Car Hiawatha (also see below), produced Off-Broadway, 1964.

Thornton Wilder's Triple Bill (includes *The Long Christmas Dinner*, *The Queens of France* [also see below], and *The Happy Journey to Trenton and Camden* [also see below]), produced Off-Broadway, 1966.

OMNIBUS VOLUMES

The Angel That Troubled the Waters, and Other Plays (includes *Nascunter Poetae, Proserpina and the Devil, Fanny Otcott, Brother Fire, The Penny That Beauty Spent, The Angel on the Ship, The Message and Jehanne, Childe Roland to the Dark Tower Came, Centaurs, Leviathan, And the Sea Shall Give up Its Dead, Now the Servant's Name Was Malchus, Mozart and the Gray Steward, Hast Thou Considered My Servant Job?,* and *The Flight into Egypt*), Coward, 1928.

The Long Christmas Dinner and Other Plays in One Act (includes *Pullman Car Hiawatha, Such Things Only Happen in Books, The Happy Journey to Trenton and Camden, Love and How to Cure It,* and *The Queens of France*), Yale University Press, 1931.

(And author of preface) *Three Plays: Our Town, The Skin of Our Teeth, The Matchmaker,* Harper, 1938, limited edition with illustrations by Dick Brown, Franklin Library, 1979.

A Thornton Wilder Trio: The Cabala, The Bridge of San Luis Rey, The Woman of Andros, Criterion, 1956.

The Cabala and The Woman of Andros, Harper, 1968.

The Alcestiad; or, A Life in the Sun: A Play in Three Acts, with a Satyr Play, The Drunken Sisters, Harper, 1977, limited edition published as *The Alcestiad; or, A Life in the Sun; The Drunken Sisters,* illustrations by Daniel Maffia, Franklin Library, 1977.

The Collected Short Plays of Thornton Wilder, edited by Donald Gallup and A. Tappan Wilder, Theatre Communications Group, 1997.

OTHER

We Live Again (screenplay; based on *Resurrection* by Leo Tolstoy), Metro-Goldwyn-Mayer, 1936.

An Evening with Thornton Wilder, April 30, 1962, Washington, DC (consists of third act of *Our Town*), Harper, 1962.

American Characteristics and Other Essays, edited by Donald Gallup, foreword by Isabel Wilder, Harper, 1979.

The Journals of Thornton Wilder: With Two Scenes of an Uncompleted Play, "The Emporium," Yale University Press, 1985.

Mirrors of Friendship: The Letters of Gertrude Stein and Thornton Wilder, edited by Edward M. Burns, Yale University Press, 1996.

Author of screenplay, *Shadow of a Doubt,* for Alfred Hitchcock, 1943. Contributor to periodicals, including *Harper's, Hudson Review, Poetry, Atlantic,* and *Yale Review.* Theatre reviewer for *Theatre Arts Monthly,* 1925.

The autograph of *The Bridge of San Luis Rey* is held in Yale University's American Literature Collection of the Beinecke Rare Book and Manuscript Library.

■ **Adaptations**

The Bridge of San Luis Rey was filmed three times, initially in 1929; also filmed were *Our Town,* 1940, and *The Matchmaker,* 1958. *The Matchmaker* was adapted by Michael Stewart as the musical *Hello, Dolly!,* words and music by Jerry Herman, and produced in 1964; it became the longest running musical on Broadway and was subsequently a popular film. *Our Town* was adapted as the musical *Grover's Corners,* by Harvey Schmidt and Tom Jones, in 1987. *Theophilus North* was made into the movie *Mr. North* by John Huston, starring Danny Huston, Anjelica Huston, and Robert Mitchum. There have also been radio and television versions of many of Wilder's works.

■ **Sidelights**

A noted dramatist, novelist, and essayist, Thornton Wilder's name is known to most U.S. high school and college students because of the fame of his play, *Our Town.* First performed before American theatergoers in 1937, *Our Town* would soon be produced across the country and abroad, its popularity overshadowing its author's many other works. During Wilder's forty-seven-year career he produced seven novels, six long plays and several short plays, and a collection of essays on literary figures. Also appearing as an actor in several of his dramatic works, Wilder distinguished himself as an educator, teaching at both Harvard University and the University of Chicago. His invitation to read his works before President John F. Kennedy and his cabinet in the early 1960s attests to Wilder's stature as one of the cultural figureheads of twentieth-century America.

In addition to widespread popularity among the general public, Wilder garnered critical kudos throughout his career. Three of his works—the novel *The Bridge of San Luis Rey*, and the plays *Our Town* and *The Skin of Our Teeth*—were recipients of the Pulitzer Prize, while his novel *The Eighth Day* earned the National Book Award in 1968. Sales of his novels broke records repeatedly—*The Bridge of San Luis Rey* sold more than three hundred thousand copies in its first two years of publication alone. In both his plays and his novels, Wilder's sophisticated understanding of literature, history, and humankind can be appreciated even by the general reader: while describing the writer as "a classicist and humanist with a profound interest with the past," *Dictionary of Literary Biography* contributor Sally Johns maintained that "Wilder has always appealed to the sentimental, yet his works skillfully avoid sentimentality."

Strict Upbringing Leads to Closet Rebellion

Wilder was born in Madison, Wisconsin, on April 17, 1897, the second son (and surviving twin) of Amos Parker Wilder and Isabella Thornton Niven. His father, a journalist, came from an old New England family proud of its puritan roots that stretched back more than a century to England, and his mother—a Presbyterian minister's daughter—descended from a Southern family, although she herself had been raised in New York. Wilder's father was a charismatic man, highly educated and also highly principled. Having earned both his bachelors and masters degrees from Yale University prior to marrying and moving west to Wisconsin, Amos Wilder, Sr. then took charge of the *Wisconsin State Journal* for several years. However, when Thornton was nine years old, the elder Wilder abandoned the paper to accept a post as consul general in Hong Kong. Accompanying his father along with the rest of his family— Wilder had an older brother, Amos, and older sister, Charlotte, as well as two younger sisters, Isabel and Janet—Wilder spent six months in this exotic land, gaining a rich exposure to the culture and philosophy of the East and attending a German school before returning with his mother and siblings to the United States.

Making their new home in Berkeley, California, Wilder and his siblings attended public school until 1909, when his father transferred to Shang-

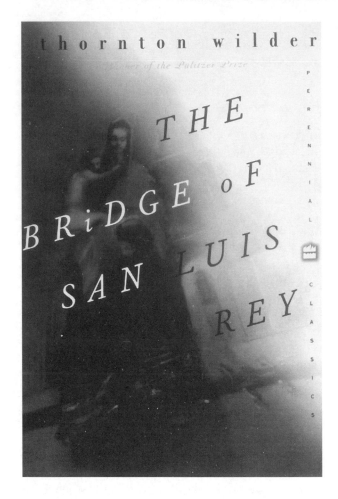

Wilder received his first Pulitzer Prize in 1928 for this work about a monk who searches for the meaning of why five people were killed in a bridge accident.

hai, China, and commanded that his family return to his side. This time it would be mission schools that the boy would attend, but his studies there were so unsuccessful that his father sent both Thornton and Amos back to California. Wilder was a teen when he and his family returned to the United States, again making their home in California.

While expressing the outward desire to be seen as worthy in the eyes of his overachieving father, Wilder appeared conflicted in his feelings. He exhibited a lack of motivation and discipline throughout his early schooling, and proved to be, by all accounts, worthless on the high school playing field as well, which did not help in his efforts to measure up to his father's exacting standards. Attempting to raise her children herself while her husband was absent, Isabella Wilder recognized that her youngest son was bright but undisciplined and that his failure to gain his father's respect could affect his feelings of self-worth. She began to take Wilder to amateur play productions while the young man was in high school and encouraged his acting efforts at Berkeley High School. She also encouraged his efforts at writing by serving as a willing audience for his stories and providing constructive criticism. Wilder also benefited from the cultural activity of a college town after the family relocated to New Haven, Connecticut, home of Yale University, following its members' second trip to the Orient.

Career Choice Made by Father

Having spent several years in mission schools while his father worked in Shanghai and other Chinese cities, Wilder came home to the United States to roost, graduating from high school in 1915. Unwilling to send his son to his own alma mater, Wilder's father instead encouraged Thornton to attend Oberlin College, a small Ohio school with a monastic atmosphere. His years at Oberlin proved to be liberating; without parental constraints Wilder was free to pursue his own interests in acting and writing. Unfortunately, by the time of his junior year Amos Wilder had returned and set up permanent residence in New Haven, Connecticut, near Yale. He demanded that his son return to the East Coast and fulfill the family tradition of a Yale degree. The remainder of Wilder's college career, which spanned the years of World War I, would be at Yale, broken only by a summer spent in the Coast Artillery Corps in nearby Fort Adams, Rhode Island.

While Wilder's days at Oberlin had made him realize that he would be happiest as a writer, his father had other ideas. A schoolteacher's job would provide stable wages, thus making Thornton able to support his parents in the coming years (older brother Amos made little money as a member of the clergy). So, after graduating from Yale University in 1920, the dutiful son traveled to Rome as a visiting student of archaeology in that city's American Academy. In addition to studying ancient ruins, learning Italian, and renewing his love affair with the classics, Wilder had the opportunity to meet and converse with modern authors such as Ezra Pound and the poet Lauro de Bosis, who would later translate several

of Wilder's novels into Italian. Away from supervision by both his parents and school administrators for the first time in his life, Wilder threw himself into several love affairs that ended unhappily, and these personal experiences, as well as his growing worldliness, would influence several of his early works, including *The Cabala* and *The Woman of Andros*. A year later, just prior to beginning his four-year stint as a language instructor at Lawrenceville Academy, Wilder again traveled to Europe, this time to France in order to "brush up" on his French. A trip to Paris brought him into the company of several noted American expatriate authors, among them Ernest Hemingway and Gertrude Stein. Stein particularly would have a marked impact upon young Wilder, and the two would remain friends until Stein's death in 1946. A second trip to Paris in 1935 to visit Stein and her partner Alice B. Toklas would provide encouragement to Wilder to commit himself to a more pioneering approach to playwriting, and *Our Town* would be the ultimate result.

Student Work Intrigues New York Publishers

While still teaching at Lawrenceville, Wilder spent his spare time hard at work on several short, one-act plays, and also experimented with longer ones that were never published. Meanwhile, his contributions to Yale's literary magazine while he was a student there had since been circulated by friends, and eventually caught the attention of several publishers. In 1925 he was approached by Albert Boni of New York City, who persuaded the twenty-eight-year-old Wilder to rewrite his "Memoirs of a Roman Student" into a cohesive work. Wilder took on the challenge and in 1926 published *The Cabala*, his first novel.

The Cabala was quickly followed by *The Bridge of San Luis Rey*, which was published in 1927. Wilder had begun working on the novel while on leave from Lawrenceville to attend graduate school at Princeton; he returned to his teaching duties upon its completion. The unexpected success of his second novel, and his receipt of the Pulitzer Prize for fiction, allowed Wilder to leave Lawrenceville a year later. His celebrity status allowed him to expand his literary friendships to include such figures as F. Scott Fitzgerald, Willa Cather, Sigmund Freud, John-Paul Sartre, and Edmund Wilson. An introduction to noted drama critic Andrew Woollcott rekindled Wilder's early love of the stage, and he began mingling with a steady stream of actors and actresses, among them Helen Hayes, Mary Pickford, Ethel Barrymore, and Ruth Gordon. At one point he even offered to marry Gordon when she found herself pregnant out of wedlock. Although appreciative of his noble offer, Gordon politely turned him down; Wilder would remain single his entire life.

Realizing that his royalties as a writer would not support him as well as the parents and sisters he was now endeavoring to care for financially, Wilder took a teaching position at the University of Chicago in 1930, shortly after publishing his third novel, *The Woman of Andros.* He remained at Chicago for six years, and then, while still writing, began lecturing, acting, and writing screenplays for both Metro-Goldwyn-Mayer and

Alfred Hitchcock, who directed Wilder's *Shadow of a Doubt* in 1943. A controversy over *The Woman of Andros* and the mixed critical reception to Wilder's subsequent novel, *Heaven's My Destination,* prompted the writer to move from fiction-writing to writing for the stage. After the production of several shorter works, *Our Town* reached the New York Stage on February 4, 1938. Running for 336 performances, the play was awarded the Pulitzer Prize, establishing its author as the first person to win that prize for both fiction and drama.

Career as Dramatist Put on Hold during War

Wilder's writing career was put on temporary hold when he was called to active duty in the U.S. Air Force during World War II. Serving as a captain in Army Air Force Intelligence after intensive training—Wilder planned the air assaults on both Taranto and Salerno and was praised for his strategic abilities—the writer was profoundly influenced by the war against Nazi Germany, and his works written during wartime and after his return to civilian life would be less concerned with the individual and more focused on mankind as a whole, as well as more controversial. *The Skin of Our Teeth* premiered on the New York Stage in 1942, and he began work on his *Alcestiad,* based in part on the works of Euripides, shortly after returning to civilian life. However, Wilder would put the play aside to write *The Ides of March,* a fictional account of Julius Caesar's last days that was published in 1948.

Discouraged by the mixed reviews accorded to his fifth novel, Wilder again cast around for a teaching position, this time accepting Harvard University's Charles Eliot Norton Professorship, for which he lectured on American classical writers. During the remainder of the 1950s he published essays, lectured, and authored a successful revival of his earlier play, *The Merchant of Yonkers,* under the title of *The Matchmaker.* He also completed the *Alcestiad,* which was performed for the 1955 Edinburgh Festival, although to less than enthusiastic critical acclaim.

In 1962, having reached the age of sixty-five, Wilder announced his retirement. After journeying to Washington, D.C., at the behest of President John F. Kennedy to present a reading from his works before the U.S. cabinet, Wilder moved

thornton wilder
Winner of the Pulitzer Prize

P E R E N N I A L

C L A S S I C S

OuR ToWN

Wilder's 1938 drama of life in a small New Hampshire village has become an American classic.

Wilder (center) goes over the script of *Our Town* with actors Dorothy McGuire and John Craven during its 1938 production in New York City.

to an isolated home in Arizona, and began once more to work on a novel. Although his seclusion was interrupted after an attack of skin cancer forced him to seek medical attention in New Haven, he worked diligently on his novel for five years, and in 1967 *The Eighth Day* was published, according to essayist Richard H. Goldstone in *Dictionary of Literary Biography*, "to the astonishment of a reading public which had seen no fiction from Wilder in almost twenty years." Wilder's mystery novel would receive the National Book Award for fiction in 1968.

While *The Eighth Day* received the now-characteristic mixed critical reception of all Wilder's works, it was read and enjoyed by many Americans. Encouraged by this show of continuing popularity, Wilder began a series of autobiographical short stories which were collectively published as the 1973 novel *Theophilus North*. Purporting to be a chronicle of the life of his twin brother, the book recounts the adventures of its title character. Again either panned or ignored by critics, *Theophilus North* proved to be an entertaining tale in the opinion of Wilder's loyal and ever-increasing readership. At the time of his death two years after the novel's publication, his popularity among readers both in the United States and around the world showed that his uneven and sometimes overtly hostile treatment at the hands of literary critics had done little to tarnish his reputation.

Wilder's work for the stage has been perceived in several different ways by critics. One reviewer, Travis Bogard, noted in *Modern Drama: Essays in Criticism* that Wilder was "a man who, along with [fellow U.S. playwright] Eugene O'Neill, freed the American theatre from its traditional forms through his experiments in *Our Town* and *The Skin of Our Teeth*." Critics such as Bogard view the playwright as ahead of his time due to the philosophical underpinnings of Wilder's dramatic works, underpinnings that seem particularly revolutionary when viewed in contrast to the trite, melodramatic fare appearing on stages around the country during the 1920s and 1930s. The playwright also rejected the sophisticated sets and costuming required by the so-called "naturalist" school of playwriting, removing sets and extravagant costumes. Comparisons have been drawn between Wilder's work in the early part of the twentieth century and the literature produced generations later by such writers as Joyce Carol Oates, Carson McCullers, and Walker Percy.

In contrast, others have perceived in Wilder a writer who was a bit of an anachronism—a playwright who drew on the style of a previous century in his work. He was dubbed by *Dictionary of Literary Biography* Goldstone as "last in the line of the New England puritan writers" because of the strong moralistic and religious undertones that characterize much of his body of work. However, his was not a restrictive moralism, and this "old-fashioned" belief in the benefits of living a good life could be seen as a positive break with the tradition of the era: the pessimism, doubt, and angst of the post-World War I generation. Indeed, some critics have maintained that Love is the central theme uniting each of his works: not only human love and the aspiration to moral standards that allow men and women to attain dignity through self-love and love from others, but also an eternal, all-encompassing love that transcends the death of mere individuals.

Our Town **His Most Beloved Work**

Influenced by Stein's naturalist philosophy as it relates to the stage—to portray genuine human emotions rather than the overacted, exaggerated emotions characteristic of traditional drama—*Our Town* portrays a timeless story of love, marriage, and ultimate loss. Taking place in a small New Hampshire village called Grover's Corners, the play features the characters George Gibbs and Emily Webb. Narrated by the Stage Manager, the story of George and Emily unfolds: Act I takes them through a single day during their high

school years, as their status as next-door neighbors and friends is clearly on the verge of becoming romantic; their growing love results in an exchange of wedding vows in Act II; and Emily's ultimate death during childbirth nine years later provides the subject for Act III. Titled "Death," Act III also finds Emily allowed to return to earth to relive one moment of her past. She returns to her twelfth birthday, her childhood home, and attempts to tell those around her how much she cares for them and treasures every moment she has with them. This final segment of the play, along with the constant asides of the Stage Manager and other technical staging devices, "guide the audience to accept the play's assertion that the most mundane elements of everyday life are almost too precious and significant to be appreciated," according to *International Dictionary of Theatre* contributor Gerald Berkowitz.

Notably, *Our Town* is performed in a spartan setting, with no sets and few if any props to distract attention from the characters' actions. As Berkowitz explained, Wilder "exploited the drama's plasticity of time and space, making full use of the ability of a stage scene to represent any place, and for time to pass with the speed of an onstage announcement or a programme note." Reviewing the play shortly after its New York stage debut, *Saturday Review* critic John Mason Brown noted of *Our Town* that the play "is concerned with the universal importance of those unimportant details which figure in the lives of men and women everywhere. . . . It burrows into the essence of the growing-up, the marrying, the living, and the dying of all of us who sit before it and are included by it . . . [Wilder] shows us the simple pattern behind all simple living. He permits us to share in the inevitable anguishes and joys, the hopes and cruel separations to which men have been heir since the smoke puffed up the chimneys in Greece." Brown's laudatory review, which was later collected in his *Dramatis Personae*, is typical; it reflects the simplicity and wholesomeness that have transformed *Our Town* into one of the most frequently performed works on the American stage, a staple of high school and college drama clubs and community theatre.

First produced in 1942, the more confrontational and experimental *The Skin of Our Teeth* demonstrates Wilder's altered focus as a result of World War II. The play introduces Mr. and Mrs. Antrobus, a couple living in the nondescript suburb of

Excelsior, New Jersey, that reflects the history of mankind over a period spanning five thousand years. Modeling his drama's dialogue and cyclical themes on expatriate Irish author James Joyce's *Finnegan's Wake*, as well as the philosophy espoused by Stein, Wilder has his fictional Antrobus family weather such events as death, the Ice Age, glaciers, floods, and warfare up to the Napoleonic Wars, ultimately demonstrating the triumph of the human spirit over adversity.

In *The Skin of Our Teeth* the characters of Mr. and Mrs. Antrobus live a simple life in the suburbs, but they also represent all men and women in a loving, committed relationship from time immemorial, from Adam and Eve up through the centuries. Wilder toys with the historical record of mankind's development throughout his play—in one scene Mr. Antrobus returns from work tired after a long day working on his latest invention— the alphabet, while later, we learn that his annual Lodge convention in Atlantic City has been disrupted by Noah's Flood—and shows that what people look back upon as incredible accomplishments as well as devastating tragedies involved "regular folk;" that we all have the capacity to achieve greatness and overcome tragedy, even if we sometimes do so "by the skin of our teeth."

"One way to shake off the nonsense of the nineteenth-century staging is to make fun of it," Wilder pointed out in his preface to *Three Plays*, referring to his 1938 play *The Matchmaker*. First produced in 1939 as *The Merchant of Yonkers*, *The Matchmaker* remains notable more for its mid-century adaptation and, later, as the basis for the

Drama students from Brandeis University perform a 1996 production of *The Skin of Our Teeth*, Wilder's 1942 play for which he received his third Pulitzer Prize.

motion picture *Hello Dolly*, starring actress Carol Channing. Based on a nineteenth-century English adaptation of an Austrian tale, *The Matchmaker* uses nineteenth-century stage devices similar to those in *Our Town*—characters directly address the audience, for example—to tell the story of a miser named Horace Vandergelder who ignores the fact that his niece Ermegarde is pining away from lovesickness. Ermegarde's love interest, as well as several other star-struck couples, become entangled in a web of madcap intrigue while widowed Dolly Levi, who has her eye on miserly Horace, plies her trade as a matchmaker. While everything from mistaken identities to daring escapes figure into its plot, the ultimate conclusion of *The Matchmaker* can be summed up in actress Judy Garland's line from the classic film *The Wizard of Oz:* "There's no place like home."

Novels Appeal to Growing Middle Class

Wilder's acclaim as a playwright stemmed from his "employment of innovative, unconventional theatrical techniques to affirm [the] conventional, humanistic values" held by many middle-class Americans, according to Johns. This acclaim tended to overshadow his equal accomplishments as a novelist. Even so, despite the mixed reception accorded to his fiction, Wilder's readership grew tenfold during his lifetime. Considered less experimental than his plays, Wilder's novels still demonstrate his creativity through their use of such techniques as allegory, mystery, parable, and epic. His fictions range in format from the *bildungsroman* or life story, to the epistolary novel, a book made up entirely of correspondence and journal entries.

In *The Cabala* Wilder tells the quasi-autobiographical story of his twenty-something protagonist, whose visit to Rome and his exposure to new religious, cultural, and political experiences results in a growth of both insight into himself and understanding of his responsibility as an artist. The uplifting *The Bridge of San Luis Rey*, which was published shortly thereafter, is, by contrast, wholly fictional. Focusing on a young monk's investigation of the tragic death of five individuals fallen from a rope bridge in Lima, Peru, during the eighteenth-century, the novel explores the unconsummated loves that each accident victim took to his or her death. The novel closes with the realization, among those left living, that while lives

---

If you enjoy the works of Thornton Wilder, you may also want to check out the following books and films:

Sue Ellen Bridgers, *Permanent Connections*, 1987.
Olive Ann Burns, *Cold Sassy Tree*, 1984.
Sharon Creech, *Walk Two Moons*, 1994.
Avalon, a film by Barry Levinson, 1990.

---

had been lost, the greater loss had been the love the victims could not now bestow upon the living.

In each of his major novels, to which must be added his final work, *The Eighth Day*, a story centered on a murder in a Midwest coal mining town, Wilder presented a consistent world view. In an essay in *Twentieth-Century Romance and Historical Writers*, Warren French framed several quotes from *The Eighth Day* within his interpretation of Wilder's philosophy. Wilder "is not interested in detailed re-creations of great events," maintained French, "but in making broad statements about the significance of the past. He believes that 'there are no Golden Ages and no Dark Ages,' but only 'the ocean-like monotony of the generations of men under the alterations of fair and foul weather.' All times and places, he feels, are much alike, usually tragically self-destructive, but occasionally magically rewarding."

Criticized for Being Behind the Times

Although the optimism underlying Wilder's works fueled their popularity among the reading public, he was rebuked in some circles for ignoring the problems of modern society and for adopting an almost patrician air in his highly styled, sophisticated prose. In contrast to authors Sinclair Lewis, F. Scott Fitzgerald, Ernest Hemingway, and Upton Sinclair, whose works reflect society's concerns over slums, tenement houses, the oppression of minorities, and dismal working conditions, Wilder appeared to thematically ally himself more with the nineteenth century. His adoption of that past era's optimism, morality, and strong sense of decorum, along with Wilder's own somewhat prim, didactic tone, chilled the enthusiasm of some critics while cementing his embrasure by the middle-class reading public. However, the criticism that Wilder was somehow "old-fashioned" is contradicted by his continued structural references to the groundbreaking works of such modern experimentalist as Joyce, Hemingway, and Stein, which showed him firmly grounded in the twentieth century.

Although Wilder's optimistic and moralistic approach appealed to middle-class readers around the world—his works were particularly popular in postwar Germany and elsewhere in war-ravaged Europe, as people sought direction in rebuilding the moral and political order—his works also contained darker themes. While he did not directly delve into life's more unpleasant aspects, neither did he ignore many of the problems faced by society. *The Bridge of San Luis Rey* focuses on death and religion; *The Cabala* deals with obsession, incest and infidelity, mock-intellectualism, materialism, and the failure of both Puritan idealism and the European decadent tradition; characters in *The Woman of Andros* range from grasping moneymakers to the morally and spiritually bankrupt; and *The Skin of Our Teeth* depicts the endless cycle playing out the failings—and successes—of humanity.

Philosophy Serves as Undercurrent to Writing

Wilder has been set in a class apart from his more realistic literary contemporaries, in part because of the cyclical view of life that continued to preoccupy him. As he reflected in "Goethe and World Literature," included in *American Characteristics and Other Essays:* "every man and woman born is . . . in a new relation to the whole"; there exists a "planetary consciousness" that reflects "the unity of the human spirit." This belief in a "unity of the human spirit" is also reflected in Wilder's other writings. In his preface to *Three Plays*, for example, he contended that "Every action which has ever taken place—every thought, every emotion—has taken place only once, at one moment in time and place. 'I love you,' 'I rejoice,' 'I suffer,' have been said and felt billions of times, and never twice the same. Every person who has ever lived has lived an unbroken succession of unique occasions. Yet the more one is aware of this individuality in experience . . . the more one becomes attentive to what these disparate moments have in common, to repetitive patterns." Although

Wilder focused on the actions of Americans in society, his main concern was with the manner whereby such actions established the place of individual characters within humanity, the "unity of the human spirit," and how to express this within literature. By imbuing twentieth-century characters and situations with age-old symbols, his work presented an interesting paradox in its attempt to transform commonplace experiences into flashes of the universal and timeless.

Wilder has been seen by many literary critics as a religious writer who used his novels and plays to renew the spiritual energy of his audience by presenting a cohesive Christian worldview unfragmented by denomination. Interestingly, he used literature rather than didactic nonfictional works such as essays and speeches to promote his religious views; as he wrote in the foreword to *The Angel that Troubled the Waters, and Other Plays*: "All that is fairest in the Christian tradition [has been] made repugnant to the new generations by reason of the diction in which it is expressed. The intermittent sincerity of generations of clergymen and teachers has rendered embarrassing and even ridiculous all the terms of spiritual life." Realizing that an overtly religious message would be rejected, Wilder searched constantly for new ways of couching it within his plots and storylines.

Through his celebration of the ordinary in life, and his ability to portray it in a way that was accessible to the average reader or theatergoer, Wilder gained international stature as a distinguished literary figure. His "importance lies in the plays themselves," according to *International Dictionary of Theatre* contributor Berkowitz, plays that are "affirmations of both theatrical imagination and faith in humanity." Respected for both the quality of his prose and his creative vision, Wilder "is distinguished also for the uniqueness of his works." In the words of *Reference Guide to American Literature* essayist French, "each is a fresh, formal experiment that contributes to his perception of the artist's reinventing the world by [revealing and illuminating] our perceptions of the universal elements of human experience."

■ Works Cited

Berkowitz, Gerald, "Thornton Wilder," in *International Dictionary of Theatre*, Volume 2: *Playwrights*, St. James Press, 1994, pp. 1045-46.

Bogard, Travis, essay in *Modern Drama: Essays in Criticism*, Oxford University Press, 1965.

Brown, John Mason, "Wilder's Our Town," in his *Dramatis Personae: A Retrospective Show*, Viking, 1963, pp. 79-84.

French, Warren, "Thornton Wilder," in *Twentieth-Century Romance and Historical Writers*, St. James Press, 1990, pp. 695-98.

French, Warren, "Thornton Wilder," in *Reference Guide to American Literature*, St. James Press, 1994, p. 909.

Goldstone, Richard H., "Thornton Wilder," in *Dictionary of Literary Biography*, Volume 9: *American Novelists, 1910-1945*, Gale, 1981.

Johns, Sally, "Thornton Wilder," in *Dictionary of Literary Biography*, Volume 7: *Twentieth-Century American Dramatists*, Gale, 1981, pp. 304-19.

Wilder, Thornton, foreword to *The Angel That Troubled the Waters, and Other Plays*, Coward, 1928.

Wilder, Thornton, preface to *Three Plays: Our Town, The Skin of Our Teeth, The Matchmaker*, Harper, 1938, limited edition with illustrations by Dick Brown, Franklin Library, 1979.

Wilder, Thornton, *American Characteristics and Other Essays*, edited by Donald Gallup, foreword by Isabel Wilder, Harper, 1979.

■ For More Information See

BOOKS

Allen, Walter, *The Modern Novel*, Dutton, 1965.

Authors in the News, Volume 2, Gale, 1976.

Berney, K. A., editor, *Contemporary American Dramatists*, St. James Press, 1994.

Blank, Martin, *Critical Essays on Thornton Wilder*, Prentice Hall, 1996.

Broussard, Louis, *American Drama*, University of Oklahoma Press, 1962.

Bryer, Jackson R., editor, *Conversations with Thornton Wilder*, University Press of Mississippi, 1992.

Burbank, R., *Thornton Wilder*, Twayne, 1961.

Cohn, Ruby, *Dialogue in American Drama*, Indiana University Press, 1971.

Cole, Toby, editor, *Playwrights on Playwriting*, Hill & Wang, 1961.

Contemporary Literary Criticism, Gale, Volume 1, 1973, Volume 5, 1976, Volume 6, 1976, Volume 10, 1979, Volume 15, 1980, Volume 35, 1985, Volume 82, 1994.

Cowley, Malcolm, editor, *Writers at Work: The Paris Review Interviews*, Viking, 1957.

Dictionary of Literary Biography, Volume 4: *American Writers in Paris, 1920-1939*, Gale, 1980.

Drama Criticism, Volume 1, Gale, 1991.

Edelstein, J. M., compiler, *Bibliographical Checklist of the Writings of Thornton Wilder*, Yale University Press, 1959.

Fergusson, Francis, *The Human Image in Dramatic Literature*, Doubleday, 1957.

Goldstein, Malcolm, *The Art of Thornton Wilder*, University of Nebraska Press, 1965.

Goldstone, Richard H., *Thornton Wilder, An Intimate Portrait*, Dutton, 1975.

Grebanier, Bernard, *Thornton Wilder*, University of Minnesota Press, 1965.

Haberman, Donald, *The Plays of Thornton Wilder*, Wesleyan University Press, 1967.

Lifton, Paul, *Vast Encyclopedia: The Theatre of Thornton Wilder*, Greenwood Press, 1995.

Kuner, M. C., *Thornton Wilder: The Bright and the Dark*, Crowell, 1972.

Papajewski, Helmut, *Thornton Wilder*, translated by John Conway, Ungar, 1969.

Schroeder, Patricia R., *The Presence of the Past in Modern American Drama*, Fairleigh Dickinson University Press, 1989.

Simon, Linda, *Thornton Wilder: His Work*, Doubleday, 1979.

Vinson, James, editor, *Contemporary Novelists*, St. James Press, 1972.

Vinson, James, editor, *Contemporary Dramatists*, St. James Press, 1977.

Wagenknecht, Edward, *Calvalcade of the English Novel*, Holt, 1943.

Wilder, Amos Niven, *Thornton Wilder and His Public*, Fortress Press, 1980.

Wilson, Edmund, *A Literary Chronicle: 1920-1950*, Anchor, 1956.

PERIODICALS

Antioch Review, summer, 1967, pp. 264-69.

Classical and Modern Literature, fall, 1991.

Kenyon Review, spring, 1986, pp. 126-30.

Modern Drama, September, 1972.

Nation, September 3, 1955.

New Republic, August 8, 1928.

New York Review of Books, November 21, 1985, pp. 31-34.

New York Times, November 24, 1986; December 20, 1987; December 5, 1988; December 11, 1988.

New York Times Book Review, December 30, 1979.

Paris Review, winter, 1957, pp. 36-57.

Philadelphia Inquirer, December 14, 1975.

Saturday Review, October 6, 1956.
School Library Journal, December, 1995, p. 56.
Sewanee Review, winter, 1987, pp. 162-68.
Times Literary Supplement, March 14, 1986, p. 281.
Twentieth Century Literature, number 9, 1963, pp. 93-100.
Variety, April 29, 1996, p. 149.
Virginia Quarterly Review, winter, 1953, pp. 103-17.
Yale Review, October, 1994, p. 17.
Yankee, March, 1994, p. 98.

■ Obituaries

PERIODICALS

Newsweek, December 22, 1975.
New York Times, December 8, 1975.
Washington Post, December 8, 1975.*

—Sketch by Pamela L. Shelton

Acknowledgments

Acknowledgments

Grateful acknowledgment is made to the following publishers, authors, and artists for their kind permission to reproduce copyrighted material.

CHERIE BENNETT. Le Grou, Michel, photographer. From a cover of *Wild Hearts on Fire*, by Cherie Bennett. Pocket Books, 1994. Reproduced by permission of Pocket Books, a division of Simon & Schuster, Inc. / Cover of *Love Never Dies*, by Cherie Bennett. Avon Books, 1996. Reproduced by permission of Avon Books, Inc. / Watts, Stan, illustrator. From a jacket of *Life in the Fat Lane*, by Cherie Bennett. Delacorte Press, 1998. Jacket illustration © 1998 by Stan Watts. Reproduced by permission of Delacorte Press, a division of Random House, Inc. / Bennett, Cherie, photograph by Nancy Andrews. Reproduced by permission of Cherie Bennett.

ROBERT BLOCH. Cover of *Once Around the Bloch: An Unauthorized Autobiography*, by Robert Bloch. Tor Books, 1993. Reproduced by permission. / Scene from the film *Psycho*, photograph. Archive Photos, Inc. Reproduced by permission. / Bloch, Robert, photograph. Archive Photos, Inc. Reproduced by permission.

LILIAN JACKSON BRAUN. From a cover of *The Cat Who Ate Danish Modern*, by Lilian Jackson Braun. Jove Books, 1967. Used by permission of Putnam Berkley, a division of Penguin Putnam Inc. / From a cover of *The Cat Who Knew Shakespeare*, by Lilian Jackson Braun. Jove Books, 1988. Used by permission of Putnam Berkley, a division of Penguin Putnam Inc. / Braun, Lilian Jackson, photograph by Patricia Beck. Reproduced by permission of Lilian Jackson Braun.

EDWIDGE DANTICAT. Roberts, Richard Samuel, and Dorothy Handleman, photographers. From a cover of *Breath, Eyes, Memory*, by Edwidge Danticat. Vintage Books, 1995. Reproduced by permission of Random House, Inc. / Clinch, Danny, photographer. From a cover of *Krik? Krak!* by Edwidge Danticat. Vintage Books, 1996. Reproduced by permission of Random House, Inc. / "Lasiren et Met Dlo," painting (detail) by Gerard Valcin. From a jacket of *The Farming of Bones*, by Edwidge Danticat. Soho Press, Inc., 1998. Reproduced by permission. / Danticat, Edwidge, photograph by Doug Kanter. AP/Wide World Photos. Reproduced by permission.

HARLAN ELLISON. Cover of *Harlan Ellison's "The City on the Edge of Forever."* White Wolf Publishing, 1996. Reproduced by permission. / Berry, Rick, illustrator. From an illustration in *"Repent, Harlequin!" Said the Ticktockman*, by Harlan Ellison. Underwood Books, 1997. Illustrations © 1997 by Rick Berry. Reproduced by permission of the illustrator. / Ellison, Harlan, photograph by Chris Cuffaro. Reproduced by permission.

LAURA ESQUIVEL. Toelke, Cathleen, illustrator. From a cover of *Like Water for Chocolate*, by Laura Esquivel. Anchor Books, 1995. Reproduced by permission of Doubleday, a division of Random House, Inc. / Pecanins, Montserrat, illustrator, and Brian Nissen, photographer. From a cover of *The Law of Love*, by Laura Esquivel. Crown Publishers, Inc., 1996. Reproduced by permission of Random House, Inc. / Leonardi, Marco, and Lumi Cavazos, in the film *Like Water For Chocolate*, 1993, photograph. The Kobal Collection. Reproduced by permission. / Esquivel, Laura, photograph by Jerry Bauer. © Jerry Bauer. Reproduced by permission.

PETER FARRELLY AND BOBBY FARRELLY. Carrey, Jim, and Jeff Daniels, in the film *Dumb and Dumber*, 1994, photograph. The Kobal Collection. Reproduced by permission. / Harrelson, Woody, in the film *Kingpin*, 1996, photograph by Jim Sheldon. The Kobal Collection. Reproduced by permission. / Stiller, Ben, and Cameron Diaz, in the film *There's Something About Mary*, 1998, photograph by Glenn Watson. The Kobal Collection. Reproduced by permission. / Farrelly, Bobby, and Peter Farrelly, photograph by Glenn Watson. The Kobal Collection. Reproduced by permission.

CHARLES FERRY. Cover of *Binge*, by Charles Ferry. Daisy Hill Press, 1992. Reproduced by permission. / Ferry, Charles, photograph by Herral Long. The Toledo Blade. Reproduced by permission.

DANIEL HAYES. Cover of *The Trouble with Lemons*, by Daniel Hayes. Ballantine Books, 1992. Reproduced by permission of Random House, Inc. / Cepeda, Joe, illustrator. From a cover of *Flyers*, by Daniel Hayes. Simon & Schuster Books for Young Readers, 1996. Cover illustration © 1996 by Joe Cepeda. Reproduced by permission of the illustrator. / Cover of *Eye of the Beholder*, by Daniel Hayes. Ballantine Books, 1998. Reproduced by permission of Random House, Inc. / Hayes, Daniel, photograph by Gary Gold. Reproduced by permission of Daniel Hayes.

JOHN HERSEY. Minor, Wendell, illustrator. From a cover of *A Bell for Adano*, by John Hersey. Vintage Books, 1988. Reproduced by permission of Random House, Inc. / Minor, Wendell, illustrator. From a cover of *Hiroshima*, by John Hersey. Vintage Books, 1989. Reproduced by permission of Random House, Inc. / Minor, Wendell, illustra-

New York. © 1999 The Munch Museum/The Munch-Ellingsen Group/Artists Rights Society (ARS), New York. Reproduced by permission. / *The Dance of Life,* 1899-1900, painting by Edvard Munch. Nasjonalgalleriet, Oslo, Norway/Bridgeman Art Library, London/New York. © 1999 The Munch Museum/The Munch-Ellingsen Group/Artists Rights Society (ARS), New York. Reproduced by permission. / Munch, Edvard, photograph. Corbis-Bettmann. Reproduced by permission.

PHYLLIS REYNOLDS NAYLOR. Cover of *Shiloh,* by Phyllis Reynolds Naylor. Yearling Books, 1992. Reproduced by permission of Dell Books, a division of Random House, Inc. / Ben-Ami, Doron, illustrator. From a cover of *The Fear Place,* by Phyllis Reynolds Naylor. Aladdin Paperbacks, 1996. Cover illustration © 1996 by Doron Ben-Ami. Reproduced by permission of the illustrator. / Moser, Barry, illustrator. From a jacket of *Saving Shiloh,* by Phyllis Reynolds Naylor. Atheneum Books, 1997. Jacket illustration © 1997 by Barry Moser. Reproduced by permission of the illustrator. / Mak, Kam, illustrator. From a jacket of *Achingly Alice,* by Phyllis Reynolds Naylor. Atheneum Books, 1998. Jacket illustration © 1998 by Kam Mak. Reproduced by permission of the illustrator. / Duda, Jana, illustrator. From a jacket of *Sang Spell,* by Phyllis Reynolds Naylor. Atheneum, 1998. Jacket illustration © by Jana Duda. Reproduced by permission of the illustrator. / Naylor, Phyllis Reynolds, photograph by Katherine Lambert. Reproduced by permission of Phyllis Reynolds Naylor.

MARY STEWART. Cover of *Thornyhold,* by Mary Stewart. Ballantine Books, 1989. Reproduced by permission of Random House, Inc. / Cherney, Lawrence, illustrator. From a cover of *The Hollow Hills,* by Mary Stewart. Ballantine Books, 1996. Cover art © Lawrence Cherney/FPG International. Reproduced by permission of Random House, Inc. / Cherney, Lawrence, illustrator. From a cover of *The Last Enchantment,* by Mary Stewart. Ballantine Books, 1996. Cover art © Lawrence Cherney/FPG International. Reproduced by permission of Random House, Inc. / Stewart, Mary, photograph by Jerry Bauer. © Jerry Bauer. Reproduced by permission.

VINCENT VAN GOGH. *La Chambre de Vincent a Arles,* painting by Vincent van Gogh, photograph by Erich Lessing. Musee d'Orsay. © photo R.M.N. Reproduced by permission. / *The Starry Night,* painting by Vincent van Gogh, (1889) oil on canvas, 29 x 36 1/4" (73.7 x 92.1 cm). The Museum of Modern Art, New York. Acquired through the Lillie P. Bliss Bequest. Photograph © 1998 The Museum of Modern Art, New York. Reproduced by permission. / *Sunflowers,* painting by Vincent van Gogh. The National Gallery, London. © National Gallery, London. Reproduced by permission. / van Gogh, Vincent (self-portrait), painting. Corbis-Bettmann. Reproduced by permission.

ROBB WHITE. Mantha, John, illustrator. From a cover of *Deathwatch,* by Robb White. Dell, 1973. Reproduced by permission of Dell Books, a division of Random House, Inc. / White, Joan, illustrator. From a cover of *Fire Storm,* by Robb White. Dell, 1980. Reproduced by permission of Dell Books, a division of Random House, Inc. / White, Robb, photograph by Joanie Logue. Reproduced by the Literary Estate of Robb White.

THORNTON WILDER. Kure, Maskazu, photographer. From a cover of *Our Town,* by Thornton Wilder. HarperPerennial, 1998. Cover photograph © by Maskazu Kure/Photonica. Reproduced by permission of HarperCollins Publishers. / Reed, Dan, illustrator. From a cover of *The Bridge of San Luis Rey,* by Thornton Wilder. HarperPerennial, 1998. Cover painting © by Dan Reed. Reproduced by permission of HarperCollins Publishers. / Voelcker, Brian, Martin Gobbee, and others in a Spingold Theater Center production of Thornton Wilder's *The Skin Of Our Teeth,* Brandeis University, Waltham, MA, April, 1996, photograph by Eric Levenson. Reproduced by permisson. / Wilder, Thorton, Dorothy McGuire, and John Craven, photograph. AP/Wide World Photos. Reproduced by permission. / Wilder, Thornton, photograph by Carl Van Vechten.The Library of Congress.

Cumulative Index

Author/Artist Index

The following index gives the number of the volume in which an author/artist's biographical sketch appears.